THE

Back from the Abyss

THE LONGEST CLIMB

Back from the Abyss

Paul Pritchard

ROBINSON
London

Constable & Robinson Ltd
3 The Lanchesters
162 Fulham Palace Road
London W6 9ER
www.constablerobinson.com

First published in the UK by Robinson,
an imprint of Constable & Robinson Ltd, 2005

A copy of the British Library Cataloguing in
Publication Data is available from the British Library.

ISBN 1-84119-477-8

Printed and bound in the EU

1 3 5 7 9 10 8 6 4 2

For Cadi Eliza

For bad fortune, I think, is more use to a man than good fortune. Good fortune always cheats when she seems to smile, whereas bad fortune is always truthful because by changing she shows her true fickleness. Good fortune deceives, but bad fortune instructs.

Boethius – *The Consolation of Philosophy*

Contents

Illustrations

The Totem Pole. *Photo Paul Pritchard*

Pritchard bouldering in the lost capital of Hampi, India, in 1990. *Photo Sean Smith*

Ascending fixed lines whilst attempting a new route on Meru Central, Garwhal Himalaya, India, 1993. *Photo Philip Lloyd*

In the chasm of the Joint Trail, Chessler Park, Canyonlands, Utah. *Photo Jane Boucher*

Snorkelling on the Great Barrier Reef. *Photo Jane Boucher*

Jane Boucher on Mount Kenya. *Photo Paul Pritchard*

Bernard Kinyua watches over me on unstable ground on the way to the summit of Point Lenana. *Photo Brian Hall*

Jane belays while Keith Partridge films and Margaret Wicks directs whilst pulling onto the summit of Point Lenana, Mount Kenya. *Photo Brian Hall*

Federation Peak. *Photo Grant Dixon*

At Thwaites's campsite in the forest. *Photo Jane Boucher*

Displaying the scar after the head plate. *Photo Jane Boucher*

Racing down Mount Wellington on the recumbent trike. *Photo Matt Newton*

Enjoying fine dining at the Lava Tower on Kilimanjaro. *Photo Paul Pritchard*

The Kilimanjaro team in the upper section of the Western Breach at 6am. *Photo David Lim*

Paul Pritchard, Bungama Hitla, Pete Steane, David Lim, Jamie Andrew, Kornelli. *Photo David Lim*

My first post-accident climb; Rincon (5.4), Eldorado Canyon, August 2004. *Photo Steve Quinlan*

Acknowledgements

In the writing of this book I have had much assistance from many people.

Thank you to Ray Kay, Joe Simpson, Mirella Tendrini, Riccardo Cassin, Maria Coffey, Doug Scott, Jim Curran, Terry Gifford, Simon Yates, Steve Dean, Pat Ament, Steve Venables, Ed Douglas, Tom Hornbein, Carol O'Brien, Ken Wilson, The Mountaineers Publishers, Kurt Diemburger, Tami Knight, Jon Krakauer, Ginger Cain, Pat Falvey, Gordon Stainforth, Ken Crocket, Donald Bennet, Al Alvarez, Shelley Hocknell, Joe Brown, Warren Macdonald, Peter Steele, Ken Rushby, Julie Summers, Leni and Peter Gillman and David Simonite for your help with the internet book auction.

Also Hugh at Delphi Graphics, Roger Alton, Noel Craine, Ali Thomas, Con Moriarty, Gwion Hughes, Trevor Hodgeson, Stew Quin, Tony Loxton, Tom Prentice, Ben Lyon, the BMC, Chipper Jones, Terra Nova Equipment, Rab Carrington, Charlet Moser, Petzl, Stone Monkey, Geoff Birtles at *High*, Wild Country, Richard Cuthbertson, Mick Fox, Ted Silvester, Pete Norton, Eddie Start, Kate Philips, Dick Turnbull and Simon Panton for your kindness concerning the Mount Kenya for Headway project.

My warmest thanks also go to Phil Kelly and Andrew Gridley for going to Djebel Toubkal with me. You needn't have!

For help in climbing Point Lenana my appreciation lies with Meg Wicks and Richard Else at Triple Echo Productions,

Acknowledgements

Brian Hall, Bernard Kinyua, Keith Partridge, Ian Howell, Gabriel and Charles for making it such an unforgettable trip.

I owe a great big dept of gratitude to Fiona Lockett, Emma and Damon Ward, Anthony Taylor and Liz Rollins for humping loads on the 'Feder' trip. And I mustn't forget Michele Callisaya, Fiona Doherty, Kerri Muir, Andrew Hunn and Bruce Taylor – my excellent team of therapists and neurologists in Tasmania.

For the Kilimanjaro trip my warmest thanks must go to my partners Pete Steane, David Lim and Jamie Andrew. Also Ben Pritchard and Richard Heap at Slackjaw Productions, the Upendo Leprosy Centre, Sue Lowe, Faye Cran, Musa Kopwe at MK Safaris, Chris Bonington for acting as patron, Chris Snook at Novartis, Paul and Cathy Casey at Mountain Works, Marmot, Vasque, Jonny Woodward at Black Diamond, Fred Hall at DMM, and Tim Sloane at Mountain Designs. I mustn't forget the heroic Bungama Hitla, guides Safiel Mteta and Kornelli and porters James, Waka, Masanja, Iddi, Mukuku, Mohamedi, Malishi, Tumainiel, Tredo, Changigi, Jeleman, KB, Tobias, Omari, George, Hamis, Elineema, Ebwadi, Charles, Ledwini and Eric Kiluwa. A resounding Cheers!

I must give praise once again to Maggie Body for being such an excellent editor and special mention must be given to Sandy Britain and Mark Garthwaite for help with technical aspects of the text and to Matt Newton, Jamie Andrew, Perry Hawkins, Sean Smith, Brian Hall, Steve Quinlan, Grant Dixon, Philip Lloyd and David Lim for photographs.

I could never omit my partner, Jane, who puts up with my memory lapses and fits of over-emotion admirably and cuts a saccharine figure as a porter.

Acknowledgements

Everyone who appears in the book was an intrinsic part of my healing and to all of you I am more than grateful. If I have omitted anyone it is not my intention, just the workings of an addled brain. Please accept my humblest apologies.

Paul Pritchard
www.headway.org.uk
www.paulpritchard.com.au

1

Sisyphus Happy

I leave Sisyphus at the foot of the mountain! One always finds one's burden again. But Sisyphus teaches the higher fidelity that negates the gods and raises rocks. He too concludes that all is well. This universe henceforth without a master seems to him neither sterile nor futile. Each atom of that stone, each mineral flake of that night filled mountain, in itself forms a world. The struggle itself toward the heights is enough to fill a man's heart. One must imagine Sisyphus happy.

Albert Camus – *The Myth of Sisyphus*

On winning the Boardman Tasker Award for Mountain Literature with my first book *Deep Play* in late 1997, I immediately spent the prize money on a round the world ticket. Taking in Borneo, Australia, New Zealand, America and Alaska, it was to be a dream trip and my then girlfriend Celia Bull and I had it all planned out.

Peering into the depths of Low's Gully on Kinabalu, Borneo, was more impressive than either of us could have imagined and the Blue Mountains of New South Wales were truly beautiful. But on arriving in Tasmania a rock monolith known as the Totem Pole, standing off the grating southern coastline of the island state, was to set our lives on a divergent course for ever.

A computer monitor-sized block landed on my head from twenty-five metres and smashed my skull. The resulting brain damage meant that I lost the use of my right arm for good and my right leg has only limited movement. I also lost the power of speech for several months and was to have severe problems with picking words from my brain for two years. (This still continues to a moderate extent.)

Celia played a pivotal role in my rescue, hauling me thirty metres to safety and running to the nearest telephone, eight kilometres away. When paramedic Neale Smith lowered me into a waiting boat I had been lying on a ledge in a pool of blood for ten hours.

Thus began my year-long journey through several hospitals. After a brain operation that lasted the whole night – the theatre nurses had to transfuse two litres of blood – I was in an induced coma for three days, which isn't very long as comas go but, when I awoke I couldn't move or speak. I didn't just think I was in some terrible nightmare, I *was* in some terrible nightmare where I feared for my life.

This horrible situation went on for a month until I was considered stable enough for evacuation back to Ysbyty Gwynedd, a hospital near my village in Wales, to await a place in rehab. Once the health service had found me a space I was sent to Clatterbridge, a neuro-rehabilitation centre, for the best part of a year. Here I very slowly learned how to talk, walk and use my brain again.

This is where I had the idea of writing a book about my accident and rehab and calling it *The Totem Pole*. It would be much more interesting than watching telly all day as the other patients seemed to do.

One day my friend Brian Hall came to the rehab unit and he found me in the garden smoking in my wheelchair.

'Hello, stranger.'

'Hi . . . ' I instantly recognized his face but momentarily misplaced his name. As I franticly rummaged through the dusty shelves and boxes of my brain there was an awkward silence. Brian knew what I was doing but didn't want to tell me his name because he knew it was good therapy to get my mind working again. He had known others with head injuries and so was not particularly bothered by the pauses. 'B. . . B. . . Brian.' I finally got it out.

'You look good. I expected you to have half your head missing from what people have been telling me.'

'You can't believe anyone these days,' I uttered more to get something out, though I knew it to be banal.

We made small talk about what had been happening on the climbing scene before Brian came out with why he had really come to see me.

'How do you feel about going back to the Totem Pole?'

'What, to climb the thing?' I was making a black joke.

'No, 'course not, to be filmed watching someone else climb it.'

Brian is a director of the Kendal Mountain Film Festival as well as a safety officer and cameraman.

'I would jump at the chance,' I blurted unhesitatingly.

That was how, two months after I got out of rehab, in February 1999, I found myself on a 737 cruising over the lakes and mountains of Tasmania bound for Hobart. Then, with a little help from a helicopter, I watched Steve Monks and Enga Lokey climb the Totem Pole from the cliff-top opposite. It was one of the most moving and profound experiences of my short life.

After the filming had ended I landed with my bags on Jane Boucher's doorstep. Jane was an intrinsic part of the nursing team at the Royal Hobart Hospital where, immediately after my accident on the Totem Pole, I spent over a month ever so slowly improving in health. Jane showed Celia and me a great deal of love when she offered Celia a place to stay in her small house.

When I was flown back to Wales we endeavoured to keep in touch. She and her boyfriend then came to Britain on a travelling holiday over the northern summer and Celia and I thought to repay them by inviting them to stay in our home. Back then, when I was still very ill, the therapists would only let me out of the rehab centre at weekends, so I didn't get to see much of her. I recall her dyeing my hair post-box red, but as my memory is sadly lacking of that departed time, this is about all I recollect.

When Celia and I parted company, in the summer of '98, I felt like the sky was falling in and for a while I toppled into a deep, dark hole of depression. Was there no end to this nightmare? How would I ever get out of the rehab centre now? These are the questions I continually asked myself. I had nowhere to call home now, though I knew my mother would have taken me in in an instant. But I considered this to be a retrograde step for me.

Jane lived in a shared house on stilts in Taroona, a semi-wealthy suburb of Hobart. The house, like a lot of homes in Hobart, was very different to the tiny terraced dwellings of Llanberis in North Wales. She had taken a week off work to show me around the island after the filming.

We visited Wineglass Bay, a popular beach with trekkers on the Freycenet Peninsula, and Jane and I enjoyed each other's company. She was a climber, mountain biker, runner and bush walker and could not visit a beach without swimming in the ocean. Although I could not participate in most of those activities any more, I did aim to and I wanted to share them with someone.

Jane had an astounding vitality about her, though without flaunting it, and that is why I fell in love with her. I always looked forward to her beaming smile coming around the corner.

Instantly I made plans to return to Tasmania for a third trip, which I made in the late spring. When we met at the airport my heart was racing to a salsa beat; it was like two strangers were meeting for the first time. We were wary and circled each other – I had only known this woman for two weeks effectively and here I was giving my heart to her. OK, so there was the month in hospital, but I was with Celia then and anyway, romance was the last thing on my mind. Being able to talk and move and getting all those tubes out of me came before any thoughts of passion.

As we drove down to her grandmother's shack on the beach in the dark, over the music of Triple J radio, a fondness for each other again soon grew.

Jane once played Mrs Pugh in a high school presentation of *Under Milk Wood* and, just as long as I didn't assume the mantle of Mr Pugh, the would-be poisoner, she would fly back to Wales with me. Soon we were strolling on beaches hand in hand, always making sure we went the whole length there and back, and bush walking through foreign rainforests with strange birdcalls. I didn't dare attempt a mountain or even a hill yet because I was just too unsteady on my leg, always falling over to the right.

Jane had arranged a romantic weekend at Cradle Mountain National Park. She had pictured in her mind azure skies and a golden sun and me climbing my first peak, but on arrival the reality was a freezing wind blasting from the Antarctic. We had designs on climbing up the impressive Cradle Mountain but the driving ice particles made our bare legs red raw. We made it about a mile up to Crater Lake and scurried back to the warmth of our chalet. Next morning we awoke to a blanket of fresh deep snow and, after a snowball fight which Jane won, we left Cradle Mountain.

Jane decided that she could just about live with me, and so we flew the twenty-four hours back from Hobart to Manchester together. It was summertime and summer in Wales always has an eternal, dreamlike feel about it. I showed her all the places that are special to me, usually cliffs or mountains, as that is where I'd spent the last seventeen years of my life.

I showed her Gogarth, a cliff towering above the sea with thousands of guillemots and razorbills, little and great auks racing through the sky. They seem out of control until they land with the deft skill that no human can emulate. We saw well dressed puffins and fulmars hovering on the wind, not to mention the streak of the peregrine.

I showed her the giant and deathly quiet Dinorwig slate quarry where men, now dead or aged, had hewn away the whole side of Elidir Fawr. Some say that the blue – grey quarries are ugly, but the ghosts that linger there entrance me and I secretly hoped they would entrance her.

I showed her Cwm Silyn with its llyn like a disc of water on a boiling hot August day, Gallt yr Ogof rising above it like a Welsh preacher, the cave a mouth bellowing out his sermon.

Straight away Jane got not one but three jobs, two waiting tables at a café and a pub and a more career-orientated venture at the local hospital, Ysbyty Gwynedd, a place whose high dependency unit I know only too well.

Jane quickly made her own friends and settled in to life in the village and my house with ease. She was soon speaking more Welsh than I was and within a few weeks Jane was an intimate part of the community.

As for me, I was beginning to feel that I was gathering together some semblance of a life again – dragging a shattered remnant from here, something completely new from there, as a bird builds a nest. It was never going to be my previous life, full of mountains and cliffs and high living, but a life nevertheless.

Walking back through the sliding doors of the Wirral Neurological Rehabilitation Unit at Clatterbridge Hospital I felt like I was going home. Proud as punch, I puffed out my chest, pulled my stomach in and tried to minimize my limp. There were patients there that I recognized and knew well after almost a year. Football-mad Kevin was still in there; after I had been there six months he began to remember my name but now there was not a glimmer of recognition. And there was Cue Ball too, still tied into his chair – if he weren't tied in he would be on the floor – continuing his mantra-like mumbling.

It had been almost one and a half years since my head injury and I was now able to walk and potter about my village with the aid of a stick. I was going for my three-monthly check-up with Doctor Pinder or Colin, as I liked to call him, though I don't think he was too impressed at this assault on his professional status. Colin takes life seriously. But then it's the serious ones who surprise you with hidden depths, like a tendency to spend the weekends covering themselves in whipped cream and flagellating themselves with eels.

Colin and Sian Hughes, my former physiotherapist, filmed me walking toward them, away from them and across the camera. They were both impressed at how I'd come along but stressed, 'You have to keep up your exercises or your progress will stagnate or even go backward.'

I was honest when I told the pair of them that after a year and a half I couldn't help getting a bit bored with these.

Colin and Sian looked at each other.

'Well, it's on your head. We can't watch over you. We can't make you do anything,' Sian said. 'And besides, it's not our problem. It's yours.'

I was taken aback by the serious tone in her voice. We had always had a giggle together; she saw the funny side. Sian could see the funny side of a car crash, literally, as that's were she gets most of her clients.

'I'll try my best,' I answered rather guiltily.

The injury to the left hemisphere of my brain had effectively given me a stroke. The right side of my body was limp – I couldn't use my arm, and I wasn't able to talk or think straight. When I arrived at Clatterbridge, two months post accident, I went everywhere in a wheelchair. The therapists and I worked for over ten months, full-time, to get me to my present state of agility, physical and mental. When I left rehab and moved into my new terraced house in Llanberis, I could walk a hundred metres with the aid of various splints.

A couple of months later saw me attempting to climb my first hill, Moel Elio, near my little house in the centre of the village. Jane and I made our effort in a horizontal, soaking fog. We set off up a dirt track in our 4x4 Panda, a hilarious vehicle, which had deckchairs for seats. The wheels spun in the mud as we approached a five-bar gate. We sat in the warm, dry car silently willing the other to go out into the storm and open the gate. This was pointless however as we were both about to get drenched. As Jane was driving I was the first to buckle under pressure and after I'd opened the gate Jane parked up in a pond.

There remained a 500-metre climb to the summit and the ground was steep, the grass slippery. We followed a fence-line the whole way but, unfortunately, it was to my right so I couldn't use it as a banister. Sheep mooched about, apparently unfazed by the lashing wind and rain.

In his book *How the Mind Works* Stephen Pinker says that walking is a miracle: 'When we walk we repeatedly tip over and then break our fall in the nick of time. When we run we take off in bursts of flight.'

My gait was the opposite of this smooth, rhythmic 'miracle'. My knee flicked back painfully into hyperextension with every step and I leaned heavily on my walking pole, my torso twisted into a horrible shape with an exaggerated Quasimodo stoop.

Depending on which way I staggered or slipped, Jane would field me from behind, dodging this way and that. At times my feet would shoot out behind me and I would pitch violently onto my face and elbows. I would then climb to my knees and, with mud flecking my wet face, raise myself to my feet in an undignified manner by pulling up on the ski pole.

The cloud was so thick we could only see a few metres in front of our feet and, with our hoods up to shield our faces from the blasting rain, the top took us by surprise. When we arrived at the summit enclosure, several sheep bounded out over the wall scattering in all directions before coming together again as a single flock.

This was the top of my first hill. I became very emotional and rejoiced. It had been a year and a half since I had been to a summit or the top of anything, and the storm was beautiful. Most people would think that we were crazy walking up a mountain in such appalling conditions but I just turned my face into the wind and let the rain mingle with the tears.

Jane unpacked a flask of piping hot tea and tinned salmon sandwiches. With my queen by my side I felt like a king at a banquet, sipping tea and munching soggy butties. Tugging at my brain, I thought back, urging it to recall the last mountain I had climbed. Suddenly I was there, sitting on top of Victoria Peak, one of the many peaks of Mount Kinabalu, alone, looking down into the depths of Low's Gully and then gazing out over the Bornean jungle.

'Well, we did it,' said Jane, raising her voice and snapping me out of my dreamy recollections.

'Yeah. And what a view.' I looked out into the mist and shouted into the wind. 'We still have to get down again though,' I added, knowing we were not in a serious situation but should need to take a modicum of care.

Wet as herrings, we skimmed back down the marinated grass, I spending most of the time on my behind. This didn't matter to me though, as my mind was working overtime busy planning which hill I would climb next. I decided there and then that I would climb all the hills in Snowdonia.

My legs ached for about a week, which isn't surprising, as they hadn't been used for eighteen months. After my knees ceased hurting and my muscles aching I ventured to climb that Matterhorn of Wales, Cnicht. Jane and I made our attempt on one of those boiling tops-off days, an intense summer's day, the kind you can smell, where you can hear the heat radiating.

We wound our way up the old drovers' road and then began climbing up the ridge until we arrived at a shoulder sixty metres below the summit. I had climbed well, I felt, up until then. But the way above rose wickedly steep. A nervous tingling began in my neck and travelled down my spine. There were rock steps up above to be scrambled, almost rock climbing.

A feeling that I knew well overcame me: that of wanting to go for it but not wanting to at the same time, then telling myself to pull myself together and not to be 'so soft'. I say I knew it well because I had experienced it hundreds of times on rock climbs when deciding to go for it way above my last protection.

'What's wrong?' Jane asked.

'Oh, I don't know. I guess I'm scared of hurting myself.'

'It does look a bit steep.'

'Too right it does. It looks bloody steep.'

The realization that I might not make it was beginning to seep through my mind as dampness does a Welsh house.

'You'd have done it with a rope.'

'Yeah. Pity we don't have one.'

We vowed to go everywhere with a short length of rope – if we remembered – from then on.

An internal game of push and pull raged in my head for half an hour until I reached a decision. I would be 'so soft'.

'I'm bottling out.'

I was worried. What would happen if I broke my leg? I had also forgotten the helmet, which I would normally wear for hill walking.

'OK. Well . . . Do you mind if I go to the summit? I won't be long.'

''Course not. You go on. I'll wait here for you.'

Jane skipped up to the summit and back in minutes, which didn't give me the time to have the nap on the warm sheep-nibbled grass I was so looking forward to. Until my next attempt, a year later, I would mull this failure over in my mind time and again.

The summer continued and so did the mountain walking exploits, though perhaps at a slower pace than I would have wished. Aching legs plagued me, especially the right one, but as the left had to work all the harder that fatigued also. On average I could manage one peak a week but I sensed that would improve if I just kept working at my walking.

At any available moment I was up on the hills. It was as though I were reborn and experiencing glorious exertion – the shapes of mountains and the sounds of them too, the wind, the buzzard or the streams of water – for the first time. I revelled in going to the less travelled places in Snowdonia; places that I had never been to, places that I had never heard of before my accident.

One such place was Bryn Cader Faner in the Rhinogau. That it should take a major head injury to get me to tread these hills I reproached myself. Some say these are the most difficult hills to traverse in the whole of Wales – there are no paths and the beauty of the purple heather dotted with yellow gorse flower belies the difficulty of the bog-wading.

Bryn Cader Faner is one of the most beautiful prehistoric tombs in Britain. It has twelve uprights that all angle out-wards at thirty degrees, mimicking the rays of the sun. The whole tomb is about ten metres in diameter but time and perhaps looters have destroyed the centre, which is now just a pile of rubble.

My mate Tone trotted through bogs that, because of my paralysed leg and drop foot splint, I became fast in. The splint, an ugly fake tan thing, goes from the tip of my toes to the back of my knee and effectively freezes my ankle in the same way a ski boot does. My ankle isn't just useless but worse than useless. It is spastic. This spasticity means that whatever way I want to move the ankle it will do precisely the opposite.

Once my right foot went shin-deep I was unable to extricate the limb. More than once I had to ask Tone for help getting me out of the bog. He would come back to my stranded position and I would put my left arm around his shoulders. He would then take my right leg and give it a good strong yank.

Some people might think that asking for help to get one's foot out of a bog would be quite humiliating. On the contrary. By asking my friends for help in everyday tasks I have moved on to a new level of warmth and kinship that I never knew existed before. Either by giving me lifts to my physiotherapy sessions or coming walking with me or simply opening a can of baked beans, they are re-affirming their love for me. God knows it must be boring having to stand around waiting for me in the cold whilst I walk at a snail's pace. But they do it. How warm inside I feel when a friend calls me to ask if I want anything from the shop.

We shared a chocolate bar, Tone smoked his roll-up, and I circumnavigated the cromlech. The tomb is situated on a saddle, giving a vista of luminous green on three sides. The low crags of the Rhinogau where behind us, Harlech, with its castle, below to the left, and the wide flood plain where the Glaslyn and the Dwyryd converge to the right. Cardigan Bay was laid out in front of us like a vast sparkling carpet that spread from the tip of the Lleyn Peninsula to St David's Head in Pembroke. Wanting this picture to stay with me forever and with stinking mud right up to the knees, I trudged my way back to Tone's car.

Recovering from my injury, I was now finding that I had all the time in the world to explore the hills without feeling pressured to work or climb. It was like being a child again, having no responsibility of any kind. It is a state that we seldom feel in this age of appointments to be kept and the constant striving for success.

On one summit, Yr Aran, in a hypoglycaemic state, I sensed I was soaring in the wind: there was a buzzard gliding below me and, in my sugar low, I was flying with her. Before the ascent I was filled with trepidation but any of my previous doubts were replaced by pure elation. I was indeed a child again.

As long as my body didn't betray me, as so often seemed to be its only vocation, I was OK; I could continue with my rehabilitation apace. But my hip joint locked painfully and my knee often felt close to disintegration. My tremendous problems walking continued and I could not lift my right foot more than a few centimetres clear of the ground.

Once during the summer I was walking around a quarry near our home and tripped over my trousers, which were very large, and face planted in the dirt just inches from a great big rock. I lay there for a long while not moving. Jane must have thought that I was unconscious.

'Are you OK?' she asked, shaking me out of my sorrow-ful daze.

'Yeah, I'm just pissed off with everything. All this falling, these injuries I keep having. This fucking cripple business is getting me down.'

Climbing up to a sitting position and resting my back against a stone wall, I continued, 'I know, I'm just expected to keep soldiering on, being brave, but I don't know how much longer I can cope with it all.'

'But you need to or you'll cave in.'

'It is so much pressure though. It's like being in prison or something. I want to run but I can't. I want to jump but I can't. I want to swim but I can't. In fact it's worse than being in prison 'cause the prisoner doesn't have to see and feel what he's missing each and every day. It stinks.'

'I know.'

'No, you don't know. How could you possibly know anything about being a hemiplegic? Sure, you know how to treat a hemiplegic or any other kind of brain injury, but actually having one is different. It's a nightmare.'

'Look, imagine that you did say, "Bugger all of this" and gave up. Then what would you do?'

I thought about this for a while, pictures of me going into a home like the rehab centre I was in for ten months flitted through my head: afternoons wasted watching daytime telly, three plates of crap food a day, being reprimanded for going to the canteen alone and terrible nights spent awake due to other patients wailing in the darkness. The blank stares of most of the other 'clients', while neurologically interesting – an electrical charge must still be firing across those synapses even in the most head-injured person – didn't make for challenging conversation. Fascinating though my time in rehab was, and it did make for an interesting book, I was truly thankful to be out of there.

What would I do then?

I pulled myself to my feet with the help of Jane and said, with lips curled up in a slight grin, 'Well, I'll just have to keep soldiering on then, won't I?'

Late in the summer Jane and I were on our way to a rock festival in Leeds; we were rattling along the M62 when black, acrid smoke began billowing out of the bonnet of our faithful 4x4 Panda. After pushing the ailing car to a garage we were informed that the head gasket had gone and there was no more they could do for her. I swear I saw Jane shed a tear as we emptied the car and under huge loads, went to the railway station.

We arrived at Temple Newton Park just in time to see the last of the Chemical Brothers set. We got star treatment because of my disability. The 'raspberry ripples' (cripples) had their very own campsite with guards around it, which meant we could relax in the knowledge that our tent wasn't getting ripped off at any given moment.

A guide showed us to our own stage. There were mohawks in wheelchairs and metal heads with prosthetic limbs – about twenty crazies – all behind railings to stop them rolling off. Or maybe the railings were to stop the crowd from climbing up, as this was definitely *the* place to be. We clambered up the ramp with our inflatable sofa. I felt honoured to be there and I danced and thrashed better than the last time I attempted such movements.

A drunk Glaswegian was jumping around in his wheelchair and being friendly with Jane. He was trying to converse with her by shouting above the deafening music, which Jane was trying to listen to.

'Wits yur nayme, hen?'

'What?'

'Ra musos ar no bad, eh?'

'What was that?'

'See Blur, thus is wit ah cayme fur . . . pure dead brullyent bu'!'

'Blur, yes,' shouted Jane, still feeling a dash of compassion.

'Av goat that MS, yur ken?'

'What was that? Have you got MS? Is that what you said?'

'This chair does ra fuckinnboxin.'

'What did you say?'

'See Divine Comedy? Therr fuckin' shite bu'.'

Jane just nodded in agreement, pretending to have heard him.

'Fancy a chong on ra doobie?' He slurred, and leaning over her the Glaswegian passed Jane a very badly rolled joint.

Jane glanced askance at the soggy joint and shook her head as if she was afraid of catching an infectious disease.

'Wit d'ya say yur nayme wiz?'

'Are you speaking a foreign language?'

'Hayaswallayorrabuckie onyego,' he garbled, passing Jane a bottle of cheap red wine.

Again she declined to share a bottle with this nutter from Glasgow.

'It's fuckin' shite sittin in this chair aw day bu'. Gorrn . . . get a slug o ma buckie wee manto,' he managed to get out before teetering over a fraction too far and toppling out of his chair and on top of Jane.

In September 1999 *The Totem Pole* was launched at the Alpine Club in London. The book concerned my accident in Tasmania in February 1998 and my subsequent year in rehab. My publicist, Gina Rozner, had a gruelling week of publicity planned out for me, with interviews on all the major radio stations in the mornings and afternoons and lectures in the evenings.

My first lecture since the accident was in a shop in Shepherds Bush. I had just finished giving my reading and had invited the first question.

A young woman stood up. 'How do you feel about never being able to climb again?'

I attempted to answer her. 'Well . . . I . . . Er . . . Don't really . . . can't . . .'

I wanted to say that I hadn't really arrived at any positive conclusion yet and still felt like a climber but, slowly, I felt an epileptic seizure coming on. I always know instinctively when it is about to happen. I become vacant and slow and this strange metallic smell fills my nostrils, like rusty iron. Since my injury it's the only time I can smell anything.

The audience was looking a bit edgy.

Finally I stammered out rather calmly, 'I think I'm going to have a fit,' before starting to hyperventilate.

Dostoyevski used to have 'ecstatic epileptic auras' and 'During these five seconds I live a whole human existence, and for that I would give my whole life and not think I was paying too dearly.'

My seizures on the other hand were painful, disorientating and disturbing and lasted at least ten minutes. I felt hard done by. Why couldn't I be like Dostoyevski? It was a small consolation that this was my very first fit in front of an audience.

One of two things can happen, depending on which type of fit I'm going to have: either a tingling begins in my hand or foot and slowly grows in intensity until it is unbearable or, more worrying for the audience, I lose the power to speak and start drooling. This is followed shortly afterwards by uncontrollable twitches in my facial muscles and a drooping of the right side of my face. Luckily this time it was the unbearable tingling of the foot, which is more painful but less embarrassing.

The audience sat there, stony silent and statue still not really knowing how to treat the situation. Luckily Jane was in the crowd and she sprinted to the front to hold me. I never lose consciousness but become unstable, unbalanced, and if the fit continues I become confused.

'Has anybody got any tissues?' She directed the question to the audience.

One could see the question whirring over in their minds. 'My God, is he about to wet himself?'

Meanwhile my foot had begun to feel like it was in a bucket of maggots and they were slowly devouring it. A creeping, fleshy tingling. It was a sensation I knew well – at that time I was having on average one fit every three weeks – though it doesn't get any more pleasant with routine. I had hold of my lower leg and was thrashing about and hyperventilating in a more vicious manner now.

A shop assistant had the foresight to break up the uncomfortable library silence by shouting, 'You are all welcome to browse around the shop. Please, this way.'

This took the attention off me, for which I was appreciative. Tiredness and exhaustion can induce seizures but so can nerves or anything that creates an atmosphere of stress or ups one's heart rate. The idea is to remain calm and relaxed always which, as I'm sure the reader will understand, is difficult for a climber.

As ever, Gina was sympathetic: 'Mind you,' she said, 'that shifted a lot of books. Can you do that every time?'

'I'll think about it,' I said weakly.

2

Candylands

> One moment you are feeling calm, self possessed,
> happy. Then fear, disguised in the garb of mild-
> mannered doubt, slips into your mind like a spy.
> Doubt meets disbelief and disbelief tries to push it
> out. But disbelief is a poorly armed foot soldier.
> Doubt does away with it with little trouble. You
> become anxious. Reason comes to do battle for you.
> You are reassured. Reason is fully equipped with
> the latest weapons of technology. But, to your
> amazement, despite superior tactics and a number
> of undeniable victories, reason is laid low. You feel
> yourself weakening, wavering. Your anxiety
> becomes dread.
>
> Yann Martel – *Life of Pi*

In October my American publishers, The Mountaineers,
had arranged for me to go on a reading and signing tour
around North America and Jane and I decided to make a
holiday out of it.

We were accidentally booked on first-class to Toronto;
the woman checking us in looked at our tickets, cast us a
glance, and asked politely, 'Did you win these tickets?'

'No, we didn't,' I answered, put out.

'Oh, I was just wondering.'

'Do we look that rough then?' I said, before noticing

what we were wearing. I had on my Nepali jumper with the Star of David on the front and a pair of massive trousers and Jane was attired in her six-year-old worn through pile jacket and a pair of Tevas. We were most definitely not first-class material and possibly the scruffiest people on the whole plane.

On landing, an American narcotics hound took a liking to me and sniffed me all over. I told Jane off for bending over and slapping her thighs and generally encouraging the hound but I knew how she loved dogs. We got questioned and searched but they turned up nothing. Afterwards Jane pulled out these giant prescription codeine pills that she was taking for pharyngitis, which were most definitely narcotic.

We then flew to Salt Lake City and were met at the airport by my very good friends Steve and Cris-Anne Quinlan. Steve is like a brother to me. Together we had made the first ascent of Adrift, a multi-day big-wall route on El Capitan in Yosemite Valley, and the first ascent of the West Face of Mount Asgard on Baffin Island.

We hired a Dodge Neon – fire engine red of course – with one mile on the clock, and took off for the desert. It was a five-hour drive down to Indian Creek in the heart of Canyonlands National Park, a place I knew well. Huge walls of smooth, red sandstone line this canyon.

We were singing along in the dark to Dwight Yokem on one of the country stations – every station is a country station in the mid-west – driving past Newspaper Rock, the entrance to Indian Creek. We were right behind Cris-Anne and Steve's pick-up when a deer came bounding out of the darkness and collided with the front of their vehicle. For me, the state of contentment at being back in a familiar and beautiful place was shattered in the space of seconds.

Steve, unmistakably angry, was running about the vehicle kicking it.

'Fuck . . . Fuck . . . Fuckfuckfuckfuck . . . Fuck!' he shouted.

The animal had taken out a headlight and put a sizeable dent in the grill but he could only think about the fate of the deer. You could see the fear in the eyes of the animal and a tear in Steve's.

'Do you think there'll be a gun around here?' Steve asked Cris-Anne.

Unlike so many Americans, the Quinlans never carry a piece.

'Maybe at that farm further down the Creek.'

No sooner had she spoken than the piteous animal hobbled to its feet and limped off into the darkness on the other side of the road.

'They do that. The poor bastards stagger off and then go and die in the woods,' said Steve.

'Do you think we should go after it?' asked Jane with water in her eyes.

'Nah, well never find it in this dark.' Steve was dismayed.

So the four of us got back into the cars, leaving only a little pool of blood on the surface of the road as evidence that an animal was dying in the woods.

We pulled into the 'Fuck Superbowl' campsite. The reason for the peculiar name is that on every Superbowl (the American equivalent of the FA Cup) climbers come here to avoid the ballyhoo. The site was full of cars and noise, the whole place like a dust bowl, the fine powder getting into our eyes, ears and teeth. It was Steve's birthday and we had come to celebrate it. There were many of his old friends there, and mine too, so before we knew it, it was late into the night.

A slight hangover greeted me on awakening. But the day had come to venture into the 'Candylands', as the climbers affectionately know Canyonlands. Enormous rock mushrooms of all hues of red, orange and white dominate the skyline. The colours have run into streaks, which give the appearance of sad rock crying.

To limber ourselves up we walked two slick rock trails, one very short and the other four kilometres. There was a brain-boiling panorama of Little Spring Canyon, shuddering in the heat. We only took half a bottle of water which we drank in one go and then struggled with thirst for the remainder of the walk. I hadn't had time to walk much for the last month and my lack of fitness was self-evident.

There are literally hundreds of kilometres of cliffs in a crumpled line of Wingate Sandstone fringing the mostly dry river valleys. These red cliffs are fractured every ten metres by a soaring vertical crack, of varying widths, each one requiring a distinct crack climbing technique to overcome. I was once again in Indian Creek! Steve, Celia Bull and I had climbed all over these walls, and even made a few new routes on a road trip we made in 1994.

As the day came to a close, the setting sun veiled the walls of Indian Creek in a deep crimson and the cottonwoods in the campsite were as if on a stage, in the spotlight. Sitting on the slick rock I could feel warmth on my cheek, radiating from it, like being blanketed in a cosy dream.

The next day we were back into Canyonlands again to try an ambitious twelve-kilometre walk up Big Spring Canyon and down Squaw Canyon. The description in the leaflet detailed some scrambling; we imagined that would mean for big, slow American tourists and that it would be fine for us, even with my gammy leg and single arm. We trudged through the soft sand in a landscape that Salvador

Dali could never have dreamed up. All melted towers of orange and terracotta, wider on top than at the base.

About seven kilometres into the walk we had to cross from Big Spring Canyon into Squaw Canyon and this required a climb over a saddle. The terrain was much more difficult than we expected and was, in my opinion, graded rock climbing. Teetering up holdless slabs, I was thankful for the sticky rubber soles on my shoes.

Then, about a hundred metres up above the base of the slab, there came a particularly steep section to get onto the summit of the pass. I tried again and again to pad my way up but each time my right leg would go rigid and I would be left doing battle with a metre-long metal girder with a boot on the end of it. Several times I overbalanced and almost fell to my demise. I imagined myself tumbling and tumbling down the slab and landing in an unrecognizable pile at the bottom.

Jane dangled a hand from her sloping perch and, like Michelangelo's *Creation of Adam* on the Sistine Chapel ceiling, we strained with all our might but our fingers never quite touched. Then, like an idea that was so obvious, we both uttered in unison, 'The ski pole!'

So, with Jane heaving from her ever so precarious roost and me trying to pull her off with just my left hand gripping the pole, we grunted and hauled.

Now, I've been in some scary situations but this was definitely the most traumatic experience I've encountered in my whole life. My head felt so vulnerable without a helmet. (I forgot the thing and anyway wasn't expecting to be climbing rocks.) And I felt useless for the first time since my accident as I'd had to rely on some one else in a life or death situation. OK, so I depended on Jane to tie my laces and clean the fire grate, but never in something so serious. I wasn't in control, wasn't responsible for my own life and felt enveloped in dread. Jane was terrified too.

With spastic limbs that wouldn't behave and a disco leg, I fought my way onto a foothold. I felt as though Jane was sending me off balance and I snapped at her, 'You're pulling me off!'

'I can't help it,' she retorted in a panic-stricken voice and then an unfinished sentence, 'You should be telling me . . . '

I didn't answer. I just fought a Herculean battle with my spastic limbs until I joined her on the little sloping ledge.

It was only afterwards when Jane was sitting shaking on top of the cliff, telling me 'I almost fell then,' that we realized how stupid we had been. For what seemed like an age I lay there on my back, thoroughly exhausted. When I finally picked myself up to survey the scene, what I was presented with was so beautiful that it hurt my eyes. In my fragile state there seemed to be a golf ball stuck in my throat and I was gagging and weeping painfully, the landscape brought out such emotion in me.

We were confronted by tens of domed and jagged horizons, all shades of the same colour, from the subtlest ochre to the gaudiest post-box red. Once again I was in awe of the beauty of this earth that I had been deprived of for a year and a half; almost deprived of for good.

Jane gave me a hug and said with a single tear in her eye, 'I felt physically sick back there and my heart was pounding like nobody's business.'

It only dawned on us that evening that the ski pole was telescopic and could so easily have fallen apart, me holding one end and Jane the other. I pictured the scene with horror, Jane crouching there holding the handle, watching as I fell away from her, wide-eyed, uselessly gripping the end section of the ski pole like some failed orchestra conductor.

The descent was easier as I could bum-slide down most of the smooth sandstone, but when we reached the bottom I took a deep breath and exhaled in overwhelming relief. We still had four miles of soft sand to traipse through to get back to the car, and my knee was hurting, but at least we were safe from harm or even death.

The Swedish knee cage sounds like an implement of torture or a Scandinavian design-winning sex aid, but it is a device to stop the knee from hyper-extending, and I had borrowed one from my physiotherapist at the last minute. It proved to be too big and kept on slipping down around my calf, so this contraption stayed in the rucsac. I would just have to deal with the pain, because the only other option was to spend a cold night out in the desert with no sleeping bag or water.

We arrived at the car park at 5.30 in the afternoon, six and a half hours after we had left. Virtually hallucinating, I was totally knackered but I had broken my distance record by a full three and a half kilometres.

That trek was the longest and riskiest I had made in my post head injury body. One thing I hadn't counted on was going rock climbing. I again discussed with Jane the use of a rope for such situations. Helmets, ropes, knee cages, splints, elbow and shin guards – one of these days we would remember all these items. We had been remarkably stupid for making such a hazardous outing, but that bit of climbing made me feel alive again.

My mind then turned to considering why I denied that I was different to anyone else. OK, so I had a limp and couldn't use one arm, but essentially I was just the same as other people. I might talk a bit more slowly but I got things out nevertheless.

There have been quite a few consultants and doctors who have told me that I won't recover as much as I think I will. In my mind this arrogance is misplaced, especially concerning head injury. How can anyone do anything but make a vague guess at the extent of a patient's recovery?

So in this way I succeeded in deceiving myself and I managed to convince myself that there was nothing wrong with me.

Some time later I read about Richard Lazarus of the University of California at Berkeley. He went part way to proving that self-deception can be a matter of survival. He showed that patients who repressed thoughts of an upcoming operation – in other words people who deceived themselves about the seriousness of their condition – suffered fewer post-operative complications than patients who dwelt on the hazards of the surgery.

In a separate study of sixty-nine patients with breast cancer, Martin Seligman of the University of Pennsylvania found that five years after mastectomy, seventy-five per cent of the women who had denied their illness were still alive and healthy as compared to only thirty-five per cent of those who had resigned themselves to their fate. 'This suggests that believing something is true maybe the first step to making it so,' stated Seligman.

Could it be the same mechanism for head injury too? If this is fact then I might be behaving in the preferred way as far as my recovery is progressing. Perhaps denying illness is the very same as denying injury.

A couple of days later, when my leg had recovered, we took a drive to the Islands in the Sky where we strolled in a gale for three kilometres along the edge of the canyon. There was an old lady struggling, fighting to walk to the lookout, about forty metres from the car. Her right arm hung limp and the right side of her face was distorted in the manner of the Munch painting *The Scream*. She'd obviously had a stroke and had a right 'hemi', just like I was carrying.

Two relatives were guiding her down the path to keep her from falling over. Jane and I overtook them and I marvelled at her courage. I asked her when she had her accident but, as is often the case, before she had time to answer, the guy she was with spoke for her, 'Oh, about three years.'

'I was talking to the lady,' I said.

This white-haired woman then began to move her lips, 'Ah . . . Ah . . . Aaah,' she got out with a struggle and then, 'I . . . I . . . Maaa.'

'It's OK,' I said, 'you don't have to say anything.'

Then she held out her hand and I took it in mine and said, 'I don't know what to say. Don't ever give up.'

The very sound of my words was banality itself to my ears and I cringed with embarrassment. But I watched her face light up as she looked me in the eye – I like to think it was a knowing look – with a directness that few 'normal' people could hold. As Jane and I went on our way the old lady proceeded to the lookout and, as I looked back, I saw her beaming as she looked over the railings and into the void below.

The scene was unimaginable. Terraces and 300-metre cliffs with rock needles and plugs all over the place, stepping down and down into the land. And there, in the depths, I noticed Standing Rock, which Celia, Steve and I had struggled to the top of six years ago. This fine needle is the most slender extremity in this vast landscape. Suddenly I was back there . . .

Down there . . . The jeep drive around the 'White Rim' to get into Monument Basin, all these crazy shapes, mushrooms and syringes . . . Sleeping on top of the cliff opposite

Standing Rock . . . Waking early in the cold morning and letting strong coffee warm us up . . . Steve playing The Pixies on the Jeep stereo and turning the volume up – just as I was getting into it, Celia told us to turn it down and that didn't we appreciate the solitude of the desert. Steve and I couldn't argue as the silence itself was deafening.

A breakfast of porridge and strawberry breakfast bars . . . Scrambling down the gully to the base of the pinnacle . . . The three of us milling around the foot of this giant monolith, not wanting to be first on. The illusion was that it was going to topple over at any time.

The rock crumbled in my hands and under my feet – this I was used to after years of climbing on Gogarth in Wales, a cliff whose looseness was infamy itself. The route wove up a huge dihedral, capped by a roof. This brought to mind the Grecian game of 'Jenga', were one has to remove wooden bricks from the base of a tower and stack them on the top until it tumbles.

As I remembered crossing the roof I could sense the rope-drag, the friction as the lines ran against the rock. I could here myself shouting down:

'I can't move, Steve!'

We were attempting a second free ascent. Steve has the crux pitch but can't cope with the difficult move.

'Oh fuck, I'm going to have to taint,' he calls down to us.

'That's the free ascent blown,' I grumble under my breath, but as I approach the crux move I fall off too. 'It's bloody hard, Steve.'

I follow Celia up the top pitch that brings us onto the summit. We pose for self-timer photos and sign the visitors' book, one of the most exclusive visitors' books in the world.

On the trail there is a 'handy' information board that

points out all the landmarks of Monument Basin, the kind that saves you the trouble of looking at and truly appreciating the landscape, so that you are left with the memory not so much of the spectacle before you as the display board with all its interesting facts on geological history, rainfall and visitor numbers. On this board I saw that Standing Rock had been renamed the Totem Pole!

'Is that a coincidence or what?' I asked Jane.

Later that day we drove to the Fisher Towers State Park in Castle Valley, a little north-east of Moab. Thunder had been threatening the whole day and static electricity hung in the air, making our skin prickle. Whenever she touched the car Jane received shocks from it. Then the sky cleared and the towers, which Jane commented looked like the drip castles she used to make as a child on Tasmania's beaches, turned, quicker than I would have liked, from orange to blood red. In the latter stages of the sunset, the towers resembled H.R. Giger's fantastic sets of *Alien*, spattered with blood.

In the night we were woken in our tent by the loudest thunder we had ever heard. These deafening claps were preceded by magnesium flashes like a scuffling crowd of paparazzi outside our little nylon dome.

Then the sound of grinding gravel as a car pulled into our isolated campsite and the headlight beam swung past our tent. Whoever was out there knew we were here and, being thirty kilometres from the nearest house, they also knew how isolated we were. News items of mass murders and killings for the hell of it were on the radio daily and we became terrified.

'Be quiet!' Jane whispered.

'I didn't say anything.'

'Your heart – I can hear it beating.'

'I can't stop my heart from beating.'

'Ssshhh.'

Not being able to run I felt completely vulnerable and, through conditioning I know, as the man in the partnership, totally unable to protect Jane. All we could do was lie there and let the killers slice the tent open and stab us to death. When all was quiet, Jane unzipped the door and saw folk putting up their tents. They didn't want to murder us because they were just campers looking for a place to sleep. Finally we fell back into slumber.

Early the following morning we attempted to walk around the Fisher Towers, about seven kilometres, but I failed to get halfway because the path was dreadful and shaley. I remembered back to the last time that I was there six years ago, when I didn't even notice the difficulty or the distance. Celia and I just ran along it, much as Jane was running along it now. I think I was fatigued and in a poor frame of mind.

I tried to cheer up before the next walk of the day by eating junk food; a family-sized bag of Doritos and two Reese's Peanut Butter Cups. We had planned to do an overnight camp in the heart of Canyonlands, my first one for a long time, at least eighteen months. I was loaded up with the sleeping bags while Jane had the five litres of water, the tent, food, stove, pans and all the other essential pieces of kit that one requires for camping on her back.

We set off late in the afternoon for the eight-kilometre hike. I tired quickly because of the walking I had done earlier in the day and was too tired to notice the splendour of the scenery we were passing through. 'Oh yeah, there are some more sandstone needles.'

The soft sand on the path was mangling my ankle as it rolled again and again with every step I took.

'Shall I run ahead and get the tent up?' Jane offered, noticing my thinly disguised torment.

'Oooh yeah, that would be great,' I said, trying to sound enthusiastic.

'Maybe I'll have time to get a panad (Welsh for a cuppa) on as well,' she added.

As I finally reached the campsite, which was protected by a smooth, towering overhung rock wall, the tent was up and Jane handed me a plastic mug of milky tea.

Without a word, I drank greedily. The few desert oaks threw long shadows on the fine sand as the night approached.

Camping out was everything I remembered it to be. The silence, the blackness, the profound feeling of peace inside, being wrapped in the night sky without a trace of light pollution. Heat was radiating from the stone, which was warm to the touch long into the night. At least that's what Jane told me – I was fast asleep by 7.30 pm. Even though I was getting tired, I wasn't having fits as Colin, my consultant neurologist, had tinkered with my dose of anti-convulsants to stave them off whilst not making me too drowsy.

If I were not so exhausted I would have been kept awake the whole night long worrying about the following day. As it was, after eleven hours' sleep I awoke well rested and excited about the long trek which, at twelve kilometres, would be the farthest I'd ever attempted post-injury. Jane prepared us breakfast, which was a shared aluminium cooking pot of muesli with hot instant milk, while I put on my wrist and ankle splints. I downed two little anti-convulsant pills with a mug full of water and stuffed the sleeping bags into my pack. The two of us paused to sup from thermal mugs of instant coffee, ones we got from some Shell garage, off which we scratched the 'S's.

A film of rime-ice adorned the tent, so chilly was the morning. Jane shook and folded the flysheet and collapsed the poles as her breath condensed in the shadows from the heavy breathing that comes with the first exertions of the day. We virtually ran across to the line from shivering shade to sunshine and approached a viewpoint, a gap in the cliffs, from which, it seemed the whole of Canyonlands lay at our feet. We each found it hard to dawdle here for we knew there was a long way to go before we felt comfortable in pausing.

As we trekked across Chesler Park, the soft sand played havoc with my ankle still. I hadn't packed the Swedish knee cage after the problems I had encountered on the descent of Squaw Canyon, which meant I had considerably less weight to lug about, but I nevertheless faced a hyper-extending knee joint when I became fatigued.

The utterly surreal landscape continued as we walked. Immense towers were gathering in to ambush us. These towers were joined together at the very top only, giving the impression of a dense forest of giant mushrooms. Only a handful of these formations have been ascended as climbing was banned here a number of years ago because, according to the National Parks Service, the rock is too soft to take the metal wedges climbers need to protect them-selves. Yes, the conventional metal gear would harm the rock but have the authorities considered knotted ropes and slings, the sandstone climbing technique of the Elbsandstein in Germany? However, there is so much rock in Canyon-lands anyway that climber's aren't unduly worried by the restriction.

Mentally weaving dream routes up these crazy minarets I was thus kept busy. Knowing that they probably had never been ascended just made me want to climb them more. Sitting on my rucsac, I gazed at my surroundings and for the briefest of moments I was oblivious to the fact that I was now unable to climb. When I am walking I am reminded by my ridiculous gait that I am disabled, but when I am seated my body permits me to forget.

After toiling across the plains of Chesler Park we dropped down into the depths of the Joint Trail. Rock walls just a single metre apart rose up for more than forty metres. Our track turned at right angles again and again with the fissures that cut down into the rock. This had the effect of disorientating us completely. The pink and orange light found its way in, somehow, trying to reach the sandy floor, but dissipated before it had any chance of landing. Occasionally, when there was a step in the level of the sandy base there would be a ladder, which I could handle with ease. But once there was just a log, tilted at forty-five degrees, with a couple of cursory footholds chopped in it with an axe. It was as if this labyrinth had flooded at some point and a piece of detritus had lodged in between the walls.

I ended up negotiating the log by leaning against one wall with my good arm and ever so gingerly stepping one foot across the other to locate with the steps. Not falling off was my proudest moment of the whole trek.

When we emerged from this labyrinthine grotto we rubbed our eyes and saw an ugly 4x4 track bulldozing its way right into the heart of an otherwise beautiful national park. We were to find lots of these and were left wondering just how the National Park Service that is supposed to be protecting the environment could assimilate such destruction into its policy.

We marched for six kilometres on this 'road' as the sun bared down upon us, meting out its punishment. We finished the last of our water on the final stagger and now my vision started blurring. I tried in vain to lubricate my suede tongue with spittle, and the soles of my feet were tender because they had had so little use these last eighteen months. Hardly even noticing the approach of the car park I ragdolled toward the car.

'Hey, that's not our car,' mumbled Jane through the side of her mouth, trying not to draw attention to us.

'It's not?' Even though I was utterly trounced, I still managed a tiny laugh.

I had broken yet another personal post-head injury record, the second in four days.

That night we slept at 'Fuck Superbowl' for the last time. I had to be at the Banff Mountain Book Festival in Canada in a couple of days so, after hassling Steve yet again to come to Wales, we bade our friends farewell.

We had one day left in the Canyonlands of Utah, so we drove up to the wondrous Arches National Monument, a short way north of Moab. A stocky, helpful, white woman dressed in a dark green uniform with matching brimmed hat assigned us a campsite number. We navigated our car past scores of RVs and found site 31 with its own picnic table.

As Jane stood on the bench to see the view, I attempted to lift her with my one useful arm. I surprised myself momentarily – for I had not lifted a lover for a number of years – at how strong I was. It felt beautiful to hold her there, she looking down and me looking up. Our eyes met in a romantic moment . . . But then I began to sway and, as my hamstring barely functions, I couldn't take a step backward to steady myself. We went down like a felled tree straight onto a tumbleweed. For days afterwards I was picking spikes out of my arse.

Later we took a stroll out to Double-O-Arch. Jane found a 'secret canyon' and beckoned me in. You had to squeeze through the entrance into a room about the size of my house with overhanging, water-worn, bowl-shaped sides. Up the back was a forty-degree slab with a trench in it, obviously the watercourse when it rained. Jane was already setting off on this climb and I felt compelled to follow.

Now, maybe I should have been put off from climbing after the walking stick incident, but that's not me. A new door was very slowly opening. In fact, it was so slow that I can only liken my recovery to that map on the screen on long-haul flights with the position of the plane charted on it. If you stare at the little plane it doesn't move at all but if you ignore it for an hour – in my case four months – and have a snooze, then look again, you'll find you have travelled quite a long way. The only difference is that I cannot ignore my recovery, I have to keep fighting every inch of the way.

I moved up as though working out moves in a chess game, sometimes being quite still for five whole minutes, at times turning around a full 360 degrees without gaining any headway. Sometimes I struggled to leave a foothold gasping and wheezing, with lungs that hadn't had to work for nearly two years, clawing single-handedly at the holdless rock. Then I would slither back down, blindly hoping that my foot was on target, getting awful road rash off the rough rock. But I knew that I was learning afresh and that the habit of fifteen years' practice had effectively to be unlearned.

Jane was a couple of metres above, encouraging me; 'Come on. You've got this far. It'll be a lot harder to get back down now.'

I hovered about seven metres above the flat sandy ground and, looking down, I knew she was right. I froze.

My right leg went rigid and my arm was bent grotesquely in the classic spastic position.

With eyes gently shut I began to compose myself. Shallow breaths . . . Relax.

When I am in a truly difficult situation I never waste my breath on such trivialities as speech so I didn't answer her. No, I thought, it is impossible for me to get back down.

There was no ledge for Jane to stand on like the last time we were climbing in Big Spring Canyon.

'You've only got another metre to this hold and then you're away,' she pointed out.

Looking up there was indeed a large flat hold about the size of a cassette tape box. If I stretched I could reach to just thirty centimetres below it. I began to fight for height, back and footing in the narrow trench for all I was worth. But unlike the last time I actually felt in control. As long as I fought slowly I knew I would be safe. There was no having to pull on a collapsible trekking pole this time.

Stretching up, my four fingers crept onto the flat hold and formed a crimp. It was in the bag. I had done my first in control rock climb. And solo. Sure, it would only be graded Easy or Moderate, fifteen grades easier than I used to climb, but it was a start.

Driving to Salt Lake, Jane and I decided to get a motel room in Price and scrub a week's dirt from our bodies. The unfriendliest landlady in the United States booked us in to what we named the Bates Motel. After sitting in a bath close to boiling point, watching *Little House on the Prairie*, the two of us emerged pink and wrinkly as babies.

We were picked up at Calgary airport and driven to Banff, home of the famous Mountain Film and Book Festival. Directly above the town are snowy mountains where skiers recreate and, if I were prone to dwelling in the past, I would have become depressed at my not being able any more; but I was always useless at skiing anyway.

Herds of elk roamed up and down the pavements and alleyways looking for hapless tourists to injure. But the only injury I sustained was slipping on an icy path leading steeply down from our hotel to the town. My feet shot out from beneath me without any warning and I landed on my back, severely winded. My spastic elbow instinctively threw itself out to save my back from damage but, as it stayed bent, it only crashed onto the floor, threatening to snap my humerus.

On looking up I expected Jane to be holding out her hand with her eyes raised, one hand on her hip. Instead she had her face in her hands and was crying. On my way down I had smacked her in the eye, accidentally I might add, with my flailing ski pole. After that I fell a further four times because Jane didn't want to be anywhere near me. So I went straight into the nearest climbing equipment shop, bought some excellent slip-on crampons and didn't fall on the icy paths any more.

Collecting the Grand Mountain Book Prize for *The Totem Pole* was a dream come true. Walking out onto the stage, the spotlights glaring upon me, all I could hear was the deafening sound of two thousand people clapping. I found myself being presented with a hideous stained-glass, wave-like trophy and a cheque for $2000 Canadian, and instructions to keep the speech brief.

'Thanks to the judges,' I spoke into the microphone. 'Without them I wouldn't be stood here on this stage.'

My leg became rigid and my arm was frozen, bent and out to the side as my slip-on crampons ruined the polished wood floor of the stage.

After I had posed for photos with the other trophy winners, I met my old mate Ed Douglas in the bar.

'That should see you in beer for the evening,' he said.

This was less about my capacity to swill ale, I might add, rather more the state of the Canadian dollar.

A stream of people queued up during a signing session afterwards, some with their own stories of trauma. One woman told me about a huge rock that had fallen on her sister whilst cross-country skiing in the Rockies.

'Was this a long time ago?' I asked.

'Goodness, no. Two weeks ago,' she answered.

'God, I'm sorry to hear that.'

We chatted for a while but I began to feel uncomfortable talking to a grieving person. Not being a trained counsellor, I wasn't prepared for this.

Then a man came by who had a very familiar condition. He was dragging his foot and had a limp left arm.

'What's happened to you then?' I asked, trying to make light of our situations and getting more comfortable in my new roll of agony aunt.

'Oh, I . . . I . . . I . . . had a stroke.'

This man was having difficulty getting his words out. He didn't have a stutter; his speech was slow as he was searching for the words in his confused brain, a problem common to many stroke people and head injuries.

'How long ago?'

'Oh, just a . . . couple of years.'

'So you've still got a lot of healing to do then.'

'I wanted t . . . t . . . to thank you for . . . writing your book,' he said. 'It really clarified things for . . . It helped me see that I wasn't the only one.'

'Thank you,' I said, as a lump formed in my throat.

Out of the hundreds of letters and emails I received after writing *The Totem Pole,* there was one letter in particular that was most moving. It was from a girl whose relationship with her boyfriend had not been working for some time. After an age of deliberation they split up and the very next day he had a car accident. He lapsed into a coma, which he was in for eight weeks, and when he woke up he didn't recall ever splitting up with her. He thought they were still together, still an item.

She did the bravest thing and stayed with him.

She wrote, 'If there's one good thing I do in my life it will be this.'

They seem to have put their differences behind them now and have found a new love for each other.

Later that day Jane and I went for a much needed walk up Tunnel Mountain, a pretty little hill on the edge of Banff. What a release it was to get some aerobic exercise and shake off the cobwebs from the air travel and high living. This was the first 'snowy mountain' I had been up since the accident and I did come a cropper several times as my slip-on crampons balled up with snow. Something I was very interested in was how I would perform on snow. If I were to be a mountaineer, I would inevitably come into contact with the white stuff. But the rubber crampons aren't like the heavy-duty crampons that I would some day need. I would have to wait a few more years – my weak right leg was gaining in strength by the month – before I could experiment with big boots and chunky steel crampons.

The climb took about two hours to the summit, from which the whole white landscape was laid out below us like a Monopoly board. The little town with its pencil line streets and dice for houses, the pipe-cleaner trees and the cars busying themselves as ants do. The only things that didn't appear tiny were the mountains. Like the serrated edge of a saw, the peaks and spires lined up down each side of the valley. I hadn't seen alpine peaks, snowy mountains, for a while and I'd almost forgotten just how much this special kind of vista meant to me. How it feeds the soul. As I gazed at this aggregate of mountains I found myself wanting to climb them all. But I knew they were too difficult. I would have to bide my time.

Tunnel Mountain wasn't a 'real' mountain. It was a sanitized mountain with a fenced path all the way to the top to prevent you from falling off the edge. As I viewed these real mountains an understanding gradually came upon me that I needed to climb them. I would have to be patient, but luckily that is something I know a lot about. We had to turn our backs on that cold little summit, one, I hoped, of many to come, each gaining in altitude and difficulty, and slid back down to the town of Banff. I was momentarily refreshed.

During the evening there was dancing and lots of it. Jane propped me up for two hours while we danced a kind of Lambada to every tune. This is the only way I can dance, holding on for dear life, and staggering occasionally, as I am twirled and spun. Later our team went in search of further dancing and frivolity.

Jane and I shared a taxi with the American bare-foot climbing legend Henry Barber and the fierce warrior of El Cap, Leo Houlding.

When we got out of the cab Leo exclaimed, 'Wait 'til I tell the guys back home that I've shared a taxi with Hot Henry Barber!'

'That's nothing,' said Jane. 'Just wait 'til I tell them he groped me!'

We were then whisked off to Washington DC for the American Alpine Club annual dinner. On landing at

Ronald Reagan airport, we took a taxi to the Hilton where, after a few sakis at a nearby Japanese bar, we hit the hay. The following day we met the President of the AAC, Alison Osius, and took the subway to do our sightseeing. The Lincoln Memorial was smaller than I imagined, and I was struck by how few black tourists were paying homage, compared to the white that were pouring out of buses in one continuous stream.

By far the most heart-rending memorial was that for the Vietnam War. You wouldn't think that 58,000 names on a wall could make you cry but it was the people, some kneeling, some on step-ladders, each with a piece of paper and a pencil, taking a rubbing of the names of their loved ones that left me choked. And then there were the vets, of course, who were now sentenced never to forget.

There were stalls run by vets selling stickers like 'VIET CONG EAT DUNG'. A bearded guy in army fatigues and dark glasses told me about Jane Fonda.

'Yeah, she went running to the fucking national press telling them that American soldiers were fucking killing babies. That's how she started a major anti-Vietnam War movement in the states. Fucking hippies!'

He was getting visibly upset as he went on, 'I bet you know all this though.'

'No, I don't.' Why would he think that I knew anything about Jane Fonda?

'If I saw Jane Fonda now I'd blindfold her an' get a few buddies to execute her by firing squad so that she wouldn't know who killed her, just as it was for all those fucking deserters.'

He was becoming very emotional now. 'Which battalion were you in?'

I couldn't believe it – he thought that I was a vet too.

'I was only three years old then,' I told him. 'I know I've had a hard life but . . .?'

'I thought you was here to remember your fallen buddies.'

He soon lost interest in me when I told him I wasn't in the war.

Feeling deeply sad for these veterans whose whole lives are still consumed by a war that took place over thirty years ago, I momentarily, just momentarily, empathized with them. I too was crippled through no fault of my own. My only sin was, perhaps, being in the wrong place one time too many. Later, back in our room, I rebuked myself. OK, I almost died, but how could I even begin to imagine what these guys had seen? My injury was minuscule compared to the psychological scarring those teenagers endured. Nevertheless the fact remains that I almost died.

At the American Alpine Club that night there was a weighty line-up of speakers, including Bradford Washburn, Tom Hornbein and my old friends Bobbi Bensman and Conrad Anker. Conrad talked movingly of his best friend and climbing partner, Alex Lowe, who had died in an avalanche on Shishapangma. Hobbling up with my too-tight braces, I nearly fell climbing onto the stage.

The reading went well, though it was interesting to discover that the Americans, or perhaps it is only the AAC, are a little more conservative than the Brits and will laugh in different places. A constrained hush reigned as I read of my fellow patient Caroline and how she loves being a spastic so that she can cause a scene whenever and wherever she likes.

> She was in a crowded bar once and she shouted out loud to her boyfriend, 'I NEED A SHIT'. He incidentally has left her. He said that she wasn't the

dollybird he went out with in the first place but a
fat cow now. She retorted that she was still good
in bed though.

When I got back to the hotel room the light on the telephone was flashing. The message was from Ken Wilson,
back in Britain; he had just attended the adjudication cere-
mony of the Boardman Tasker award.

'Well, what can I say,' began the message. 'You've done
it again kiddo. You've cleaned up at Banff and now you've
cleaned up on this side of the Atlantic as well.'

This normally outspoken man who published my first
book *Deep Play* was sounding quite emotional. I was
touched and intoxicated with excitement. Dancing around
the hotel room as well as I could, I gave Jane a one-armed
hug and a smacker.

Jane and I arrived home and as soon as I stepped through
the door I had a seizure; my first in two months. It was as
if my brain was saying, 'Now you're safe, now I can allow
you to have a fit.'

These seizures were becoming less frequent but I didn't
want any at all. When you have a head injury the Driving
and Vehicle Licensing Agency revoke your driving licence.
As long as I was having seizures driving was out, indeed I
had to spend a year fit-free before they would even consider
giving me my licence back. Any jobs that involve driving
or operating machinery were out too. Not that I was particularly interested in a job operating a JCB or being a train
driver, not since I was seven years old anyway, but I wanted
my driving licence back.

All that time in America and Canada I spent fit-free and
then this has to happen. This particular seizure was incredibly

painful; the vat of maggots again. I lay on the bed hyper-ventilating for ten minutes until it slowly disappeared and then I fell into a deep sleep.

The very next morning Jane went to the newsagents to get a morning paper. She returned with an armful that they had saved for me.

'Look at these!' she said. I could sense her anger as she threw the bundle down on the table.

My toast was hanging from my mouth as I gawped at headline after headline. 'CRIPPLED CLIMBER'S LOVE FOR NURSE WHO SAVED HIM', 'SAGA OF MOUNTAIN MAN AND AUSSIE ANGEL OF MERCY', 'KISS HANGER', 'I'VE FALLEN FOR YOU', 'THE SUMMIT OF LOVE', 'ROCKY ROAD TO ROMANCE', 'NURSE FALLS FOR CLIMBER', 'THE INJURED CLIMBER WHO FELL FOR HIS NURSE'.

The media publicity machine had been in full action while we were in the States and our story was in every tabloid and broadsheet. Although I wanted some publicity to promote my book, some of the tabloids didn't even mention *The Totem Pole* or the fact that I had written it.

Jane shook her head and asked, 'What are we going to do?' more to herself than to me.

She hadn't been involved with the media before and was shocked.

'We've been made to look like right plonkers here,' I agreed, shaking my head in dismay.

'Yeah, we look like fame-seeking idiots.'

'I know, we'll write a letter!' This was my answer to everything, from dog shit in the park to global warming, but I seldom got it together.

Then Jane noticed the *Daily Star*'s 'BOULD'ER OVER' headline and began to giggle. Once we had started there was no stopping us. With Jane knelt on the carpet and I sat at the table, the papers strewn across it and spilling onto the floor. We erupted into uncontrollable laughter at the absurdity of it all.

3

TAB: *The Human Condition*

> The years of searching in the dark for a truth that
> one feels but cannot express, the intense desire and
> the alternations of confidence and misgiving, until
> one breaks through the clarity and understanding
> are known only to him who has experienced them.
>
> Einstein – *Ideas and Opinions*

In the summer of 1988 a friend of mine named Ed Stone
suffered a head injury when a rock fell on his head. He
was up climbing on Clogwyn Du'r Arddu, a hallowed dark
cliff on the shoulder of the highest mountain in Wales,
Snowdon. A party of what we full-timers used to call weekend climbers knocked the rock off a ledge, about fifty
metres above him.

He was hanging there for a while until our mutual friend
Ben Pritchard (no relation) managed to lower him to the
ground. The Royal Air Force evacuated him by helicopter
off the mountain. Ed spent just a couple of days in hospital
for observations and was then discharged.

Very slow mentally for months afterwards, sometimes he
would pause for whole minutes just to answer simple
questions and sleep overcame him at the slightest inclination. I remember being quite unsympathetic; mocking his
docility was a favourite pastime of mine.

In the early nineties Ed died in a long fall, from the opposite flank of the same mountain. He went out for an afternoon's ice climbing, on his own, and fell 200 metres. We never quite knew how it happened. Maybe he hit a patch of rotten ice or made some mistake. Maybe a rock or piece of ice fell on him from above. In this final fall, Ed suffered severe head injuries.

How I wish he were here now so that I could apologize for my micky-taking and to empathize, saying, 'Yes it's terrible, isn't it. Now I understand.'

A bizarre feeling overcame me. It was like when I first had my accident; I would fall asleep in a crowded café or, more than once, on the bus, thereby missing my stop. When I went to my bed in the evening I would sleep eleven hours, where I would usually only need eight. I could only put this down to having finished everything to do with *The Totem Pole* and all the publicity for it. I now found myself at a loss for something to do.

The Climbers' Club were expecting that I would be editing the upcoming climbing guidebook to Gogarth, a giant sea cliff and my favourite place to climb in the whole world. But I became easily confused and couldn't get interested in the project. I used to love Gogarth more than girlfriends but I hadn't been there for six months and I could feel myself wondering why.

The cliffs, I was sure, would still look very impressive and I could still appreciate the immense swathes of sea pink and bladder campion but there was something missing now and I couldn't quite put my finger on what that was. As difficult as it was for me to admit, I just didn't feel a part of the climbing community any more. In fact, from time to time, I would become jealous of that community, all the climbers going off for their day's exercise and me, who was once at the fore, now left out.

Jealousy doesn't serve any purpose, at least that's what I kept telling myself, but I couldn't help myself sometimes. If I was to get better and preserve what sanity I had left, de-cluttering my life was essential, down-sizing the amount of 'stuff' in it. So, painful though it was, the Gogarth project had to go.

Having said that, I agreed to present a photographic exhibition with Nigel Shepherd, an alpine guide and author, at the Electric Mountain Visitor Centre in Llanberis. 'Through a Climber's Eye' was the title of the exhibition. We each showed our best mountain and climbing photographs. After a month, when we were taking the photographs down, Nigel saw something written in the visitor's book. Amidst an anonymous ranting monologue was this sentence: 'Just because you have a hole in your head doesn't mean you have an appreciation of nature and images.'

For a moment I felt hurt and confused. Vindictive bastard, I thought.

Everyone is entitled to his or her own artistic opinion but I hadn't even had my head injury when I shot those images. In fact I had not taken any pictures since my accident because all cameras are right-handed so unuseable for me. I was left pondering the identity of this insanely jealous wretch and angered by the comment. Tens of thousands of people visit the Electric Mountain every year, so it was impossible to say who wrote those seething words.

Hatred is a common response to persons with a dis-ability. Some members of the able-bodied public, more than we would like to admit, have a fear of what they consider to be abnormal or what they do not understand and this fear comes to the surface as hate.

Quite a few times I have been verbally abused, called a 'spaz', or boys will mimic my walk and then laugh between themselves. It is exactly the same mechanism at work with racism, homophobia and misogyny. At least on this and another occasion, when I was physically attacked in my wheelchair, the hate was obvious and out in the open. Anyway, the anger from this visitor comment soon passed and was replaced with a sad feeling, for those words were written from a lack of understanding.

It is the more sinister, unconsciously patronising attitude of some people, of which the 'Does he take sugar?' syndrome is only one aspect, that I find truly offensive.

A chap in the pub, who obviously thought he was paying me a great compliment, said, 'I think you're really amazing to have overcome so much and to do so well.'

I wondered why I had become angry. His comment might sound harmless enough in itself and it did take a whole year to unravel the knot of why it produced this effect in me.

I used to say that that accident was just about the best thing that ever happened to me, for it gave me a new mission in life and taught me how to treat people more humanely. Most of all it taught me to cherish life and never ever waste time. I used to say that I was not just putting a brave face on things and that was how I felt. I just 'overcame so much', as the chap put it, because I had to.

At the root of his remark and countless others, for I get them just about every day, is the unconscious, deep-seated opinion that my injury must be appalling and my state pitiable. But it isn't appalling and I don't want anyone's pity.

Apart from the funny walk, I am not a different person. Inside I am still a climber, still think like a climber, still study five metre high rubble pile cliffs by the side of the road, and I will continue to climb, at whatever level, Easy, Moderate, Difficult, disability or no disability.

It is the hidden assumptions about me by some people that really jar. I can hear these people who stare asking silently, 'Don't you yearn to be normal? 'Can you even get an erection?' And others saying, 'I bet he's incontinent,' and, 'Don't give up hope, a cure might be just around the corner.'

There have been several remarks made to Jane about how handy it is being a nurse because she can clean up my mess. She hates that and says, 'Why can't some people see that I married you for love and not for any dodgy motive like neurosis?'

Obviously these are the people who do not know Jane or me very well. But others who know us almost better than anyone have said to her, 'You must be a saint in disguise.' Even my mother has commented on how great it is that Jane is looking after me.

I have heard some friends say that they would rather be dead than disabled. I say to them now, wait until you are disabled, because you will be some time in your life, that is almost a certainty, then decide. There is a name that the disabled have for everyone else, TABs, meaning Temporarily Able-Bodied, which is the ideal description of the human condition. Pain is normality. We are all destined to become a cripple at some time or other. The best we can hope for is that we evade suffering until we are old, and some of us might but not many. Anyhow there are very few that can't get some kind of fulfilment with, or even from, their disability.

The visitors' book mysteriously disappeared shortly after we noticed that entry.

* * *

One day I saw a fellow with a mullet, riding what looked like a machine from the future. This was a tricycle with a difference. With two wheels at the front and a single drive wheel at the back, one rides it practically lying on one's back. A tingle of excitement passed through me. I felt I might be able to use one of these recumbent tricycles. I saw this fellow riding by again and again. One could only see the yellow flag, used as a signal to traffic, above the window level as he pulled up outside Pete's Eats, our local café. One day he came in and over a pint of tea I learnt the rider's name was Robin. After our brew he took me to the car park for a test drive.

Reclining in the bucket seat, I tried to work the pedals but, because the hamstring was so weak on my right leg it repeatedly fell from its pedal. But I noticed these were cleat pedals that special cycling shoes clipped into.

'Can I have your shoes, mate?' I appealed to Robin.

Leaving him on the tarmac in just his stocking feet, off I went. Working up to speed I cycled to the end of the car park and back again and then there and back and once again there and back. I could do it! I could ride this strange contraption!

Quite suddenly that feeling in the pit of my stomach, like when one goes to the end of a high diving board and peers over the edge, gripped me. I was falling for this invention. There and then, I knew that I was on the verge of something fresh and stimulating.

'How much do you want for it?' I asked Robin, unable to conceal my excitement.

The question was in jest of course, so I was taken aback by his answer.

'Well, it is for sale. I'm upgrading to a new racing model.'

'Wow, I'll buy it. I don't care how much it is.'

'Five hundred quid?'

'Five hundred it is.' I would have to sell some more of my redundant climbing equipment.

'That's settled then. It's yours.'

A few days later, after buying myself a pair of cleat shoes, I rode the recumbent tricycle to the Cromlech boulders, just a few kilometres to half way up the Llanberis Pass. But it is uphill all the way. The wind blowing through my hair on the way down was as if I had been released from prison. Speeding around corners my old climbing mate Gwion had difficulty keeping up with me as he was riding a normal sit-up-and-beg bicycle. These recumbents can freewheel down-hill much faster because of the more aerodynamic shape.

I have since met numerous riders of recumbents, some disabled, some not, though they are ideally suited to people with spastic limbs. When one recumbent passes another there is an understanding that we are riding superior machines.

There was a cycle race that I'd heard people talking about for years. The Snowdon Bike Hike follows the Snowdon marathon route for fifty kilometres up the gruelling Pass of Llanberis, down the Nant Gwynant, a freewheeling joy, and up to Rhyd Ddu. I had never taken much interest in this charity cycle race because I was so obsessed with climbing but now I would take it seriously.

The race in aid of the National Children's Home for Wales was going to take place on 8 March. It was 10 January already so I had my work cut out to gain the fitness required to complete such a feat. Next time I wanted to go to three-quarters of the way up the pass. But on 17 January I made it all the way to Pen-y-Pass, the very top. It was an unexpected success, as I imagined I would turn back at the three-quarters point but I felt strong and just had to go for it. The ride up did take a long-time though and we arrived at the summit of the pass in the dark. Two other long-time climbing friends, Noel and Trevor, escorted me. (I need an escort: if there is a right-hand corner I cannot signal.) We were in such a rush to get out there cycling that we'd forgotten our bike lights and we didn't have a lamp between us.

Noel joked that it wasn't the first time we had got to the top in darkness. We were forever getting to the top of climbs in the dark. It was a common story for us to get benighted at Gogarth and have to climb out by the flashing beam from the lighthouse, which only swept around every thirty seconds. So one would have to use the couple of seconds of light to make a move and study the rock ahead, and then stay stock-still for half a minute on tiny holds. This way climbers would ascend in increments and top out in complete darkness.

It was a Sunday and one of those rare blue-sky days in Wales. I recall it was a Sunday because all the chapel bells were ringing as Tone and I drove to Malltraeth on Ynys Mon (Anglesey) where we had decided to do a ten-mile cycle through the woods. It was to test the trike to the limit, getting bogged down in soft sand and having to ride a kilometre through axle-deep sea water. Tone was on a normal bike and he got his feet wet above the ankles. I was completely drenched, effectively having to sit in the water and get sprayed from three wheels.

There was many a time my wheels just spun in the silt and Tone would have to push me along, me helping, for what it was worth, on the pedals. But perhaps the crowning moment was him having to pull me backward through the knee-deep water, me with a sodden backside and not knowing where I was going.

In mid-February it started to rain and rain and rain, as only it can in Wales. Living in one of those dark terraced houses that don't seem to let any light in, I thought I was going mad. Seasonal Affective Disorder had begun to creep into my state and added to this was the fact that I couldn't do any exercise. Never mind the climbing wall, I couldn't even go to the gym or swimming pool.

I could feel the paranoia creeping into my mind. 'Why doesn't anyone come to see me . . . They're all in the pub without me . . . I haven't got any real friends . . . They're all just acquaintances that I used to climb and socialize with.'

Deep down I knew this not to be the case and that it was just the rain and the fact that I couldn't go out training on my tricycle. I knew it would pass but I still missed climbing desperately. I supposed I always would.

Then one day the sun shone. Jane escorted me up Llanberis Pass as far as the boulders and then cut me loose on my first solo mission. I was worried because indicating is impossible with one functioning arm, which always has to stay on the controls. I ended up nodding frantically to a bus that had stopped in the oncoming lane because I wanted to turn across it. The driver must have thought I was seriously ill or having some kind of attack; he wouldn't have been far wrong.

I had a pile of fried food and a chocolate slice at the café on the summit and raced back down the pass. It never ceased to thrill me, banking hard on corners in a sometimes desperate attempt to stop myself from crossing the white line into the oncoming traffic. My yellow flag was all that was visible above the chest-high dry stone walls, so if a motorist failed to see it I could get squashed. Still, I thought it was worth the risk to get a little adrenaline rush. It is what makes me tick, even after all I had been through.

The cycling successes continued as, late in February, I travelled thirty-five kilometres over mountain passes and down dales. An entourage, the keen team of Jane, Noel, Ann, Gwion and Sandy, escorted me. The day was crisp and sharp, bright and snowy on the tops. As I was pedalling furiously a special clarity settled upon me and I became intensely happy. I could still participate in some activities with my friends. It was what I had been longing for. Not just gentle strolls in the hills, for that isn't what I was built for, but adrenaline-filled activities like downhill biking at sixty kilometres per hour.

This tricycle had revolutionized my life. It made it possible to get out there and go visiting, feel the G force of cornering fast, get some wind through my lank hair and, dare I say it, compete. I always scorned competition but now I was disabled I rather fancied the idea of pitting my skills against able-bodied folk. Perhaps it was an inferiority complex on my part, having to prove my worth in society. I really didn't know. And still don't.

I was aiming to make it to the Cwellyn Arms, a pub in the Rhyd Ddu valley, which hosts the Bike Hike. As I struggled up the final long hill out of Beddgelert, I gasped to Gwion, who was hanging back with me, 'Bloody hell, this is hard going. I'll never manage the Bike Hike.' I was tiring so quickly.

'Just take your time. This isn't the race yet.'

When I got to the pub Ali brought me out a pint while I was still sitting in my bucket seat.

Gwion then brought something to my attention: 'Do you know that you've been pedalling with your parking brake on all the way up that hill?'

I felt like a right tool.

Just before my precious cycle race I had an appointment

with Colin in a clinic in Clatterbridge. He pushed and pulled my ankle and knee, elbow and wrist and then scribbled some notes in my file. He prescribed Tizanidine for me, an anti-spasticity drug, which relaxes *all* ones' muscles. But I didn't want *all* my muscles relaxed, just some of them on my right side. I was willing to try anything though, if there was the tiniest chance of regaining some lost function in my right arm.

Why I didn't have access to Tizanidine the previous year I didn't quite comprehend. Learned paralysis is very real and, after a few months of not moving, a muscle can forget how to function. The synapses in one's nerves lose the ability to fire through neglect. A good example of this is the Indian yogi who put his arm above his head twenty years ago and swore never to bring it down as an act of supreme will power. After a year of the arm being elevated he would find it nigh on impossible to get his arm down again. He forgets how to use the limb.

Researching on the Internet (doctors hate a know-it-all patient) I could find no reference for the use of Tizanidine on TBIs (Traumatic Brain Injury). As I studied the screen, I only read of its uses for multiple sclerosis patients. It was only made obtainable in Britain in 1999, even though it has been available on the continent for ten years. So maybe that is why it was so new to brain injury cases.

Collecting the yellow box of Tizanidine from the Llanberis chemist, I began to feel uneasy and, on reading the list of possible side effects, I started to panic. There were the usual nasties: nystagmus, ataxia, diarrhoea, somnolence, hypotension, nausea, neurologic seizures and anorexia. These side effects I was used to reading on drug packets: they like to cover all possible chances, however unlikely, just in case.

But then there were some extremely bizarre conditions; megaloblastic anemia, agranulocytosis, hirsutism (thankfully 'rare' was bracketed alongside this), severe exfoliative dermatitis, psychotic reaction, moon face and buffalo hump. I had to start with three pills per day for a week and slowly work up, week by week, to thirty-four pills a day!

Popping my first pill, the feeling was as if I was coming up on magic mushrooms, the stomach-cramping pain, slightly altered reality and a vague fever. We were due to go out for dinner to a relative stranger's house. Neither Jane nor I knew Cathy Woodhead very well and there's me feeling like I'm on a hallucinogenic drug. Jane started to have one of her panic attacks while I gazed at the room in amazement as it changed dimensions before my eyes. Cathy served a half avocado for a starter and watched with consternation as I chased it around my plate.

That night, about 4 am, I awoke to an incredible pain in my right foot. I knew this pain well. That foot in the bucket of maggots again. Since Colin had upped my dose of tegretol, my epilepsy control, I hadn't had a seizure for three months and I thought, foolishly in retrospect, that I would never have one again. It sometimes takes years of tinkering with a patient's dose before they get it right.

It was the Tizanidine that caused the fits. I knew it was. How else could I go for three months without and then this? Worry gripped me as I thought about the cycle race in less than a week. I vowed to stop taking the little white pills there and then after I had only taken two. In the morning Jane and I laughed about how we could get rich selling the tablets on the street as the new party drug. I threw them in the rubbish bin.

Clatterbridge was a place to which I vowed never to return but I found myself drawn back for all sorts of reasons, this perhaps being the oddest. I was to perform my reading from *The Totem Pole* in front of an audience consisting of the nurses, doctors and therapists who aided my recovery. There was Vera, the head nurse, Lise, my Norwegian occupational therapist, Ann, the social worker, Shirley, the kick-boxing nurse, Dr Shakespeare and Paula who took me to Liverpool for my CAT scans. There were other nurses too, whose faces I recognized but couldn't quite place, though I knew they were instrumental in getting me well.

I hadn't done my reading for a while and was unprepared for the hysterical laughter in the audience as I talked of the 'Big Nurses' at Clatterbridge. Even 'Spherical Man' who I described lighting the summer barbecue at the unit, was there.

He came and talked to me afterwards. 'I'm Spherical Man,' he said. 'Pleased to meet you.'

For a moment I didn't quite understand him. My confused mind didn't know what he was talking about. Then the penny dropped. All the people I'd basically insulted in *The Totem Pole* were in the audience and there was nothing I could do about it. But judging by their laughter, most of them were amused by it.

Someone from the darkness asked me if I was accident-prone. One could say that I was because of my two other misadventures: smashing myself up at Gogarth and falling sixty-metres and breaking my back on a Scottish icefall. But really the Totem Pole catastrophe was a fluke. It could have happened to anyone who was in that position. It was a one in a million chance, at least. However if you put someone at the bottom of a cliff as often as I have been mooching around at the base of cliffs or mountains then it is more likely that something will occur than if you had stayed sitting on the sofa.

I know you're thinking that is obvious. But this is just one of those things that an accident victim keeps going over and over in the mind until he or she arrives at some sort of calm rationale.

'How could you smell the seaweed on your first ride out of hospital without a sense of smell?' came another poignant question from the back.

I couldn't answer her. Then a slow realization forced itself upon me that the smell of seaweed on the dockside during my first ride out in my wheelchair was an elaborate mental illusion.

'Wow! I must have imagined it.'

Ever since that rock split my head open my brain has had no concept of smell and I can only taste food if it is heavily spiced. It took me some time to work this out, as I think I can still discern the scent of flowers; plucking the perfume from a map in the mind in a sort of mental hypothesis. The briny, musty seaweed smell was so real that I thought I could smell it but in reality I could not. If I do not have the visual prompt as to what aroma you present me with then I couldn't tell you.

It was about that time I had a most curious visitation. There was a weak knock at the door. I opened it and was confronted by a couple, completely drained of colour, standing there on the pavement. The woman blurted out nervously that her son had had a climbing accident and he had been in a coma for three and a half months. I hurriedly put my duvet on and escorted them to the café. They told me of how he had his brain injury in Scotland in July 1999 on the North Face of Ben Nevis.

They described how they were in a state of despair as a consultant told them their son might not wake up or a doctor told them not to hold their hopes too high for him walking. This smacked of my injury and of how certain members of the medical profession reacted to my situation.

They were blind to a single ray of hope. Is this complete and utter negativity something they learn in medical schools? Give the worst possible scenario so that the hapless relatives will be let down softly if what they want for their child or brother or mother doesn't come about? Or are some of them just in need of a few basic lessons in communication?

Don't get me wrong. I'm not saying all in the medical profession are bad communicators and I have had some very thoughtful nurses, doctors and consultants.

It would have been far more acceptable for a doctor or consultant to say to me, 'It is more than likely you will recover some function in your limbs,' than what one told me: 'You should be glad that you have two moving limbs because some people cannot move all four of theirs!' What right has a doctor to play God like that? OK, so they may know more than us but they don't know it all. It would be an impossibility to know everything there is to know about the brain.

I found myself getting angry on the couple's behalf but took care not to show it. By way of support I tried to put their minds at ease a little, telling them that it was still very early days as far as recovery for the brain goes and that he would *never* stop improving. Giving them a reading list, I told them to let me know how their son was getting on.

People came to me now from all over Britain and even further afield expecting advice and counselling. I have to tread very carefully because I do believe that, by example, I do have something to say to these grief-stricken people. But, on the other hand, I am no professional in anything, except writing, so what I say could be dangerous.

As if to substantiate the claim that improvement never ceases 5 February 2000 was a day that will be with me for as long as I live. I moved my pinky. On this auspicious day I was sitting in the armchair in my little house and checking how much movement I had on my right side. This I do frequently, several times a day. Toes . . . Ankle . . . Knee . . . Shoulder . . . Elbow . . . Wrist . . . Nothing. I then started with my thumb, no. Index finger, no. Middle finger, no. Ring finger, no. Little finger. . . I couldn't believe my eyes! Ever so slowly and with great strain on my part, the finger straightened and curled and straightened and curled. One, two and three times.

When I yawned I was used to my fingers extending, an associated reaction that I have no control over, but this! I had achieved extension in my little finger, straightened it out and bent it in again under my own volition. I was doing it. This may not sound like much but after two years of straining and achieving only flexion this was a big step. I was blown away.

Excitedly I went to show Jane. 'Jane, Jane, look at this. I can move my pinky. I can wiggle it.'

'OK. Go on, show me,' she said, kneeling down in front of me.

I went to demonstrate my achievement to her but nothing happened. There was nothing there. I felt like a fraud.

'I knew something like this would happen,' I remarked. When I go to show Jane or my physiotherapist, limbs either go to sleep or get stage fright.

'Oh well, don't get sad. Even if I didn't see it move, it's still a sign of things to come.'

Not that I could do anything with just my little finger but, as Jane said, I did think of it as a sign that, one by one, the other fingers would 'wake up'. Five years later this is the only such 'event' I have ever had. The extension of my pinky only took place on the one occasion and, as for my other fingers, there has been nothing but spastic flexion as there always is. But one can still live in hope and keep trying.

People were repeatedly telling me what an inspiration I was and saying to me, 'Just stick at it.'

But it wasn't easy being an inspiration all the time and I became sick of having to 'just stick at it' every minute of every hour, for two years. Sometimes I just wanted to say, 'Bugger this,' and slob out, become a couch potato, but there was something in me, a little homunculus in my brain, that kept on repeating, 'One step at a time. Take it one step at a time.'

When I wavered I had a memory of one Steve Fonyo, a Canadian metal-head, who lost his leg at age twelve due to cancer and to prevent himself becoming a couch potato, as so many amputees do, decided to run the breadth of Canada. And so he schemed and he trained and he planned and eventually, in 1985, he ran 8000 kilometres across five and a half time zones. From the East Coast to the West he ran, across vast plains and the Rocky Mountains, winning the hearts of a nation and raising thirteen million dollars for charity.

But once he had completed this gargantuan feat he felt at a loss for what to do next. He had achieved more than he or anyone thought possible. How could he better that? He grew bored and lazy and put on weight. He started to drink and fell foul of the law. There is always a risk of losing direction for any disabled person; it takes a huge amount of will power just to look after yourself.

It took a fair amount of will power to get out of bed on the day of the Bike Hike. A mild fever and headache gripped me, I was so nervous. This ride had become a mental albatross around my neck; I had trained so hard, and I was terrified by it.

Nightmares of having to pull out of the race plagued me. In one particularly gruesome dream I crashed on one of the tight hairpins that lead down the mountain pass. Not able to hold the road – I was travelling at a ridiculous speed – I went out of control on the tight bend. My body scraped down the stone wall flenching the skin and muscles from my face and revealing the white bone of my skull. A hideous dream. From ominous beginnings the fever turned out to be psychosomatic.

I had never been in a race before. Though it was in fact just a charity ride with no pistol-shooting start or ribbon to punch through at the end, I liked to think of it as a race. At forty-five kilometres the Bike Hike was the longest distance I would ever have cycled thus far in my life, never mind post-head injury. I was never much of a cyclist. Before my accident I was never much of anything except a climber.

As we set off from the Cwellyn Arms, Gwion, Trevor and Noel stayed back to escort me, as I set a leisurely pace, while the girls sped off in a peloton. We formed a rear peloton. There was no sign of my fever now as I chatted to the guys about all things inconsequential. The first challenge was the steep but short hill of Ceunant but, as this was a ride I performed regularly, it didn't pose any particular problems. If anything was to be an obstacle it was the sizeable Llanberis Pass. From the village of Nantperis, at the foot of the pass, to the top, Pen-y-Pass, is approximately 600 metres over two kilometres. 'The pass', as it is known to locals, is steep by anyone's reckoning.

Whilst grinding up the pass we were abused twice: once by a motorcyclist who obviously thought we were going too slow. On a tight blind bend he suicidally sped past and I was convinced that his leathers brushed me. When he had overtaken us he made thrusting movements with his limp, gloved hand, as if to shout, 'WANKERS!'

'Bloody Suzuki rider!' I shouted back, much to Gwion and Noel's amusement, but I doubt whether he would have heard me over the lawnmower whine of the engine.

Trevor tried to catch him – Trevor is know for his volatility and if he had done, God help him – but even a Suzuki is too much for a push-bike.

A little while later a mini bus full of squadies overtook us with the 'very funny' bare arses poking out of the side windows routine.

I shouted to Gwion, who was twenty yards ahead of me, 'Slap one!' But he didn't hear in time. Probably a good thing, as if the bus had decided to stop and the squadies all piled out we would have been cycling back down the way we'd come up.

When we rounded Pen-y-Pass it was unseasonably fine in the mountains; the perfect day for a bike race. Now for the fun part – 700 metres of downhill to make the descent of Nant Gwynant into Beddgelert. The boys couldn't keep up with me as I hurtled along – in control at all times of course – sometimes struggling to keep the trike on my side of the white lines.

'Slow down! Slow down!' I could hear Noel cautioning as I sped around another hairpin, down into the depths of the valley.

Gwion just laughed his dirty Sid James laugh. It was just great to see him and everyone sparkling with happiness, diamonds in their eyes as they burnt down the hill. The challenge of life, in my opinion, is to make all days like this and to always take the road of greater difficulty, for happiness and difficulty so often go hand in hand. The tricycle got up onto two wheels whilst rounding more than one corner.

As we thought we were coming last, we forewent the traditional delicious ice creams in Beddgelert and raced straight through the busy village. I lost control of my leg as we climbed the long hill towards Rhyd Ddu and Gwion continued to laugh. The knee just fell out to the side and, when pushed back to a more normal pedalling position it, would then fall the other way.

Noel became bored with riding so slowly and blasted off to catch up with the girls. I expected to be last, nobody there to welcome us in, tumble weeds blowing across the deserted street, that sort of thing. But by a miracle we weren't. There were two fourteen-year-old girls behind us who, Gwion joked, were probably snogging some local youths under the bridge at Beddgelert when we cycled past.

Gwion helped me out of my bucket seat and said in his North Walean accent, extending the vowels and going heavy on the consonants, 'Bloody good effort, Paul.'

Meanwhile Noel handed me a pint of Speckled Hen. 'Cheers,' he said, clinking my glass 'And well done.'

The Hen didn't even touch the sides.

We collected our certificates in the pub and I moulded myself into the ever-so-comfy seats. By the third pint I couldn't walk, so with an arm around Gwion I spilled out into the car park. The Bike Hike was a milepost in the long road of healing for me.

Just a couple of days later I had to visit London to sit on the MEF Screening Committee. The Mount Everest Foundation was created in 1954 and is a grant-giving body that sits twice a year. There was so much money created by the first ascent of Everest, with book sales and lectures, that they had to do something with it and what better than to give the interest to exploratory expeditions going to all parts of the earth. The MEF has been responsible for handing out cash to needy expeditions ever since. It feels like one is being incredibly altruistic, as giving twenty-eight thousand pounds of someone else's money away usually does.

When I'm in London I stay with my old friend and climbing partner Sean Smith and his partner Tori Bridges; this time the occasion was a special one. The couple had just been blessed with a new daughter and this was cause for celebration. Knocking on the door, bottle of champagne in hand, I was welcomed inside. After dining and toasting baby Maya, Sean brought out a bottle of vodka from a recent trip to Poland.

At first I was wary. The last time I had had a night out with Sean – in Patagonia – it ended up with us getting kicked out of some late night bar in someone's front room because we couldn't pay for Sean's drinks. I had to drag him out into the dawn and leave him on the pavement.

But he lured me into his web and the next thing I remember it was 8.30 in the morning and I was supposed to be at the Royal Geographical Society at eight o'clock.

I hurriedly pulled on my pants and ran, as well as I could, out of the house without even my customary two cups of tea. The tube is always confusing to me, more so with a massive hangover. Bursting through the door at 10.30 I apologized for being late and said that I'd had a fit on the street. That produced the effect of the whole room feeling sorry for me. I took my place at the table and Shane Winser, representing the RGS, brought me a glass of water. Guilt flooded over me. It was too late to change my story now.

The next thing I knew I was attempting to hold a conversation with Chris Bonington but I was very aware that I must be breathing vodka fumes all over him. It was only later that I found out that vodka doesn't smell, unlike gin, which is why it is good for secret drinkers. Anyway, I could feel myself beginning to sweat and to turn green. Suddenly I knew I was going to vomit on him and had to extract myself from the conversation and rush out of the room. The next minute I was driving the porcelain bus in the hallowed bathroom of the RGS.

That evening on the train journey home I had a long talk with Lindsay Griffin, the Chairman of the MEF. We discussed our injuries: Lindsay had a huge rock fall on his leg in Mongolia and was trapped for several hours.

'The rock smashed my tib and fib,' he explained. 'I had to rig up a pulley from the slings and bits of rope I was carrying and lasso the top of the boulder and then rig up a pulley system to try and escape. Anyway I couldn't.'

Lindsay now walks with a pronounced limp and we made a comical sight hobbling down the platform at Euston station. We were looking through the windows, faces pressed against the glass, trying to spot table seats that weren't taken. Neither of us is very good at sitting in normal seats. Lindsay towers above me and I'm over 180 centimetres tall. He is possibly the tallest, thinnest human being in Britain and cannot bend his right knee. My right hamstring doesn't work, so I have trouble bending my right knee. Anyway, we eventually found one.

Lindsay started talking about how there was no incentive for your normal 'man in the street' to get better after an injury.

'I'm talking any kind of injury but especially industrial ones. In many cases it is the first time these blokes can relax. Just think about it, you've been working flat out in a factory all your life then wallop, a machine lands on you. You instantly see pound signs. You can start drawing benefit while you await your court case. You may get a hundred K or more and never have to work again, but just as long as you don't get better.'

'So what you're saying is that it would be better if the government didn't have Severe Disablement Benefit, Disability Living Allowance and Industrial Injuries Compensation?'

'In some ways, yes. There'd be more incentive to get better. But that would be Nazism, wouldn't it?'

After spending so much time in cities recently, I really needed a mountain hit. So Jane and I went to Bethesda and parked high up in Gerlan, a village on the edge of a vast high moor.

The first half of the trek into the heart of the Carneddau was like wading through treacle. I told Jane it was a good path and that she didn't need to bring her hiking boots. But when we arrived, it was very different to what my ailing memory had remembered. At least a mile of bog lay before us. Now this wouldn't normally be of much concern to me. I would have eaten knee-deep bogs for breakfast but I now found bogs very difficult, in fact the most laborious terrain I could imagine (well, other than scree). But I thought, that's OK, it'll be good training if nothing else. A challenge; that's how I saw the bog and how I saw everything now.

Cloud that was wreathing the gendarmes of Ysgolion Duon slowly lifted to reveal the climbs that I'd once ascended with athletic ease.

'There, look!'

We gazed at the great cliff of Llech Ddu and the classic line of the Grooves, which I had climbed just before I flew off to Australia on that ill-fated journey. I was draped momentarily in melancholy, as if the cloud that had minutes before wreathed the cliff had now descended upon me.

On the walk back home I fell a few times on the sodden earth and in my feather jacket I became hot and bothered. I tried to hide my anger from Jane but in my paranoid state I believe she noticed. Seeing these cliffs again brought back some good memories and that was painful. Try as I might, I was finding it incredibly difficult to accept that I wasn't going to be much of a climber ever again.

On the return I noticed seven dead sheep and a Carneddau pony carcass. It was strange how I hadn't noticed these on the way in.

More than ever now I threw myself into my cycling, determined to improve. On an old railway line on the shore of Llyn Padarn, a lake by Llanberis, I would sprint for a hundred metres and then relax for a hundred and then sprint again and relax to the end, about two kilometres. That really got the quads working, especially my lazy one. I also trained on hills. There was one hill, one of the steepest in the area, at the top of our street. Clegir is the drunk driver's route back to Llanberis after a night out in Caernarfon and is a winding, single-track surfaced lane.

On the first attempt I managed just over fifty minutes to the summit but quickly reduced that to half an hour. Most of Snowdonia was laid out before me from the top of this hill. There, to the east, were the hazy rounded mams of the Carneddau, and to the south, the flat tops of the Glyderau. The shapely peaks of the Snowdon massif lay to the south-west. Between the Snowdon massif and the Glyderau was hewn the deep gash of Llanberis Pass, which I pitted myself against with renewed vigour.

In mid-March I made my best time ever, sprinting up the pass on my trike, just over six kilometres in ninety-three minutes of sheer drudgery. That may not sound very impressive until one has seen this hill, and me. Admittedly there was a gale blowing from behind me all the way up, which aided my ascent somewhat. Coming back down again, which is usually the best, most relaxing element of these hill trials, was unusually difficult. Pedalling down a one in three hill, indeed!

Bernard, my dad, lives in Blackpool, Lancashire and Jane drove me up there to visit him. He invited us to the Club, which was an education for Jane.

In the beginning I thought it sweet to watch my dad twirling Jane around on the dance floor but then, as my eyes glazed over, I remembered all at once all the occasions that I had danced well with a partner. With Jane I would never be able to dance fluidly. Sure I could sway slowly around, leaning heavily on her, but that was about it.

When the dance was over and my dad sat down, Jane, unable to stop as ever, came over and asked me to dance. For the first time since my injury embarrassment overcame me and I found myself frozen in my seat. I had a hideous picture in my mind of how my body actually presented itself to other people, especially my dad.

Dad was always the epitome of physical fitness; as a kid, I remember him playing football with us in our driveway and swimming in the Mediterranean in Spain. At over seventy he still looks extremely fit and works all hours on 'the plot'.

And here was I, a cripple in his eyes. How could I dance in front of him? I couldn't bear to have this very proud man feeling sorry for me, so I told Jane that I would sit this one out. I think she was in tune because she didn't try to push it, she just let it drop and came and sat by me.

Interspersed with the dancing in the Working Men's Club were tombolas and bingo and a sexist, racist comedian. My dad and Anne, his wife, won eighty quid while Jane and I fumbled blindly about the bingo card.

Later that same month I had to do a reading for an outdoor shop in Brighton. After my presentation I invited questions from the audience.

'Why were you not wearing a helmet?' a woman asked rather aggressively from the back of the audience.

Somebody invariably questions me on this matter and for the first few times I answered rather guiltily that I did not know. Now I had an answer to give them.

'I wouldn't have been wearing a helmet on a sea cliff anyway. I never did before so why would I suddenly start then? I would wear a helmet in the mountains where there is a greater danger of a chunk of ice or a rock falling on my head. Sometimes, in the Himalaya, it feels like you're in combat, dodging pieces of ice every few minutes, from dice-size to milk-crate-size. Even a dice-sized rock can go straight through your skull if travelling at terminal velocity.'

I was rather proud at the fluidity of my speech. I thought about Alex MacIntyre on the South Face of Annapurna but omitted to mention this example. On that occasion the stone went straight through his helmet and he died almost instantly.

'I can't remember ever wearing one whilst rock climbing. I'm not saying you shouldn't wear a helmet. It all comes down to personal choice. It's just that I chose not to.'

I was pleased with my answer.

There are two opposing arguments about helmets: the first is that if you wear a helmet it can restrict movement, make you less aware of your surroundings and generally take more risks. The second argument acknowledges these points but states that it is better to have slightly restricted head movement than to be just another statistic.

The truth is that you cannot foresee a rock or a piece of equipment falling from the heavens, whether it is in the mountains or on a rock face.

Some climbers, including James Van Gelder, the guy in Tasmania who performed surgery on my brain, thought that, had I been wearing a helmet, I might have broken my neck. The argument goes like this: a rock falling from twenty-five metres is travelling at nigh on terminal velocity and judging by the position of the hole in my head, left parietal area (left-hand side), it could have struck a glancing blow. A glancing blow could have pushed my head severely to the right, thereby snapping my neck and maybe my spinal cord. This in turn could have given me quadraplegia (a paralysis from the neck down) with no hope for recovery, a much more serious outcome compared to hemiplegia. Alternatively, the rock breaking my neck could have simply killed me outright. No one will ever be able to answer that question.

The same debate rages over the wearing of cycle helmets. If you wear a cycle helmet some cyclists say that you ride more dangerously, disregarding traffic and obstacles. Whereas if you don't wear one you will ride more safely, killing your speed. But just like rocks from heaven, a drunken motorist can appear at any time.

At the same show a guy in a wheelchair asked if I had become more spiritual since my accident and my answer was a bit weak I thought.

Certainly I didn't believe in the classical, white-bearded, white-skinned old man, either before my accident or now. But I did believe in a karmic system whereby the net amount of good done in the world all adds up to a lump sum. If you show someone an act of kindness it will be remembered and that person will think twice about being selfish and so on ad infinitum.

But that isn't being spiritual. That is just common sense.

Returning home to Wales on the train, I sat and pondered were my beliefs lay.

My upbringing was a religious tug-o-war. My mother was on the one side taking me and my sister to church every Sunday and my dad on the other, telling us there was no God and that we would be better off going a walk in the country every day of rest.

Long boring sermons I do recall. The vicar, Mr Bacon, would preach not in words but in a low hum, like when I was in my bedroom and my mum and dad were arguing downstairs. I could hear something but I couldn't quite make out what he was saying. Then I would come round with my mum ticking me off in a harsh whisper for daydreaming again.

My sister Tracey, a fluent Arabic-speaker, went on to become a missionary in the Middle East. Tracey always believed in a Christian God and tried to convert Muslims to Christianity. She has lived in Jordan, Israel, Morocco and is currently living in Lebanon. She was once stoned by Berber tribesmen because she tried to convert them to Christianity; it does take a lot of courage to be do what she is doing.

Preferring not to put all my eggs in the one basket, I, on the other hand, wanted to see what was out there. It was about then that I found climbing. That was religion enough for me. It gave my life some meaning, gave me an identity, and I went about it with the same missionary zeal as my sister went about her work.

I worshipped the rock without expecting anything in return, well, apart from the rock allowing me to perform my gymnastics upon it. The great cliffs, Gogarth, Clogwyn Du'r Arddu and Sron Ulladale, were my houses of worship and my prayer was my movement. Climbing books were my religious texts and certain older climbers were my prophets.

But that was when I was younger.

Today my beliefs are very different and very simple. Passe as it may seem, I believe in a vital force. Everyone knows that the central nervous system runs on electricity, neurons firing tiny electrical pulses across synapses, to oversimplify the process. Perhaps that is what is known as Chi. It is my belief that there is only so much energy in the world and, when someone dies, that energy has to go somewhere, so it returns into the earth to reappear as a wave or wind or a bird or animal, maybe even a new-born baby.

So, if I had died on the ledge that day, my energy would have gone into something else eventually, the rock or the sea. A little like reincarnation, and I suspect I share this belief with millions of Buddhists and Hindus. The great Buddhist and Hindu texts of *Tripitaka* and *Bhagavad-Gita* confirm this.

I do think that the many lucky breaks I have had were just that, lucky breaks, and that there are a lot of coincidences in this world. The evolutionary biologist, Richard Dawkins, describing the timescale evolution works on, states that if you wait long enough even the Statue of Liberty will wave to you.

However, I am always willing to have my beliefs challenged.

A lady in the front row said rather eloquently, 'Your guardian angel must be pulling her hair out in despair.'

As the puplicity and eactures were beginning to slow we began planning a trip to Australia. This meant that I had to forgo any occupational therapy and physiotherapy sessions at Ysbyty Gwynedd for two months. I was going to miss Tracey's radiant grinning face. She achieved movements of my arm that no one else could by saying in her musical Welsh accent, 'Just think of yourself as a flower opening up,' or, 'Try and imagine your arm as a piscod-wibbly-wobbly [jellyfish], all loose.'

It may sound silly but it worked and my normally spastic arm relaxed and opened out, just for her.

She was always telling me, 'What you need is an OT to come with you to Australia.'

As for my physiotherapist, Penny Croxford, it was going to be one of the greatest tests of my post-injury self, being without her for two months. For two sessions a week I would go to see Penny and learn how to improve my gait or to learn invaluable new stretches. What would I do if I got into trouble, seized up or something? Deep down I knew my worrying was unfounded but I had been having physio now for over two years and it had become a way of life.

Whilst in Australia, I wondered, would I have my first, post-injury, true perfect moment? That is what I search for when I climb. Notice I use the word 'climb' still, not 'climbed'; that would be defeatist and unhealthy. It is worth more than a golden nugget, a diamond or a million pounds in the bank. You can't put a price on a perfect moment. I roamed the world for fifteen years in search of such moments and found no more than handful.

The first was at Gogarth, near Holyhead on the north-western tip of Anglesey. The year was 1986 and I had just got to the top of a new climb that I named The Enchanted Broccoli Garden. I was bringing up Mike Thomas, or Moose, as he hates to be known, on the rope, second. There was this storm light all around, when things appear to be glowing, the grass, the lighthouse, the heather humming purple, my bony hand lit up red.

There was electricity in the air, not much, just enough, and the odd fulmar hanging by a string. I didn't know it then but I had just done one of the most intricate and dangerous routes I would ever climb and the endorphins were coursing through my veins and affecting my view of reality. That moment was so serene, so perfect that it didn't seem real at all.

Baffin Island in the Arctic was another moment. We were halfway to doing the first ascent of the West Face of Mount Asgard by a weaving yet perfect route: a thousand metres of vertical granite on a mountain with a completely flat top, as if Odin had swiped at it with his hand and knocked the top off. I was hanging belaying Noel Craine, I think, with low Arctic light – the light seems to be of some import in these perfections – looking across the wall. The wall was an apocalyptic red with shiny verglas that you could see your face in. My bare cheek was resting against lichen and there was a ceiling of grey cloud, through which the sun was squeezing between that and the horizon.

It suddenly struck me like a flash that the closest human beings were in Pangnirtung, a small settlement about fifty kilometres away. Out west the Penny icecap exerted its tight grip on the earth for 300 kilometres and to the east the nearest humans would be in Greenland. It was the most isolated I had ever been. If something were to go wrong, we were completely alone. This should have terrified me, but it didn't. This loneliness had the opposite effect and made me want to experience more of the same.

As March drew to a close Noel and his partner Ali invited me to their house for dinner. As Ali was taking me home afterwards, about midnight, I saw a familiar figure struggling on sticks along the main road.

'Stop the car,' I urged Ali.

Out of the darkness came a ghoulish soul so covered with blood it took me a while to recognize him as Duncan, a guy I often have a drink with in the Heights, a pub in Llanberis. He smashed his leg up in a car crash the month previously and was sporting a full-length cast.

It turned out he had got on the bus on his way home from the pub and was sitting there minding his own business when three thugs set about him. He didn't even see the first punch coming; it was to the back of his head. The blows then rained down on him as he tried in vain to keep his attackers off. Even the bus driver was too scared to tackle them.

Filled with dismay, I could hardly believe what he was describing to me. It was precisely this kind of thing I was escaping from when I had moved away from the big city to live in Wales. I remember feeling refreshed and proud of the fact that one can leave the house wide open and the car door unlocked, and I did so frequently, almost feeling that it was my duty to prove a point.

The bus pulled up for Duncan to get off and it happened to be right by a police patrol car. The driver motioned for the WPC to get out and she walked around to the front of the bus.

When she saw the state of his face she was horrified and asked him, 'Who did that to you?'

Duncan took a step back up onto the bus and pointed at the drunken louts. They were just kids. The policewoman took their names, though they were well known to the coppers. It was a cut and dried case but she didn't give him a lift home!

The cowardice and brutality of the event he was recounting sent a shiver down my spine. They obviously had no respect for a temporarily disabled guy on crutches. If that were me on that bus, with my head that was then in an extremely delicate state, I probably would not have survived such a pummelling.

4

Seeing Stars

Joy and woe are woven fine,
A clothing for the soul divine;
Under every grief and pine,
Runs a joy with silken twine.
　　William Blake – *Auguries of Innocence*

'Don't forget Mother's Day. Don't forget Mother's Day,' I kept repeating to myself for weeks before the day.

This Mothering Sunday was more important than all the others ever were. My mum had just come out of hospital; she was in there for a reconstruction operation after breast cancer. But in my self-absorption – I had a trip to Australia to pack for – I forgot all about it.

She felt that she would not have contracted cancer had it not been for worrying about me. I was hurt, taking it to mean that she was blaming me for her illness. I found it difficult discussing how I could be culpable in her cancer but she told me that she didn't blame me. It was the accident she blamed.

I had heard that there was evidence that stress and worry could cause cancer, but there was no empirical confirmation. I felt gutted that I could have had a hand in my mother's cancer and I didn't seem to be able to disassociate myself from the accident. After all I was the one that had the accident. Without me there would be no accident.

Anyway, I still got to give her flowers on Mother's Day as the Australian Mother's Day comes a month later than British Mothering Sunday.

I sat next to an elderly Irish couple on the aeroplane to Australia and the man asked me what had I done to my leg.

An innocent enough question one might say, but I must get this question ten times a day and it does become wearing. How can I get down to a decent conversation about the world bank and third world poverty, the South Pacific whale sanctuary or logging in south-west Tasmania when all everybody wants to know is, 'What have you done to your leg?'

I found myself wishing I had a facial disfigurement; I wouldn't have heard a peep out of them then. It is strange to observe just what intimates a socially acceptable injury.

What I do appreciate though is honesty. Upon seeing me for the first time a garage-owner near Hobart told me, 'If you were a horse I'd have you shot,' and I valued his forthrightness.

A drunk propping up a bar on Bruny Island, off Tasmania, and tucking into his second bottle of red wine exclaimed simply, 'You're facked you are.'

Looking him up and down I thought, but didn't voice, not as much as you, mate.

He then went on to inform me that, 'There's somethin' wrong with ya hip and ya shoulda-blade!' and then slumped back onto the bar.

I now make a point of asking someone who has a facial disfigurement how they got it and discussing that taboo and the resultant journey of depression and acceptance they inevitably take. I feel I now have a concern for a stranger's wellbeing, because we both know a little bit about what the other has been through.

When I pass a disabled person in the street I will smile and they will normally return my friendly gesture, but sometimes the person will look dead ahead as if he or she hasn't noticed me. It took me a few years to figure out what was going on; the negative way we are made to feel about ourselves when we are out in public.

The cult of the perfect body and beautiful young looks has been in vogue for centuries in some cultures. In recent decades though this fashion has taken a step up. It has now become quite normal in Los Angeles to have calf or breast implants, collagen lips and botox injections into ones forehead and crow's-feet. The disabled are being pushed to the very fringe of society.

If you are in your mid-forties in Los Angeles you will struggle to get a good job, you will be deemed too old. This is ageism taken to the extreme. But what if someone is in a wheelchair or is facially disfigured? What chance do they have?

Tasmanians run to a different clock from the rest of Australia and the pace of life is always supremely relaxing. After visiting friends and mooching about Hobart for a few days it was time again to get back on the road.

My first encounter with the Southern Ocean was a scary one. Nat, a childhood friend of Jane's, joined us for the six-hour drive from Hobart to Ocean Beach, a gently curving arc over thirty kilometres long, which one can't see the end of.

Great waves were dumping onto the pristine white sand and, as the others braved the breakers, I made my excuses not to go near the freezing water. These tumbling waves would push me over as soon as I set foot in the surf. I would be pulled under. I might have a heart attack. They wouldn't be able to hear my cries for help. Then I suddenly said to myself, pull yourself together man, this might be the only chance you get to swim in the Southern Ocean.

So, like an automaton, I lay my sunglasses on my clothes, put on my sandal, which holds the splint to my foot, and slowly walked down the steeply sloping sand. The first thing I noticed upon goose-stepping into the water were the mesmerizing patterns that the sand made as it rushed back out to sea in the inch-deep water: just like the clouds that were screeching overhead. Jane waded into the shallows towards me as the first wave hit me. There was no time for breaking myself in gently. The water was already up to my chest. It wasn't the shock I thought it would be. The autumn sea was warm: even the Southern Ocean.

The next moment, as the water became shallower again, I felt an immense power wrenching at my feet, taking them from below me. The surge of the undertow was terrific. In a horizontal position I hung on to Jane. If I didn't have someone to hang on to I would have surely been swept out to sea. There was only ocean, twenty-odd thousand kilometres between us and Patagonia, in which to get lost, should I have gone under.

When the water wasn't rushing out and waves weren't hitting me, I took the opportunity to submerge myself completely. It felt like a baptism, with Jane holding tight on to my arm as I toppled sideways into the momentarily still water; 'Find the Lord and he will heal you!'

Back in Hobart I took time out to be alone, just to contemplate the events of the last couple of years. I found myself walking the streets, up one block, across one block, attempting to lose myself, but always arriving at the same place, the Royal Hobart Hospital where I had been rushed after the accident. A queer chill overcame me. I had been back only once when we had made the Totem Pole film and it felt strange then; all those ghosts.

An apparition, right there in front of me was Nurse Moy who, in my drugged mind, had attempted to murder me. There was the burning of the naso-gastric tube being forced up my nose, the catheter being shoved up my penis. The monitors and their monotonous bleep . . . bleep . . . bleep . . . the wailing of the other patients. I could sense it all as if I were experiencing it there and then as I hurried by the accident and emergency unit.

There were undoubtedly still nurses and therapists I knew working on the neuro-surgical ward, some of whom I wanted to see. But I couldn't take the step through the door, couldn't cross the threshold a second time. I stood below the balcony where they had wheeled me out on warm days. I remembered the stifling heat through the windows. Burning, I would just sit there, unable to ask to be wheeled back indoors. After gazing up there for what felt like hours, wanting someone, anyone, to appear I shuffled away to finish my wandering.

Swimming and bush walking were two exercises I told myself I was going to do as much as I physically could during the month I was going to be in Tasmania. After all, I didn't know when I would be back. Now that I wasn't able to be obsessed with climbing any more, I was getting into hiking, bird-watching, cycling, gardening, golf in fact all the interesting things that normal, un-obsessed people do.

Mount Field is a place that holds fond memories for me. I recalled the painful slowness and unsteadiness with which I tottered through the pandani grove around Lake Dobson the year before and now I halved the time for the three-kilometre round trip, and that wasn't rushing. This forest was like something out of prehistory, populated with weird plants and animals. Potoroos, pademelons and wallabies hopped between giant pandani trees, which look like massive pineapples atop lampposts.

At a picnic everybody played frisbee between rain-showers. Everybody except me. I dipped out and then silently berated myself for not experimenting; I had never thrown a frisbee since my accident and may, just may, have been able to. I wouldn't know until I tried. What grace they all had in launching the frisbee and especially in jumping up to catch it. I recalled, perhaps unrealistically, how I had been quite good at frisbee once and I pondered on how no longer being able to do something, be it frisbee or running or swimming, instantly makes one an expert, 'once'.

I now strongly feel that you should never shirk that which you have never tried. Glenn Robbins, an Australian friend of mine, once said, 'All things in life should be experienced at least twice!'

It was with Uncle Tom in mind that I attempted my first Tassie summit, Clemes Peak. Uncle Tom, I was told by my dad, had climbed Everest. This stuck in my five-year-old brain and I imagined him battling through the snow, up the final ridge to plant a flag on that blunt summit. About five years later I met him. He was a big man to my ten-year-old frame and to this day, whenever I think of him, his face has morphed into Edmund Hillary's.

I found out years later, when I began to climb, that he hadn't been to the top of Everest at all but instead had made the trek into the Base Camp. Uncle Tom, and his feat, got wedged in my mind and it is to this singular incident that I credit my whole climbing career.

We arrived at Waterfall Bay on the Tasman Peninsula and there over the railings I saw a large cove of enormous brightly coloured cliffs. The waterfall, which had found another route through the earth and rock, used to fall over a hundred metres of yellow horizontally bedded rock. I let a glob of spittle fall from my mouth but it disappeared and fragmented in the twisting updraft long before it reached the sea. The Totem Pole was very close by and I had a nervous feeling about the climb.

I tried to prise out of Jane just what the climb entailed but she was behaving pretty shiftily.

Jane pointed out the route. 'It's fairly steep at the beginning,' she fingered the forest, 'then it flattens out for a while until it rears up for the final climb up to the peak.'

The brontosaurus sketch by *Monty Python* came to mind.

For the first time in weeks I was feeling strong and fit, which I put it down to the oysters we had been wolfing down. I raced off up the steps and thought, 'Wow, if these steps go all the way up I'm in there!'

There were fifteen of them. I counted.

If there was a mission, then I was on it. I hardly noticed the tall stringy bark eucalyptus trees towering above us and it took Jane to point out the native cherry which, she told me, her family used as Christmas trees. Sooner than I imagined, the path flattened out and, the first third over with, I allowed myself to relax my pace a little. Again, sooner than I expected, we came across a sign saying 'CLEMES PEAK. STEEP'.

This is where the real excitement starts, I thought.

Jane started off and I followed, struggling, losing ground until she was out of sight in the dense forest. I slipped on leaf litter and mud repeatedly in the first fifty metres and instantly became dismayed as I spent more time on my behind than on my feet. It seemed that a thirty-degree hill was fine for walking up but a thirty-five-degree hill was near impossible.

Pulling up on the trunks of dogwood and she oak I made better progress, although I repeatedly tripped over large clumps of cutting grass, which lay tripwire-like, across the path. The sweat was soaking my shirt and brimmed felt hat as I tore myself upward, with only my left hand, from tree to tree. I regretted not bringing a helmet as I teetered backward on a precariously balanced stone and, after regaining some composure, I urged Jane to walk behind me. This way she could field me in the event of a fall, although realistically if I toppled backward on to Jane I would surely have taken her with me down the slope in a Laurel and Hardy tumble.

Eventually, after two hours, we made the summit block. Two three-metre steps of near vertical rock challenged me in a way I would never have dreamed of two and a half years ago. Had I come so far only to be repulsed by this final obstacle? Previously I would have skipped over these steps literally without noticing them. Now Jane had to hold my foot on greasy holds as I scrabbled and scraped up toward the top. As I hung on a sapling, I pondered how ridiculous I must have looked and was thankful that no one was following us.

Finding a dirty crack, I placed a left-hand jam in and pulled up further. Then, finding a bridge in the corner I was in, I released the jam and reached up. Stretching to my limit, I crept my fingers onto the actual acme of this small plateau until I had it in my grasp. Then Jane guided my foot a step higher and I hooked the top with my elbow. Another sapling grew on the flat summit which I grabbed hold of for all I was worth. Hooking my chin on the plain top, I now had my whole arm on the peak but that was it. I could not climb any higher.

For thirty minutes I tried everything to get my body on to the top. I had Jane go round to the top so that she could haul me up. But I was terrified. We weren't going to employ my telescopic walking pole on this occasion. Because Jane was not behind me, spotting me, I felt more at risk. If I fell I was going all the way. It was no use; I just couldn't get the rest of me up there.

'Well, your arm's topped out,' said Jane with a giggle.

'So, does that justify an ascent?' I asked, grinning, whilst appearing, I imagined, like a mole emerging out of its hole.

'No. It doesn't,' she said and then continued, 'Wait there.'

She went back down the other route to beneath me once again. Feeling much safer now, I began to down-climb. Jane placed my foot on the holds and I used the jam and the sapling to lower back down to the steep muddy ground.

We walked around to a shoulder just three metres from the top. I had never seen a forested summit before. From Wales to the Himalayas one can see 360 degrees but here you had to look out through slots in the trees. Still, to the north we could see all the way to the distant Schouten Island and the dark wedge of Maria Island and to the south, the Hippolytes and the Candlestick. I could even make out the tip of the Totem Pole, which gave me an eerie sensation, like insects crawling over my body. For some reason I could not reveal many of my darkest innermost feelings about what this piece of rock meant to me. I still have trouble expressing the anxiety I experience, of which an increased tempo in the beating of my heart and sweating palms and back are the external symptoms, upon viewing it.

After lunch, which we were saving for the top, we commenced our uneasy descent. Discovering that it was far easier to let myself go out of control, I almost fell and then caught on to a passing tree again and again. I still lost count of how many times I did fall on the steep slope.

When I find myself in dangerous circumstances requiring intense concentration I invariably take to quiet meditation, perhaps to take my mind of the danger. I don't know why this is but it happens without fail and can cover all manner of subjects.

As I fell from tree to tree, I got to contemplating why doctors are often so pessimistic. I had lost count of the number of these professionals who had given me the worst possible prognoses without foundation.

Originally I thought that these doctors learnt this manner in university so they might not raise false hope, that they should come in to your room and tell you the worst possible outcome to let you down slowly and ease you into grief. Now I tend to think that there are just a few cold and unfeeling doctors who don't know how hurtful they're being, a mirror of society really.

It must be against the Hippocratic oath to punish someone when they are down so far, but some doctors do. Obviously not all though. There are many profoundly humane doctors, of whom I know many. Maybe I don't understand just how stressful being a doctor can be but if a doctor is being rude and hurtful to his or her patients, then it might be time to find a new profession.

Caked in mud and with twigs in my hair, I reached the ute, sated in the knowledge I had achieved the most demanding ascent since my accident and at least my head and left arm had topped out.

Ralph Waldo Emerson said, 'When it is dark enough men see the stars.' I was now seeing whole spiral galaxies. Shortly after Clemes Peak I attempted a hamstring curl like

I usually did during my hellish daily physio sessions. All I had to do was lie on my front and bend my right knee so that my heel moved toward my buttock. Nevertheless it had been two years, twenty-four months, of heaving and fighting since this was a possibility for me, so I didn't expect anything. I had given up hope. Screwing up my eyes and holding my breath, whilst tensing my whole body, much the same as you would if you were attempting to bench-press 100-kilograms, it was the same old story . . . Nothing . . . Again.

Without a hamstring one is forever tripping and falling over, so this really did mean a lot to me. My hamstring had been flaccid and useless ever since the accident.

With great exertion, I went blue in the face as I forgot to breathe and my right fist clenched ever tighter in an unavoidable associated reaction. The palm of my hand bled as my fingernails made deep depressions, cutting me.

Then, ever so slowly, my foot began to rise up off the floor as I fought for all I was worth, slapping the lawn in front of me with my hand. Ten degrees . . . thirty degrees . . . forty-five degrees . . . sixty degrees . . . my spastic hand made a fist of iron.

But here I was using my 'hammy', as my physiotherapist liked to call it, though the muscle was incredibly weak still. When the lower leg gets to ninety degrees from the thigh the exercise is basically over as the hamstring doesn't have to work any more.

After a sedentary week, itchy feet began to plague me and I knew it was time for an adventure. That jewel in Tasmania's crown, the Southwest National Park, was a place I had never visited and I persuaded Jane to take me.

We began our trudging across a buttongrass plain known as Blowhole Valley. Australians have a habit of putting planking wherever they can and often this is raised to a height of two metres. These duckboards are to prevent a deep muddy trench from being ploughed across the buttongrass. Unfortunately, after rain they become slippery and I felt like I was walking a tightrope in roller skates. It took enormous concentration to fall off them as little as I did. Luckily there were no falls from the highest sections of the duckboard. Extending my telescopic pole down to the swamp below effectively gave me a third leg.

After three and half hours had lost themselves to my stumbling daydreams we came out on to a headland, which afforded a truly awesome spectacle. A thousand feet below us there was a bleached beach, bone white, with a tangled mess of giant waves rolling in from a storm brewed up in Antarctica.

On the steep descent I fell several times and, plunging out of the forest and on to the sand, I felt liberated from the prison of trees.

Traversing the sand, my leg became leaden and I tripped several times. Because of the angle of a beach and my difficulty in lifting my leg I can only walk in one direction comfortably; left to right is problematic for me. Two hours trekking remained to get to the next bay and the time was 3 pm.

'I think we should camp here.'

Jane replied teasingly, 'I agree. It'll be dark by the time we reach the next campsite and I'll have to do all the work – putting up the tent, blowing up the mats and cooking dinner.'

Next morning we walked, well, wallowed really, to South Cape Rivulet. The mud on the path was shin deep at times. There was one two-metre wall of brown porridge to be surmounted and Jane, being always ten yards in front of me, was already on top when I got there. I had slipped on my backside six or seven times before I arrived at this mud step and was not in good humour.

'God, why do I punish myself? This isn't hill walking. I'm used to wandering up peaks on blue-sky days. I haven't even seen the sky today. This is misery, claustrophobic misery. You don't even get a view as a reward for all this miserable labour. I hate Tasmania.'

Begrudgingly I put my left hand in Jane's. She heaved and I ho'd. With my knees muddied, she hauled me onto the path above. Soon the sun shone and we were walking down to the beach of South Cape Rivulet.

As I descended on to the beach I remember thinking, 'This is the business. Amazing island. I love Tasmania.'

More washing powder white sands contrasted with the black waters of the rivulet at the furthest reach of the beach. The dark gum forest abutting the sand had the appearance of an exotic desert island. I half imagined seeing the dark skinned faces of Lyluequonny people, the tribe who used to inhabit this part of the island, peering out at us from the bush. Alas the British saw to these people over a century ago.

With mask and flippers Jane was going to dive for abalone but the waves weren't just big, they were huge. In the absence of these incomparable shellfish instant noodles would provide us with a tidy lunch. All too soon it was time to leave this earthly paradise and return to the camp-site.

After a rushed breakfast and a rainbow that we could see both ends of we set off walking. The light filtering through the tea trees and native heath had the appearance of stage lighting or walking through a well lit tunnel. We caught glimpses of, and heard the out of tune squawkings of, black cockatoos.

After two and half hours of walking it started to rain . . . Torrentially. We donned raincoats and trooped on, wading through muddy puddles.

Unlike walking in Britain, where you avoid getting your feet wet at all costs, here you get your feet wet as soon as possible, then you don't have to worry about precariously edging round deep puddles of mud, of which there are millions. Everyone has wet feet for the whole duration of the bush walk. The first thing in the morning, even before a brew, Tassies boil their socks and then, after wringing them out, they put them straight on to their feet which are then put into wet boots.

Then we saw a sight that defied imagination. Two blokes wearing wetsuits and carrying surfboards came out of the dense jungle towards us. Jane knew them and stopped for a chat in the pissing rain. They were heading for the same beach I had just spent two days walking to and they were going for an evening's surfing. The two of them didn't seem to be having any problem carting their surfboards through the thicket.

I continued trudging because I knew Jane could catch me up. At one point there was a considerable drop on the left of the path with a tangle of brambles and spiky bushes at the bottom. With my bad leg I went to step out and my foot slipped on a greasy slab of rock. Hurtling down the bank, I rolled several times before I came to rest with my face pressed into a spiky bush and my head pointing down hill.

'Hmmmph . . . Mmmmph . . . Mmmm,' I mumbled, unable to turn my head. I should never have gone off on my own like that.

But then came, 'What have you done now?'

I heard Jane's worried declaration from my coffin-like restriction.

I managed to vocalize a 'Heeelph'

Jane took off her pack and scrambled quickly down to me.

'Can you turn me over?' The muffled tones were quite urgent now.

First Jane took my pack off, then she rolled me over and I gulped in a deep draught of air. When I fall on my front, only having one usable arm and a faulty leg means that I can't turn over on to my back very easily. I then had to fight my way out of the spiky clutch of the brambles with Jane giving me a hand from above.

In mid-May, Jane and I took a stopover in Queensland on our long, winding route back to Wales. It had been an ambition of mine for years to swim on the Great Barrier Reef and now it was becoming reality. I knew I couldn't actually swim but with the help of floatation devices I might be able to float around and gaze down into the illuminated depths at the reef. In preparation I had been spending as much time as I could in the pool or in Tasmania's cold seas.

But the morning we arrived in Port Douglas, whilst descending a steep street, I fell. My feet shot out from underneath me in loose gravel and flew up in the air. Landing flat on my back and winding myself considerably – my spastic arm refused to straighten – my elbow took the full force, hitting the tarmac with a sickening thud.

Jane looked at the elbow and with undisguised horror said, 'You've got to see a doctor for that.'

'Do you think so? It doesn't feel that bad.'

'Trust me, I'm a nurse.'

So I agreed and we found a surgery just at the bottom of the hill. Coincidentally Jane knew the doctor from Royal

Hobart. He entered the room wearing a colourful Hawaiian shirt and shorts. 'Hello, I'm Doctor Georgeous.'

Just managing to stifle a giggle, I shook his hand.

He inspected the elbow with a few prolonged 'Hmms' and said, 'I'm afraid I'll have to operate to remove the bursa.' He then left the room.

'What the hell's the bursa?'

'Oh, just the sack containing the sinovial fluid,' Jane said quickly, seeming more interested in the doctor's nom-de-guerre than my elbow. 'The nurses at the Royal used to call him Gorgeous Georgeous.'

Gorgeous Georgeous put thirteen stitches in the elbow. He didn't see much action in sleepy Port Douglas and so relished the operation. With the sweat dripping off the end of his nose and a manic look in his eye, he finally got the bursa out and held it up in his tweezers like a trophy proclaiming, 'Yesss! Got it.'

Then he added, 'You weren't thinking about going out on the reef, were you? That would be foolhardy.'

How could I not go out on the reef? That is precisely why I had come here to swim amongst the blues and greens, curtains of sunlight filtering down through the water. I smiled a fake smile of agreement and walked out of the door thoroughly dejected. It didn't take long for determination to overtake me and I soon convinced myself that the doctor didn't know anything. He was full of it.

Jane took a little more convincing. 'Well, it's your arm,' she said.

The day arrived. The boat was a tiny affair compared to the giant cruisers that carry hundreds of tourists. *Wavelength* carried twenty-five people and had a safe feel about it. We raced over ninety minutes of ocean to the outer reef, the clouds seemed angry and the wind was getting up. Most of the others took seasickness pills but, always having been a good sailor, I knew I wouldn't need them.

The sea had become choppy as I threw myself off the dive platform at the rear of the boat. Even though I was wearing a short wetsuit I momentarily sank. This had the effect of producing in me an instant panic. I spluttered and waved my arm about and sank again briefly. A sense of dread gripped me as I surfaced again. Gasping and choking violently, I stared wide eyed out onto open ocean, not a soul in sight.

Where the hell was the boat?

Then I splashed around and there it was, as anyone in their right mind would expect, behind me, just a couple of metres away. Splashing towards the platform, I gripped onto it as if my life depended on it. I thought it did.

It had all been so natural before, when I had snorkelled on coral reefs in Borneo. I had dived down with ease to pick up a spiral shell three metres under the surface. There would be none of that now. I squeezed hold of the rail at the back of the boat for all I was worth. And then that inner voice that told me not to be such a wimp when I was having a mental debate about whether to go for a run-out or not during my climbing days called out to me again: 'Go on . . . Do it . . . Take the plunge . . . Let go.'

'No, I . . . I can't.'

'Yes, you can . . . Just . . . Let . . . Go.'

'But I'm terrified I'll drown.'

'You will not drown.'

'How do you know?'

'Look. They're all watching you, ready to dive in after you should you go under.'

'But what if they . . .'

'They won't.'

'OK . . . I'm going to do it on the count of three . . . One . . . Two . . . Three . . .'

Jane and Fleur, a Californian guide now living in far north Queensland, took me by the wrists as I loosened my grip on the platform. With a webbed neoprene glove on my left hand and the one flipper on my left foot I slid into the warm water. But the noodle, a buoyancy aid worn under the armpits, didn't stop me spluttering when a wave came over my snorkel.

Salt water was continually pouring down the plastic tube, which fed into my mouth and I was becoming despondent. I wasn't even seeing any fish, which is, after all, what I had come for. After drinking what felt like a pint of the Pacific Ocean, I said enough is enough and hauled myself back on to the boat, which was surprisingly easy, so I thanked someone for small mercies.

Afterwards Rod, our skipper, said in his nasal Queensland accent, 'It's bad enough conditions for anyone to snorkel in, let alone someone with half a body. It's not often this choppy out here.'

With skin like leather and a very laid back attitude, Rod appeared to model himself on Bogart's Charlie Allnut in *The African Queen*. My only doubt is whether Charlie wore budgie smugglers.

Back on board, there was an ageing couple speaking a strong dialect of Spanish and they were having some difficulty making themselves understood so, with my knowledge of Castillian, I offered to translate.

'*Si te queres puedo a traduciar para vosotros*,' I shouted across the boat.

All twenty-five faces turned to look at me and the couple just stared blankly.

I repeated my offer in halting Spanish, '*Si te queres algun traduciendo, yo puedo.*'

Again blank stares. Since I had my accident I'm not as confident as I used to be and in the wrong situation I can become crippled with embarrassment. My face began to change colour from the pink that it normally is to a shade of crimson. If there was any place else to be, I wished I could have been there.

Rod then turned and asked me, 'You know some Finnish, do you?'

The next site was definitely calmer and, determined to give it another go, I allowed Fleur to tow me away from the boat to where the coral reef was. She then anchored me on a rope to the reef, so that I wasn't going anywhere, and proceeded to dive down and show me walking coral, a giant clam and cleaner wrasse. Marvelling not only at my surroundings but also at how Fleur's lissom body glided through the water, I stayed out as long as anyone did.

The third site was better still. Jane towed me this time, about fifty metres from the boat, and anchored me to these peculiar conical-shaped underwater mountains. I wanted to see a shark or a grupa but, alas, I would have to make do with myriad of other colourful fish, coral, anemones, octopus and conger eels. All I could do was hang on to my rope and gawp as this underwater world passed me by. This gravity-free world was such a delight and I wondered could it be that topside life, life on land, is disabling for everyone. When we were called back in I gave Jane the anchor and swam in to the boat, with the noodle, under my own propulsion.

Speeding back to Port Douglas, being tossed about on the waves and clutching my sore elbow, I felt like another part of my healing had just taken place. I had had this feeling on numerous occasions in the past and would have it again. And as we pulled into the harbour, I found I was smiling with a warm knowing.

But the elbow was swollen with an infection and I wondered whether I had made a mistake in not heeding Gorgeous Georgeous' advice. After a couple of days the joint had ballooned out to unusual proportions.

On my last night in Queensland, at 5.30 am, I awoke in a hotel room to a strange wetness under my body. In my sleepy daze it took me a few moments to work out what was going on. Had I wet myself? The bedside lamp revealed a mass of blood and puss. My elbow had to choose this most inopportune moment to burst.

I had to fly across the Pacific Ocean in an hour's time for I was to partake in another reading tour of America. Jane was flying in the opposite direction, back to Britain. She quickly patched me up with some stick-on sutures and covered the whole lot with Second Skin, a clear, sticky and highly durable bandage.

Later Jane revealed how she had rather a lot of difficulty explaining to the Malaysian maid, who didn't have a very good command of the English language, why the bed looked like someone had been murdered in it.

After sixteen hours on the plane my lower arm had swollen to twice its normal size. I was frantic with worry and every bump to my elbow shot an excruciating pain right down to my toes. When the aeroplane landed at LAX I had to take a taxi from one terminal to another. I loaded my rucsac into the boot and climbed in the back. About midway through the short journey I felt a dampness on my torso. My T-shirt seemed to be wet.

Terrified of finding what I most feared, I glanced down

for only a split second and then with greater scrutiny. Once again my elbow had burst but this time the juice had soaked into the velvet upholstery on the back seat of the taxi. When we arrived at the correct terminal I slipped out of the door, only opening it as much as I needed to squeeze out. Quickly closing it behind me, and smiling politely, I hoped the driver didn't notice the elbow dripping on to the pavement.

I was to read in Denver, Telluride, Chicago, Portland and San Francisco. A small tour really but exhausting enough with a septic elbow. Besides a book signing alongside Julie Andrews – the queue was at least a hundred metres long for Ms Andrews and I would consider myself lucky if one person happened by my desk – my visit to Chicago was made more special by a remarkable taxi journey.

I flagged down a cab and got in. 'The Book Fair, please.'

'Whatever you say, boss,' said the driver, without looking at me.

After a while he asked the usual, 'What the hell happened to you?'

I am used to this and just to keep him happy I said, 'Oh, I had a stroke.'

'Some stroke!' he exclaimed turning around.

On seeing his face, I couldn't help but stare. 'What the hell happened to you then?'

Just below his left eye socket, on the cheekbone, was a huge crater that engulfed his eye too. His face was a mess; he didn't have a left eye.

'Well, it was a tiny bit more violent than a stroke. I was shot in the face at close range.'

'God, who would do such a thing?'

'You want to know?'

Now he came to mention it . . .

'Can you use all your arms and legs OK?'

'Oh yeah, it took me a few years to recover but recover I did. I just have a very short fuse now, I mean a *very* short fuse.'

'I better not wind you up then. Tell me, where do you come from 'cause, with that accent, you're definitely not an American.'

'No. I'm from Ghana but I moved to Chicago fifteen years ago and five years later I be shot in the face. It's real strange the hand life deals you.'

'It definitely is,' I sighed, looking out of the window at the towering downtown office blocks passing us by.

When I arrived in San Francisco Kevin Starr, a doctor friend of mine, looked at the elbow.

'How long has it been like this?' he asked wearing a worried expression.

'Oh, maybe ten days.'

'Look, if you leave it any longer you could lose your arm. Let's see if you can bend it.'

I bent the elbow and a mixture of sinovial fluid and pus squirted out a full two metres through a tiny hole.

'That really is pretty gross,' commented Kevin with a sick grin.

Pakistan is where the two of us had first become acquainted. We were attempting different climbs on Trango Tower, a famous rock monolith on the Baltoro Glacier, just a few kilometres from K2. He was with a loud boisterous all-American team that achieved a new route on the North Face, while Noel Craine and I bumbled around on the same face and lost our gear in an avalanche. I later succeeded on getting up Trango with another friend, Adam Wainwright, though not by a new route, which is what every climber wants. Some wouldn't tell you this, but we all harbour a secret desire to make our mark. Spraying, that's what Kevin calls it, like dogs marking their territory.

'What can you do for it?' I entreated.

'I'm going to give you a course of a broad spectrum antibiotic and prescribe a peroxide bath twice daily.'

'Thanks, Kevin. What would we do without friends?'

5

Botulinum Toxin Is Good For You

And when I break I will heal. And when I fall I will
stand up again. Stand up. Stand up.
Senser – '*Stubborn*'

Back home in Llanberis, two friends from Tasmania, Ali
and Adam, paid us a visit. Together we made plans to
ascend the highest mountain in Wales, Yr Wyddfa, or
Snowdon, as we English call it. I had butterflies. What if
we didn't make it before dark? What if I fell and broke a
bone? Though not seriously hurting myself, I had fallen on
nearly every walk that I had attempted recently.

Perhaps I would have to be rescued by helicopter again.
How embarrassing would that be? I knew most of the
rescue team quite well after seventeen years living in
Llanberis and had been rescued once at Gogarth. Anyway
we had a head-torch, a bivvi bag, blister pads and emergency food. We hadn't left anything for bad luck to sink its
fangs into.

The Pyg Track begins steeply and I was having problems
on the first kilometre, almost peeling backward on the
massive stone steps numerous times. But I had three atten-
tive fielders whose sole purpose was to catch me should I
fall.

Botulinum Toxin Is Good For You

I had chosen a busy summer Sunday on which to attempt my climb, along with the seething mass of humanity snaking its way up the path in a continuous train.

There were noisy, muddy children getting told off by their disgruntled parents. There were the numerous groups of students all hell-bent on getting to the top first. There were smooching couples sporting matching fleeces. There were the skinheads with paramilitary combat trousers, racing down the track towards us and almost knocking me over. There were the two old women, perhaps in their eighties, descending the steep rocks with some if not all of the agility they used to have.

There were all the people who insisted on informing us how long it would take us to get to the summit – 'About two hours to go' – even though we never asked.

There was a young teenager called Jenny who didn't want to be there at all and was lagging behind, although she had just overtaken us.

Her dad was shouting at her, 'Don't be a slow coach, Jenny.'

And there was the man who stood aside to let me past and when I thanked him said, 'Your need is greater than mine, mate.'

I'll bet he felt good about himself all day for that 'good deed'. It is very interesting the concept of 'help' for a disabled person. Every time I go out someone invariably opens a door for me, I'm not just talking about politely holding a door open after the man, and it is invariably men who do this, have passed through it but actually making a scene about opening a door when I am thoroughly able to open it myself.

If I need help I ask for it. It is the assumption that I need assistance that I find most distasteful. Being patronized by people who think they are being helpful is just another form of prejudice.

As we wandered up into the clouds and crowds I felt happy that all these folk were here, when once I would have felt intruded upon; a how-dare-they-walk-on-my-mountain kind of approach. It dawned on me that these people, from the gurgling babies in backpacks, through the boisterous teenagers sprinting up the path to the ladies in their eighties just taking their time, all had just as much right to be here as I had. I'd never felt that before, never experienced the oneness of being a part of humanity. I'd always kept myself one step to the side, a little aloof from the rest of mankind. Now I saw how ridiculous I had been all these years. I was now just another character wending his way up Snowdon, the one with the limp, the one that had something wrong with his leg. This crowd needed a cripple.

The temperature dropped as we climbed into the gloom and soon we were in a whiteout. After racing toward the summit ridge I had to sit, exhausted. Having been up this path at least three dozen times I knew it well and was aware that the summit's triangulation point was approaching, even if I couldn't see it.

Five hours after I had so nervously begun, and in heaving mist, I was the highest person in Wales, both literally and figuratively. Occasionally we would catch a glimpse of green summits far below: Yr Aran, Moel Cynghorion and Crib Goch. Tourists who'd come up on the train ambushed the summit trig point at thirty-minute intervals. I heard a man in a T-shirt and shorts complaining about the damn cold and saw a trendy woman struggling in high-heeled shoes.

A shell-suited kid, reading some graffiti thoughtfully scratched on the rock, exclaimed excitedly, 'Ey, our dad, there were people 'ere yesterday!'

After a cup of tea in the summit café that looks like a toilet block, we set off down the Llanberis path. The easiest, lowest angle, path up the mountain, it follows the railway all the way to the top. I was floating in my descent, carried on a cushion of joy, and didn't notice any pain until very near the bottom. The one thing I had overlooked was that I had forgotten to cut my toenails before I left home and the toes of my right foot were being driven into the ends of my boots with crippling annoyance. But I'd climbed Snowdon and I wasn't going to let a hurting toe ruin this day. I marched through the village, down the high street and all the way to our front door. The aching took five days to dissipate.

In my ever-expanding quest for an alternative way of life to climbing rocks I dabbled in lots of activities. Cycling, hiking, swimming, bowling, photography (I now had a specially adapted camera), I did them all, though some not very well. I had a huge amount of energy inside me and no way of burning it up. I even tried golf.

Some of my friends were appalled to learn that I had taken up golf and so would I have been not so very long ago. If someone said to me that I would be a golfer four years ago I would have told him or her in no uncertain terms not to talk rubbish. I always pictured golf clubs as posh places, rife with classist snobbery, and I am sure such places do exist, but not on the course we went to.

Meirion, the owner of the course, sat in the 'club house', a static caravan, all day, watching us make fools of ourselves. Meirion himself had only one functioning arm, so I felt an affinity with him. But he was as such from birth, which made him much more comfortable and able with his body than I was. He had a crippled grace about him when he moved.

I would offer him money every time I went there and it was always the same: 'You are just a beginner. Once you get your par to under five over for every hole, then I'll start taking your money.'

Meirion told me about the Society of One-Armed Golfers and said he himself had played a round with the British champion. But he would always shirk my efforts to get him to play a round with me, saying that he had to man the club house.

The links has nine holes and looks like a building site, piles of rubble everywhere. There's always one fairway or another being bulldozed and the greens are like undulating ranges of green hills in miniature. Meirion was a farmer who was keen on golf and decided that he could make a little more money creating a golf course on his fields than farming sheep and cattle. I say a little more money because, at three pounds, it was absurdly cheap to play and he had a policy of letting 'ladies and cripples' in for free to encourage them to play more.

A round of golf was good exercise, I was knackered after nine holes, and it was excellent for the hand-eye co-ordination that Penny Croxford, my physio, was always telling me about. It's the neuro-plasticity thing again. The more you practise the better you become.

Swinging a club with one hand is much harder than with two and I hadn't co-ordination or power in my stroke. I still haven't. It took me four swipes down the fairway, the ball going in the rough and all over the place, to my old climbing mate and recent golfing partner Crispin's one. But I do putt quite well with the aid of a couple of bands of Velcro attaching the top of the handle of the club to my forearm. The club is then just an extension of the arm.

It was a sad day, the day that Meirion's heart packed up. One day he was there, a cheeky grin and a diabolical yet graceful limp – like a disabled Rudolf Nuryev – if such a thing were possible. The next day he was gone. I suspect that is why he always made excuses not to play.

During the long summer Jane and I went on a cycling trip to Ireland on which we achieved two kilometres of cycling (my tricycle packed up). So we had to modify our travels to include more mountaineering.

First we would go to the Magillycuddy Reeks. These are the highest mountains in Ireland – the Irish simply call them the Reeks – and whilst walking in them Jane and I had a minor altercation. We had walked up a turf-cutters' road, which zigzagged its way on to a broad ridge. Once at this ridge, we were expected to beat cross-country over a bog to a distant hill. It wasn't the distance that bothered me but the terrain.

My heart sank. 'Sorry, but I'm not walking over that.'

'Just give it a try,' Jane countered.

'I know this ground and I know that I won't be able to cross to that hill,' I insisted.

Jane strolled out on to the bog and jumped up and down. 'It's not as bad as it looks,' she shouted and then added, 'honest,' as an afterthought.

It was a humid, hot afternoon and the desert of a bog shimmered in the distance. She approached and sat down next to me looking at me with 'those eyes'.

'It's easy for you to say that it's not as bad as it looks.' You're not a cripple,' I snapped, feeling sorry for myself.

When Jane is offended she goes deathly quiet and this was one of those moments. I was feeling guilty now but also had the feeling that she was trying to force me to walk across the bog and I was about to cave in to pressure. It couldn't be easy for Jane, always waiting for me, but if I rushed or attempted something I knew I couldn't do, I could get out of my depth. We could both get benighted and I could end up hypothermic or break a leg or something.

Then I thought, get a grip on yourself man. It can't be that bad, and, muttering an apology, I stood up.

After twisting over on my ankle and tripping and wading for half a mile, the pain became unbearable and I threw the towel in.

'I really can't go any further,' I said, fighting the urge to add, 'I told you so.'

Then we heard a soft bleating and, on searching about, we came across a ewe stuck in the bog. It was sunk up to its neck and seemed to have resigned itself to its fate. Now Jane is a real softy when it comes to animals (I only pretend to be otherwise), so she ploughed in, sinking to her knees and grabbed the poor wretch by the horns. She pulled with all her might but the sheep didn't budge. I came up behind her and took her hand so that I could help her in hauling the sheep and this time the ewe started to slide slowly out.

'At times like these you're lucky that your head injury has left you without a sense of smell,' said Jane. 'It stinks!'

'She must have been in there a few days.'

Mud and faeces where matted into the ewe's wool and it weighed an inordinate amount. She was too weak to stand because her legs had been submerged in the wet, cold bog for days. We dragged her free but that was all we could do. We turned around, having failed on the walk because of me, and on the way back I felt helpless. I was no help to the sheep and no help to myself.

On 23 July Con Moriarty, a great big Irish-speaking Celt and true friend of mine, escorted us up the most difficult peak I have climbed since my injury; perhaps the most difficult of my life. I say perhaps because it rests on the toss of a coin whether the multi-day climbs of my previous life were more painful and tiring. In Patagonia, following twenty-one days ascending the Central Tower of Paine, I had slept for three days. And on climbing to the top of Mount Asgard on Baffin Island, after eleven days and nights (in the Arctic summer there is no distinction between the two), I fainted, collapsed, and bashed my head on a sizeable chunk of moraine.

Mount Brandon, or Cnoc Bréanainn, at 953 metres is but a blip on an ECG to both these mountain's spikes, but in the upper reaches it has its own technicalities.

'How can a footpath be technical?' I can hear you asking.

But a ten-centimetre difference in the size of a group of steps can alter, for me, what was to be a fairly straight-forward day into a complete epic. The size of the stones on a flat path can also be relevant. Up to golf-ball size I can handle but tennis-ball size and I persist in rolling over on my ankle. Or, most importantly for me, there is the angle. If it is beyond forty-five degrees I cannot get up it without a rope. Needless to say, we omitted to fetch a rope on this occasion.

The path began with a gentle twenty-degree slope of short, sheep-nibbled grass to cross a farmer's field. Then, after two miles, we rounded a ridge and looked down on the Fourteen Lakes in the valley of the Eisc. We had to take Con's word that there were fourteen, as we couldn't see them all at the same time. Nevertheless their beauty was self-evident.

As we traversed a slope running up to our right I felt that I was walking well and making good progress. We threaded our way in between glassy tarns and rocky outcrops, the classic *roches moutonnées* I had learned about in my geography lessons at school. That now seemed a world away. There was a handful of other walkers out enjoying themselves, dipping and diving off the rocks, and a dog splashing in and out of the water.

We crossed that line from the warm sun on our backs to the chill shade of mid-morning that was cast by the summit. This was where the hill really began. The path became loose with scree, which kept threatening to slide and sweep the feet out from under me, dumping me on my face. There were strange anvils that jutted out from the hillside, as if the mountain had undergone a rocket attack, and these needed a variety of techniques to be overcome. Tackling them head on was no good for me, with or without a rope. I could only either crouch down underneath them and scuttle to one side or lean back in a kind of limbo dance, hanging on to the flat top, slapping my hand across, left or right.

It was the latter method that I chose, with Con telling me to, 'Stay on the path, why don't you? Stay on the path for Christ's sake.'

After I ignored his pleas for a while, he saw that it was easier for me to leave the loose path and wend a route through the missiles where the vegetation was. Con and Jane did a skilled job of making sure I didn't go the 200-odd metres down to the tarns.

The angle gradually eased until we arrived at the ridge and sunshine again, where I hung limp on a rock for ten minutes to catch my breath. All that remained to the summit was a stroll along a broad ridge of about a kilometre, which plunged almost 1000 metres down to the Atlantic Ocean in the west and, in the east, near vertically down to the Eisc.

When we reached the summit I knew I was only halfway there, but to put things in my favour I told myself two-thirds. Even good climbers know that when one gets to the summit one is only halfway through the hardship. And the following half of the day is often the most dangerous: you are tired, descending is often the most hazardous part of the climb and, of course, if you are late at the summit, you risk spending the night out on the mountain. Though Brandon was a molehill compared to other peaks I had climbed, I was now worried on every summit.

But before I felt too sorry for myself I had to consider what Con had told me: when the Bishop of Kerry, the Most Reverend David Moriarty, celebrated mass on this summit on the last Sunday of June in 1868, 20,000 pilgrims were in attendance. The old, the blind, the lame, they needed mass just like anyone else. I thought of the strife that they must have gone through to climb up Brandon, just as I had done, but they wouldn't have had the twentieth-century comfortable footwear, warm pile jackets and the adjustable walking pole.

In my mind I pictured an old woman in her big dress with her ankles bound in bandages. I pictured a veteran of some battle or other, with one leg and a crude wooden crutch, hopping along. And I pictured children teasing a blind man, as they do, on the way up. My ascent of Mount Brandon was by no means the most radical to date.

A few disabled climbers like to lay claim to the 'first disabled ascent' of a mountain and I am no different, especially if it gets me some sponsorship. Mount Everest has had its first amputee ascent, first blind ascent and first transvestite ascent. One wonders what firsts are left and if it really matters.

After we arrived home Jane went back to work in Ysbyty Gwynedd while I, with my rediscovered confidence gained on Mount Brandon, thought it was time to attempt Cnicht again. With every peak I climbed I could feel my self-assurance growing incrementally stronger. Almost three years I had used up chasing that elusive bird called confidence but knew I was closer to catching it and taming it now.

It was a year since I last attempted Cnicht with Jane on the boiling tops-off day and I sensed I was ready for it again now. Tassie Liz and Tassie Stew, a couple of friends who had travelled from the other side of the earth to stay with us, accompanied me.

Without Jane behind me, spotting me, making sure I didn't come to any harm, I was naked. I hadn't thought about it before, just how much I had grown used to her being there, ducking left and right to guard against me falling or above, helping me, coaxing me on. Not knowing me so well, the Tassies couldn't sense my nervousness until I requested help on a particularly steep and treacherous section.

Above the shoulder, where I had patiently waited for Jane to return exactly a year previously, the path went up a series of steep rocky steps. These seemed too difficult for me so I chose an alternative route, which soon became quite involved, with some puzzling rock climbing. It began with greasy slabs and by the time I reached a vertical step, of about one and half metres, I knew I couldn't reverse. We had no rope and I had forgotten my helmet. Pulling up with my one useable arm, I grasped the top of the step but found to my horror that it was shaly and loose, like a stack of playing cards.

Stew began digging the shale out from above me and throwing it behind him to make the ground more solid. When he had dug down to the cards, I tried to use the footholds. It was no use. I was terrified.

Liz scrambled down to below me and held my foot in place on a hold no bigger than a matchbox edge as I made progress upwards in tiny shuffles and bursts. All I could see was her flaming red hair down below me. The top of the step was now level with my waist as I grabbed on to a rock planted in my path. Luckily the rock was solid and, heaving and grunting, I hauled, first my torso over the edge . . . Then my head started swimming. The mountain began to spin.

'Stew? I'm having problems. I think I'm going to faint.'

Stew was all distorted and his face pulsated pneumatically.

'Here. Grab on to my arm,' he offered immediately and without deliberation. He was that kind of lad.

I didn't think I could let go of the rock but I had to. From that point on I kept my mouth shut, attempting to maintain concentration.

Noticing my unwillingness to let go he said, 'I'll just pull on you're wrist, shall I?'

I nodded trying not to display the urgency of my situation.

Just to make the ascent more difficult for me Colin had put me on Baclofen, a second anti-spasticity drug, and I had been taking it since returning from Ireland. The drug had some horrible side effects, as I was now finding out. Later, when I got home, I read the leaflet about these, which included severe weakness of all the muscles, disorientation, dizziness, light-headedness and nausea.

These little white pills that appear so harmless enfeebled the whole of my body. That would have been unacceptable in the extreme, even if I didn't have a passion for the mountains. My love of climbing always came first before, and even more so now I wouldn't be able to do it so often. I couldn't let any little white pills get in the way of one of the few things I could still do. That would be asking too much of me.

With Tassie Liz pushing at my feet and Tassie Stew hauling on my arm, I was pulled out of danger. Propped

The Totem Pole.

Bouldering amidst ancient temples in Hampi, the ruined capital of the Vijayanagar Kingdom, India, in 1990.

Ascending fixed lines whilst attempting a new route on Meru Central, Gangotri, Garwhal Himalaya, India, 1993.

'Once there was just a log tilted at 45 degrees with a couple of cursory footholds chopped in it with an axe.' In the chasm of the Joint Trail. Chessler Park, Canyonlands, Utah.

'This gravity-free world was such a delight and I wondered could it be that topside life, life on land, is disabling for everyone.' Snorkelling on the Great Barrier Reef.

Jane Boucher and giant groundsel on Mount Kenya.

'As my feet dislodged stones I watched them tumble and bounce 400 metres to the less-steep hillside below my feet.' Bernard Kinyua watches over me on the way to the summit of Point Lenana.

'I remember Jane giving me her hand and I taking it, and accepting her help to stand precariously.' Pulling onto the summit of Point Lenana, Jane belays while Keith Partridge films and Margaret Wicks directs.

Federation Peak. Eastern Arthur Range, Tasmania.

At Thwaites's campsite, Eastern Arthurs.

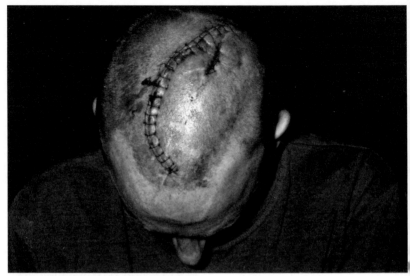

'Like an indelible, long abiding stamp of misadventure, that ditch in my skull serves the past.' Displaying the scar after the cranioplasty.

'That which took four-and-a-half-hours to climb up took 15 minutes to descend.' Racing down Mount Wellington on the recumbent trike.

'We ate a late breakfast, mango and weird tinned sausage, on a wooden table erected in the snow, in burning sunshine.' Clockwise from left: Richard Heap, Jamie Andrew, Ben Pritchard, David Lim, Pete Steane, enjoying fine dining at the Lava Tower on Kilimanjaro.

'The guidebook reads that the climb is "somewhat exposed" and "trekkers will feel a bit out of place on this route".' The Kilimanjaro team in the upper section of the Western Breach at 6am.

'There were no "whoops of joy" or any "punching of the air", nothing like that, just a contented bunch of blokes much the same as any other.' Left–right Paul Pritchard, Bungama Hitla, Pete Steane, David Lim, Jamie Andrew and Kornelli.

'So with the rock face always to my left and mugging it with violent kicks I found I was actually climbing.' My first post-accident climb; Rincon (5.4), Eldorado Canyon, August 2004.

up against a rock, I composed myself over a few gulps of water and got to my feet. The Tassies attempted to dissuade me from continuing but my inventive nostrils could smell the summit on the breeze and I wasn't about to descend for a second time.

Steadying my body on the ski pole, I continued my upward journey. The seagull hovering about and begging for pieces of sandwich off the lone hiker signalled the approach of the summit. The summit was in cloud and a chilly wind scraped across its sharp point. I don't think I even sat down on the top, turning around almost immediately, as I was again feeling dizzy and was more than aware of the difficulties I would have to face on the descent.

On the down-climb I attempted the steep rocky steps I had chosen to avoid on the ascent. On my backside I slipped and slid from step to step, eventually reaching the safety of the shoulder. By accident I had discovered a new technique to add to my repertoire – bum moves. From now on I would employ these unorthodox moves often. When learning to climb, some teachers say that one should never to use the backside or the knees. I myself have never been of that school, preferring to believe the whole body an organic climbing machine whereby, if it's easier to use your bum, then you should. As I write this both my knees are a mass of scabs and my arse is grazed from sliding down dolerite slabs.

A few days later I was leaving Pete's Eats after breakfast and was due to walk up Moel Siabod with the Tassies. This mountain stands above Capel Curig and I had been promising Jane that I would take her up it ever since she arrived in Wales. The fact that it would be her taking me up it hardly crossed our minds.

Anyway, in my weakened state, since the Baclofen, I tripped on the lip of the step and dived out of the doorway on to the pavement, hitting my head on the concrete, skinning my knuckles and grazing my knee. I rolled onto my back and stared up into a sea of face. After persevering with the Baclofen for a few more days the awful pills went the same way as had the Tizanidine; in the bin.

After the Baclofen was finally out of my system it was time for the next remedy: botulinum toxin! Now I was all for the botulinum toxin injections as it didn't mess with my whole mind and body, only one muscle or group of muscles. But it did last for three months. In the beginning I was worried that I wouldn't be able to walk properly for a quarter of a year.

I had great plans to climb Jebel Toubkal in Morocco and Mount Kenya and was fearful that my trial of botulinum toxin might interfere with those mountains. If that was the case then I vowed not to have the injections until I was done with Mount Kenya in the January of 2001. I had a life to lead and I wondered sometimes if the consultants realized this. For two and a half years I had been forced into attempting this remedy or that. That's how I felt anyhow and I was tired of playing the guinea pig.

Getting used to my strange gait, I was settling in to my new body; my leg abducting outwards, my arm always having a crook in it and my wrist forever turned in. At that time there seemed little point in doing anything that would interrupt the normal passage of my life.

I travelled up to Clatterbridge by train to see Colin. He said he only wanted to put the botulinum toxin into my arm and that my leg wouldn't benefit from the injections because there was very little life in my hamstring anyway. I disagreed saying that there was life there, but he seemed not to be listening.

He invited me to extend my fingers, which I tried with all my might until I was blue in the face. They only flexed, as usual. He wasn't looking at my fingers but my forearm for flickers of life in the extensor tendons, which there weren't and never had been since the accident.

When I asked him if these injections would get my fingers going again he replied, 'If there are no flickers in your muscle then it is completely paralysed. If there was even the slightest flicker that would mean there was some hope.'

So the associated reactions I had every day in which my fist clenched was just that; a spastic response to outside stimuli that I had no control over, a little like pulling the tendons on a severed chicken's foot.

I sat dejected while he went on, 'The most we can hope for is that by giving the injections into your arm we can improve your gait. Your walking is affected by your arm being spastic, stiff and sticking out so far.'

Colin put the injections straight into the muscles of my spastic arm. He rigged the needle up to a fuzz-box that made a white noise sound when he was in the right place, deep in the muscle. The sweat was dripping from my nose as he stabbed the wide gauge needle into my arm for the seventh time and I winced as he skewered my humerus. But I was happy, as I had been fighting the health system for this treatment for two whole years. The NHS considered botulinum toxin injections too expensive at hundreds of pounds per millilitre; I had twelve millilitres in total.

It was the same old problem, money. I could have gone private and had the best treatment around if I'd had private insurance but how could an unemployed climber afford the premiums? Well, you may be waiting for years to get treatment, and you might not get scrambled eggs and smoked salmon for breakfast, but the nurses and therapists in the public sector had my welfare at heart, as did my consultant. They just had hundreds, if not thousands, of clients and a limited amount of cash to spread between them. Perhaps it was for this reason that he didn't want to inject my leg.

Botulinum toxin has rather interesting origins. It was developed from botulism, which is a rare and severe form of food poisoning. This nasty micro-organism lives in soil and manure in large numbers but if it is cooked it dies. So don't eat raw meat. The disease attacks the central nervous system and the onset is swift, resulting first in double vision, then paralysis and, after much agony, death.

In recent years botulinum toxin has been found to have literally hundreds of uses, some therapeutic, some more sinister. In addition to the reduction of spasticity it also has a cosmetic use in the ironing out of crow's-feet and other facial lines by paralysing the muscles around the eye and forehead. A few tiny injections are all it takes to give the client a characterless face with all the attributes of an insipid mask.

In biological warfare, one billionth of a gram can kill a person. The victim inhales the airborne toxin, which completely paralyses the body. Cardiac arrest soon follows.

The car park attendant at Broadhaven Beach in Pembroke, went on, 'I used to be a builder's foreman on a bloody great building project but that was before . . . Before the stroke.'

He didn't tell me his name. It didn't matter. This man had a very dense 'hemi'. His arm hung heavy and he could barely raise his leg off the ground.

He carried an almost embarrassed manner about with him. 'That was three years ago and when I lost that job I went into a real depression. I thought, what the bloody hell am I going to do now?'

He recounted his tale in surprisingly well pronounced language and I wondered whether, like me, he had had speech difficulties. We felt comfortable telling each other our stories. We didn't need to explain about spastic muscles. We didn't need to answer embarrassing questions about going to the bathroom. We didn't need to explain about lability and why we may start laughing or crying at any time or why we often choke on our food. We just knew.

'I had wished I were dead on more than one occasion,' he said. 'And then just this summer I landed this job for the National Trust and I'm rebuilding my life, albeit slow like.'

I let him know how I had longed to be dead also, just to slip out of life with my dignity intact. But now I too had everything to live for, and I don't worry about my dignity in the slightest.

'He that would eat the fruit must first climb the tree,' the man said.

The words seemed incongruous coming from a man who most would look on as a simple, ignorant cripple.

'That's very true,' I agreed. 'Who said that?'

'Oh, it's an old Romanian Proverb.'

I was impressed. But I shouldn't have been as I, disabled myself, was only projecting the stance of a non-disabled society on to him. By these thoughts I was patronizing him. The images of 'cripples' that we are all so used to become ingrained. When you have an accident later in life these prejudices are with you still and it is very difficult to shake them off just like that. It is the strangest thing to look at another disabled person, when you yourself are disabled, and feel grief and pity for them. This incongruity may take years to shake off.

Later that night, lying in a small tent, I was waking-dreaming of my great aunt Ada, long dead now. She worked in the Pennine Laundry in Bolton, Lancashire, washing soldiers' uniforms during the second world war. When her hand went through the huge industrial mangle, used for squeezing every last drop of liquid out of the khaki clothing, she didn't faint. They stopped the machine, opened the rollers up and her hand was a pancake flat, red, indistinguishable shape. She didn't cry even though she must have been in agony. She wasn't acknowledged for her contribution to the war effort but soldiers had to have clean uniforms. Though she never wanted any fuss and didn't like to be a burden to anyone, I thought she deserved a medal.

The doctors of the time used her as an experiment and stitched the flat crushed hand inside her abdominal wall for several months. When it came out she just had a smooth, white club for a hand. They decided to make a thumb by splitting the club to fashion a boxing glove affair. She used to hide it by wearing a mitten without the thumb. Birthdays and Christmas weren't a problem for aunt Ada; the whole family knitted her gloves 'for her hand'. I still remember looking in the sideboard drawer of her terraced council house and seeing piles of mittens.

For years after the war doctors would come and test the 'hand' for life and, so the story went, if she ever jumped when they stuck their needles in she would lose her disability pension.

In some ways I feel like my aunt Ada; disabled but not disabled at the same time.

When you are in a wheelchair, as my friend Warren Macdonald from Melbourne is, you are very obviously disabled. The wheelchair says, 'Hey, look at me everybody, I'm disabled!' Warren had a huge boulder roll on him on whilst trying to climb a mountain on Hinchinbrook Island in Queensland and as a result is a double above-knee amputee.

Another acquaintance, now become friend, Jamie Andrew, had been terribly frostbitten in the French Alps. Jamie, who became a quadruple amputee, isn't in a wheelchair any more but his condition is so obvious it gives the game away in an instant. I know lots of people who are permanently confined to wheelchairs. These amputees and MS people each have something obviously disabling about them whereas me, I have something more nebulous.

Like aunt Ada, the disability isn't so obvious. When I sit down you can't tell I'm disabled unless you look very closely. I don't look any different to anyone else and neither did my aunt Ada. It is only when I stand up and I am left shuffling about like an old man – I am still young and like other young people I want to be places fast – that my disability, becomes apparent. Though I am only too aware of my disability, I am sometimes unsure that I do fit into the disabled camp.

Amidst a dense crowd of people, such as in a bar or train station I will routinely have doors slammed in my face by people who don't notice I have anything wrong with me. If I were in a wheelchair they would be climbing over themselves to be helpful. But I'm not in a wheelchair and I'm glad for it, if only for the simple reason that when I go to a pub or café, I can piss whenever I want to.

On 30 September Jane and I were married in Caernarfon. It was a magical moment, watching her come down the stairs in her Flamenco dancer's dress, into the council chambers – the seat of the council had moved and it is now a registry office. We then drank champagne at Dolbadarn

Castle, a small keep built by Prince Llewelyn in the thirteenth century to imprison his brother. Rain had poured through the month of September and then, as if by a miracle, on the day the sun shone bright. The very next day rain flooded the village for a whole month.

In the evening 250 well-wishers came to a pig shed, decorated the previous night, and danced until five in the morning. One friend said it was like he had died and gone up to heaven, as everyone he knew was there having a good time; that is certainly how I felt. As was our prerogative we retired to our hotel at midnight.

Shortly after my accident, like many that have had a near death experience, I found myself making the most of everything in life. It was unavoidable and seemed like the obvious thing to do. I thought that life was just too short to sit around. In the rehab unit, instead of staring in a trance-like state at the box like the others – one couldn't blame them, as many were severely head injured – I wrote *The Totem Pole*, tapping over one million keys with my single finger. I saw the true beauty and symmetry of anything before me, from flowers and clouds to frying pans and wheelchairs. I began cycling and hill walking. I read avidly and cooked and gardened and experimented with my new sexual being. Then, and I didn't even notice it at first, I slowly reverted back to the same old humdrum of life I had known something of before.

That true adventurer Helen Keller wrote, 'Life is either a daring adventure or nothing.'

I would say the worst thing to do with this life is waste it.

To fritter one's life away through torpor and sloth is perhaps the greatest sin. Whatever happened to that spark I had discovered for the first time so recently?

I wanted desperately for my life again to be filled with that radiance. I yearned to be shot out of the cannon, hurtling through the clouds towards the sun. I longed to ride with the wildebeest on their great migrations. And I would go to the high places again.

A thousand mountains danced in my head.

6

Travails with a Mule

Only a god can tell successes from failures without
making a mistake.

Anton Pavlovich Chekhov

More than three years after my accident I found I was
lacking ambition in the very core of my being. I felt
empty. All I could see was emptiness. All I could hear was
emptiness. I could even taste the emptiness. I had been
going on expeditions for fifteen years; fifteen years of intense thrills and insight into life and death, and now I was
in a desert of hollowness, a vacuum in the excitement that
was going on all around me.

Like the nourishment of food and water, I needed a
challenge soon, it was vital to me. I guess it's in the blood,
once a climber always a climber. The big mountains were
calling. I could hear them in my sleep. The hills of Snowdonia,
although beautiful, were relegated to a distant murmur.
Beloved though they were, I wanted more now than just to
stroll among the hills.

Being a hemiplegic meant that the actual nuts and bolts
of climbing a mountain would be far more complicated
than they had been three years ago. I would have to develop
whole new ways of approaching the problem. What if I had
an epileptic fit at 4000 metres? What would I do then? I

had to make sure that I never became over-exerted or taxed my body too much. This meant walking even more slowly than I usually did, which was about the pace of a hedgehog anyway.

I had to make sure that I never became over-excited. Staying calm was imperative. This proved to be the most difficult task for a writer has to experience events like a sunrise or emotions such as anger, to the full. Or what if I couldn't make a camp spot that day because I wasn't swift enough on my feet? The one certainty was that nothing was certain.

Whatever mountain I did climb now would take a hell of a lot more planning than I was used to. In the past, for a trip of nine months duration, I would pack the night before; throw in my rucsac a rope, boots and hardware, sleeping bag, stove, billy and food and just taking off around the world.

Now it would take several months of planning to tackle only one mountain. Even a day hike, depending on the hill, might take weeks. With the mountains in Wales, I knew the nature of the terrain. It is extremely important to have prior knowledge of the state of the paths as a one-metre step that a 'normal' person wouldn't even notice could take me a quarter of an hour to negotiate. A few of these will seriously lengthen the duration of a walk for me.

On an expedition there will be many mountains and treks that I would have to do 'on-sight' and I must take potluck on these. I had to be prepared, mentally, to fail, to just say, 'Let's forget it,' again and again and treat whatever I came up against with detachment.

As a climber I was used to pushing myself right to the edge but now this was too dangerous. I had to leave myself with the physical reserve to return home safely, and also the time. Time is a very important factor, as it is on every climb, but now I had to be precise, be over-cautious. At the present I have about a thirty per cent failure rate, which isn't too bad, considering what I've done to myself.

The time of year is something else that I am forced to think about, as the autumn and winter are much more dangerous seasons to walk in than the spring or summer. One may laugh, and I will excuse you, for it does seem ridiculous, but autumn leaf litter when wet can be treacherous, as British Rail used to be fond of telling us, and winter ice means a certain fall and maybe broken bones.

I began designing the 'Grand Plan' in 1999 after returning to the Totem Pole. I realized that with determination and lots more healing I could make some treks in the Himalaya. Maybe I could even climb a few mountains. The very thought of it filled me to overflowing with excitement. I would just have to make my choices very carefully if I wanted to avoid torturing my ego, squandering my money and wasting everybody's time, for I couldn't go and climb alone anymore. From now on I would rely on many willing people, not least Jane.

My idea was first to climb a mountain of 4000 metres, and then I would tackle a 5000-metre peak a few months later. If the hole in my skull and my brain could take it, with delicate, precise planning, there would be no limit to what I could achieve. In the dark and dusty recesses of my mind I even had secret designs on going to 6000 metres again or, in the future, even higher.

I wanted to prove to other people like myself that you don't have to lie down and give up on life just because you have a head injury. You can still follow your passion. OK, so I wouldn't be hanging from my fingertips with hundreds of metres of air below my shoe-soles any longer, but I could still do easy rock climbs and treks that would get me into the heart of the mountains. In fact, I am becoming aware that these escapades are every bit as challenging as anything I have ever done, in their concept, planning, training and technicality, through to their execution.

After my accident I harboured a desire to climb the highest mountain in the Americas, Aconcagua. The climber and journalist David Roberts wrote of me in the May 2000 issue of *National Geographic Adventure*, 'It was not the prospect of slogging up Aconcagua that once set this adventurer's heart singing: It was the chance to dance among the angels on some unknown wall in Patagonia or the Karakorum.'

After finding out that the only route on Aconcagua I had any chance of ascending was a crowded, shit-covered rubble pile, I changed my mind. Still, I beg to differ from Roberts, flattering though his words were. 'Dancing among the angels' can be just the same as walking up a mountain; it all depends on the way you look at those mountains and your level of ability. Who's to say that the weekend mountaineer shaking up an easy ridge does not feel exactly the same sensations as an extreme wall climber? With my present incapacity, and frailness of body, I am exposed to greater levels of risk teetering on a one-metre step than I was taking a thirty-metre fall and being saved by the rope.

Whatever activity, be it walking, climbing, biking or tending sheep; they all transport you into the grandeur and beauty of the mountains. What I did miss for a while was the yogic, meditative element of climbing but I have learned that I can still get this through disciplined, careful movement on scrambles. Trying to pick a way across a boulder field, with dreadful balance and without one of those boulders rolling on your legs, I soon found the yogic element I had misplaced.

The recovery from brain injury is slow. Many people can't see an end to their anguish and their resolve to continue battling weakens. They give up on their physiotherapy or neuro-psychology and, worse still, their families give up on them. After a couple of years have gone by the wife might visit the husband in the rehab centre less and less. A father might slow down on his visits to his son because he's tired of getting abused. Mum gets fed up with the 'loony' member of her family and thinks she's putting it on. But that's not the case. The son or daughter in the rehab centre is more confused and tormented than any visitor or family member can know.

There is an end, a conclusion, of some kind for most head injuries but it just takes a lot of time, sometimes years. Families need to keep the patience of a marble statue. I clung on, waiting interminable hours, sometimes days, between visits from friends and family. But those many visits kept my spirits high and aided my recovery.

Researching which would be the most suitable 4000-metre peak to climb, the obvious choice was the 4807-metre Mont Blanc, high above Chamonix. I had never ascended the highest summit in the European Alps, but two things worried me about this mountain. Firstly, it was glaciated. As I hadn't been on snow since my accident, I was naturally worried. What if my foot dragged, as it was prone to, through the snow and I couldn't manage the climb? My foot was also susceptible to the cold and I was scared of getting frostbite in it. No, the four-thousander would have to be mostly without snow. This would then give me time to adapt crampons and develop an electric insole for my right foot, which now has inferior circulation.

Secondly, there would be crowds of tourists attempting to ascend the honeypot mountain of the Alps and crowds don't agree with me. Some people stare and this makes me feel freakish. Once an Australian woman on the trail came up to me and said rather loudly, 'I think you need to see a doctor.' Keith, who was walking with me, has a wicked and sharp sense of humour and, speaking for me answered, 'Well you need to see a plastic surgeon but we wouldn't have told you that to your face!'

I thought next about the Spitzkoppe. This mountain, in Namibia, although not remotely a four-thousander, would have had buckets of adventure. But this could have been too technically difficult for me at this time, as it looked like a steep ascent, and a setback at this stage would do nothing for my mental health.

A steep scramble, that's what I needed; something that would test my endurance but on which, I would still be reasonably safe. A mountain on which, if I fell, I wouldn't fall very far and on which I could test my gear adaptations, my walking helmet and my skateboarder's elbow guard, my footballer's shinpad, my boot-lacer, my strapless rucsac and my knee support.

After a week of pondering I settled on Jebel Toubkal, the highest peak in the Atlas Mountains of Morocco, at 4167 metres. In the photographs that I studied it looked ideal. Although sometimes the mountain could get a sudden dump of snow, people who had spent time there assured me that, if I went in the right month, this would be most unlikely.

My reasons for choosing Jebel Toubkal were also skewed by the fact that I had never been to Africa. There was a whole continent waiting for me, filled to its dark heart with adventures. Friends who'd been to Morocco on climbing trips warned of gangs of pickpockets swarming the unsuspecting tourist and spiriting away your bags and money belt. They advised me to keep out of the souks.

However, after three years of sitting on my behind, none of this discouraged me. On the contrary, it all added to my romantic image of Morocco. All that was left now was to choose my team-mates and book the flight.

I hadn't been away with my earliest climbing companions since I was a teenager and it was with some trepidation that I asked Grids and Phil if they wouldn't mind coming along. I say 'some trepidation' because their prodigious alcohol consumption was well known throughout the Lancashire climbing scene. Each one of them could sup gallons back in the eighties and could well have managed the same now. I used to join in but with my epilepsy I risk having fits now every time I drink alcohol. I hoped that they would say yes before realizing that Morocco was a Muslim country and therefore mainly dry.

Grids used to be a boozing bar fighter, a real alpha male, much like many northern British men. But, unlike other northern males, he was an excellent gymnast and a brilliant climber 'when he could be arsed'. I remember us standing there, bewildered, as he came flick-flacking down the middle of the Black Dog, our regular. I hadn't really seen him in over a decade and wondered how much he had changed. I knew that he had got himself sorted out and now did something with computers.

Phil, back then, sixteen years ago, was a binman with shoulder-length black hair, a headband and he listened to Led Zeppelin and Pink Floyd a lot. We used to hang out in Bolton town centre together and go to the Mad Cider House at lunchtime. This preceded the legendary Thursday evening sessions on Bolton climbing wall where we would boulder till our fingertips bled. Everyone who was famous on the Lancashire climbing scene was there; Hank Pasquill,

Mark Leach, Ian Lonsdale, John Monks. Phil and I were frequently awe-struck.

Phil, unusually for a northern bloke, had a sensitive side to him, which he kept well disguised unless you knew what you were looking for. He was moody and back then I didn't know when I was offending him. But our friendship endured and I saw him regularly over the years. He married another good friend, had a family and moved down south to do something with computers.

In October 2000 Grids, Phil and I boarded a plane at some unhealthy hour at Heathrow airport. It was miserably cold and raining. We flew to Casablanca and on disembarking the heat was so stifling, we couldn't breath. This was what we had come for (well, besides wanting to climb Jebel Toubkal). It is an Anglo-British tourist's prerogative to want to transform into a beetroot when on holiday.

When we came to collect our bags from the carousel, mine was open at the lid. I searched inside and found that my Walkman was missing.

Grids was dumfounded. 'We've only been in Morocco ten minutes and it's already started.'

By the time we arrived at Casablanca railway station we realized that we had forgotten about food, gone without dinner, and were starving hungry. We went into the only café on the platform and Phil, who was the only member of the team who knew French, ordered three coffees. We inspected three cheese sandwiches, which appeared to have our names on them.

'Don't fancy yours much,' said Phil.

Any exposed cheese had a clump of flies feasting on it. The sandwiches rested inside a mesh fly cage, which appeared to have the purpose of confining the flies in a kind of fly prison.

'If you think I'm even touching one of those things you've got another think coming,' declared Grids.

'My thoughts entirely,' agreed Phil.

Unable to overcome my pangs of hunger, I said, 'Well, someone's got to go for it.' And then, in an unparalleled display of world traveller behaviour, added, 'I've eaten much worse things in Delhi.'

So I lifted the gauze cage and, brushing away the flies, took the sandwich back to our table and tucked in under the watchful scrutiny of my two friends – third-world virgins I liked to call them. It had to be said the thing tasted distinctly rancid and the bread fell apart, it was so stale.

We took the Marrakech express from Casablanca; Phil made us travel first class. He had read in the guidebook that even in first class it was wise to employ a guard. But the train was virtually empty and, as we had a locking compartment, we could afford to sleep the whole journey.

We arrived in Marrakech at midnight and took a taxi to the hotel, which Phil, being the most organized holiday-maker in the world, had pre-booked. Phil had also read that there are some taxi drivers that aren't taxi drivers at all and they lure you into their cab, then drive you down a back alley and that's it, you're never seen again. So he had to look at the cab driver's card, which the driver duly showed, though it could have been any piece of scrap paper.

The hotel was a dump, but I kept my cool. 'I've stayed in much dirtier hotels in Rawalpindi.'

'Bully for you,' growled Grids.

'Look, we haven't been on holiday a day yet and you're already starting to do our heads in,' added Phil.

The first thing on the agenda for Grids and Phil was to find a bar which, much to their delight, they discovered only two blocks away from the hotel. This bar was one of only two drinking establishments in the whole of Marrakech.

After two beers I went exploring. I had to be extra careful not to fall in holes down the dark streets. I stumbled upon a busy plaza. There were buskers and fire-breathers, mathematicians chalking problems on the ground, fortune-tellers with cards and peregrine falcons, transsexual belly dancers, acrobats, snake-charmers, snail-vendors and fruit-juicers, water-sellers spinning tassels on their hats with a most peculiar head action, tortoises-racing with brightly coloured numbers painted on their shells, men in turbans betting noisily on the tortoises, men in turbans eating sheep's heads, boys in turbans begging, holding their hands out to you, and all of this taking place to the overwhelmingly high-pitched din of Moroccan flutes.

That evening I told the others of my experience in the plaza and so the next morning, after a cold omelette, we returned. It was the same insane scene in the morning and I remember thinking, does this madness ever cease?

A group of snake charmers spotted us and homed in like true professionals. They must know the green tourists who have only just arrived. I like to describe what took place next as being robbed 'at snake point'.

'You take picture of snake, yes,' said the man in the skullcap, as he approached us wielding several cobras.

There was that high-pitched whining of Moroccan pipes again played by his partners sitting cross-legged on the ground. Snake-man walked towards Grids and me, all the time keeping his eyes on Phil who in turn had his lens trained on the scene.

As the shutter clicked, Snake-man became more aggressive. 'You must pay for your photos.' Then he added, seeming to me to be calculating off the top of his head, 'Twenty dirams one photo.'

Suddenly Grids and I had the snakes hung around our necks. Now I'm pretty cool when it comes to scaly things around the neck but Grids, he started to sweat and was shouting to the man, 'Get this fucking thing off me or I'll stamp on its head!'

I appealed to him to calm down. 'If you stamp on the snakes we'll be in for a right mobbing.'

There was nothing else to do. I limply handed over twenty dirams. Something told me we were getting ripped off. Grids ended up forking out a hundred dirams to get the snakes off him and Phil coughed up fifty.

Someone told us later that the average weekly wage of a policeman in Morocco is twenty dirams. So it doesn't take a mathematician to calculate that the snake charmers got nine weeks' wage for a copper out of us in as many minutes.

We escaped into the first taxi we saw. '*Combien à Imlil?*' asked Phil.

'*Cent cinquante diram,*' answered the driver.

'*Cent Diram,*' retorted Phil.

'*Non, non, non, monsieur. Cent quarante.*'

We had no idea what a good deal was but we did know that it was three hours away,

'*Cent trente, et ça c'est finale. OK?*'

'*OK.*'

We were off in the big Mercedes Grand Taxi. As soon as we had left the red city walls we could see the Atlas Mountains straight ahead. The mountains were close, a long range covering the whole horizon. There was snow on some of the higher peaks.

Presently we introduced ourselves. Our driver's name

was Ahmed; he pointed to himself and with a wide-eyed smile exclaimed, '*Votre conducteur!*'

We asked Ahmed if he knew which one was Jebel Toubkal, for many peaks confronted us. With his hand held out, palm up, fingers splayed, he simply said, 'Toubkal,' with a sweeping gesture and a shrug of his shoulders.

We stopped at the village of Asni to buy petrol for the stove and were instantly besieged by pedlars selling everything from trinket boxes and crystals to knives and antique guns, and the shop-owners were desperately attempting to get us into their shops. I began to drool and twitch and this, added to my spasticity, had the required effect. The sellers became uncomfortable with me and only hassled Grids and Phil. At first I felt bad about this but since then I have used this technique to good effect on numerous occasions and don't feel bad about it any more.

At length we arrived at the village of Imlil. The apple season was obviously upon us and some kind of grain grew in the dry riverbed. Arriving in Imlil was a relief. There were a few hustlers but not so many that we couldn't have a civil conversation with. They were Berbers and very different to the Arabs of Marrakech and other cities.

A friend from Wales had been to the Atlas range and worked as a guide with a man named Lahcen, so we knew whom to ask for. Phil put a question to the waiting group. '*Ou est Lahcen?*'

'*Ah Lahcen!*' exclaimed the group of Berbers in unison and, amidst the chattering, one of them paced off hurriedly. He returned with a small, hooded character. You couldn't see his face. Only by the white stick of a burning cigarette did one know he had a face at all.

I nudged Grids. 'The Man with no Name in *A Fistful of Dollars*.'

Lahcen shook our hands in turn saying simply, 'Hello.'

He was a man of few words but one could tell that whatever he said went. He clicked his fingers and a pot of mint tea arrived. He mumbled something and we were served lunch, over which we learnt a little about the man. He spoke good English, as well as French and a little German. He was the son of the mayor of Aremd, the village we were about to walk to, and as such was next in line for the position. A mere gesture of the hand had our bags lifted into a wagon.

We had six kilometres to walk while our bags were delivered to the guesthouse by four-wheel drive. On foot, up switchbacks in the forest, we got lost and only regained the path with the help of some goat-herders. But it was a joy to finally be on foot and breathing hard. I was already aware of the altitude, even though we were only at 1500 metres, not gasping for breath, just aware.

As darkness was encroaching we arrived at the village of Aremd. It was like we had gone back in time to a medieval place with two-metre wide cobbled streets, no electricity or telephones. There were shutters on the windows and the smoke of burning dung filled the air, stinging our eyes.

Dusk tucked the village up while we were studying the houses. Then Grids decided to help two men who were struggling to manoeuvre long concrete reinforcing rods around a tight corner on the narrow street and from them learnt were Lahcen's house was.

Lahcen was awaiting us on the steps when we finally made it. I felt strangely exhausted and, putting it down to the altitude, had a brief nap. After all, 1840 metres was far higher than I had been since my accident and I had to be very careful.

Over a dinner of traditional lamb tajine Lahcen seemed pensive and I tried to guess what he was thinking. Was he having misgivings about having anything to do with me?

Was he saying to himself, 'What if this guy falls and dies? This might be very bad for business.'

Attempting to salve my interpretation of his negative thoughts, I let him know that I too was a guide.

'I've been over 6000 metres lots of times so this mountain should be easy,' I blurted out.

Though not the intention, this little speech made me sound like a braggart, which in turn caused me to turn red in the face, wishing I hadn't opened my mouth.

Lahcen said straightforwardly, 'There will be a guide meeting you on the steps at eight o'clock tomorrow morning.'

Then he stood up and said in fine English, 'Please enjoy your meals and good night.'

I had decided to renounce my vegetarianism for this trip as I was told that it was nigh on impossible to be a vegetarian in Morocco. I wolfed down lamb and whole carrots and aubergines while my two friends, carnivores both, played around with their food, grumbling that they'd rather have pizza and chips.

We arose at 5.30 am and had a breakfast of bread and jam and powdered coffee on the balcony.

'Look, there's Toubkal.' I pointed to a dramatically lit mountain basking in the first rays of the morning sun. The others agreed with me unquestioningly as I was the 'experienced mountaineer'. It was certainly a big hill and the only one with snow on it, but I didn't know what I was talking about.

Eight am came and went. When the guide we had hired failed to turn up we decided to start walking. The path was very obvious, as it was a pilgrim trail and mule route. We had put our rucsacs on the back of a mule and Mohamed, our mule-driver, waited behind for the guide. It would be easy for them to catch us up.

The landscape was desertified. It was as if God was busy designing the place and then the phone rang and afterwards he forgot all about it. It intrigued me that we were walking past dry stone walls in the middle of an immensely wide yet dry riverbed. A teenager passed us, trotting the other way and carrying a live goat about his shoulders. He smiled and said, '*Ça va.*'

'*Salut, ça va, dude,*' answered our linguist Phil jauntily.

We climbed up the side of a valley, which became progressively steeper. After several kilometres of traversing a hundred metres above the Mizane River we saw, in the distance, a giant boulder painted white. This was the shrine to Sidi Charamouche at which an assortment of pilgrims were assembled.

I had noticed the looks they were giving me along the way but wasn't thinking much of it, for I always get strange looks from people, until I met this short, fat bespectacled man with greasy black hair. Judging by the way that he spoke English, with a fine accent, I guessed he was well educated. He was mounted on a mule, led by a boy, and his left leg was bandaged.

'I notice you have a bad leg too,' he said as he trotted past.

'Yes, I do.'

'How did it come about?'

'Stroke,' I said, as I didn't want to get into extended explanations.

'Are you hoping that Allah will absolve your pain?'

'What?'

He motioned to the boy to stop the mule and repeated himself, looking back to me. 'Are you going to the shrine to pray that Allah will make your leg better?'

'No, I'm going to climb Jebel Toubkal,' I answered perplexed.

Sensing my perplexity, he asked me, 'Don't you know about the shrine to Sidi Charamouche?'

I didn't.

He informed me that a long time ago Saint Charamouche healed a great many people, especially those with leg ailments. If I made a pilgrimage there I would most certainly be healed.

'Wow,' was all I could say, feeling under-educated.

'There is only one catch,' said the man on the mule. 'I am guessing you are Christian and not Mussulman. Am I right in coming to this conclusion?'

'Yes, well, I was baptized a Christian, but I would be interested in seeing what Saint Charamouche could do for me.'

'Then you will have to renounce your former religion and embrace Allah. That is your only chance of entering the shrine.'

'I'll think about it,' I shouted after him as he rode off on his way.

The shrine in its compelling setting on the side of a glacial river reminded me of Hindu shrines I had seen in the Himalaya. A rickety bridge led across the river to Sidi Charamouche where crystal-sellers accosted us, but all I wanted was a cup of tea.

Guarding the shrine was a wrinkled ancient-looking woman who snapped at us in Berber when we approached. There, on the entrance, was a message that we could all read, 'MOSLEM ONLY'. It was painted in English for the benefit of the tourists.

I was saddened for a moment. Maybe, just maybe, Saint Charamouche could have done something for me.

It was here, disdaining even to shake our hands, that our guide approached us and, by way of a pleasantry, made a harsh guttural grunt. Mohamed told us his name was Sid. He wore a blue polyethylene ski jacket with go-faster stripes down the arms and a tea cosy hat and the expression on his oak-coloured face said he would rather be at home playing checkers with his mates.

After several tiny cups of sugary mint tea and a bottle of something bright orange and even sweeter, we went on our way. The track now zigzagged up an enormous scree slope and, for me, the going was very slow indeed. For every two steps up the loose hillside I descended one. I began to feel curiously and depressingly weak, though I had trekked much further than this in the last year. I felt like I was wearing concrete boots and I began dragging my foot, which repeatedly hooked under stones and tripped me up.

What was wrong with me? The feeling I was now having could conceivably be from the altitude: it was nearly one in the afternoon and we had already gained 600 metres. Maybe the hole in my head was causing me to function much worse at altitude than I had previously. I remembered back to a conversation I had had with Charles Clarke, the leading high-altitude medicine specialist and Harley Street surgeon. I was attending an Alpine Club symposium when I noticed him at the back of the lecture theatre. I shuffled over and asked him what he thought my chances were of climbing a high mountain again.

'Cerebral oedema is caused by a build-up of pressure in the skull. It could be possible that you will function better at high altitude because you have a natural valve in your skull for the pressure to escape,' said Charlie with a wry giggle.

'Do you really think so?' I was almost overcome with excitement.

'It is hard to say, as I've never come across a case such as yours before,' Charlie back-pedalled, and we joked about patenting my condition for ambitious climbers. I could see the ads already: 'Want to get high? One little hole is all it takes.'

It is true that when I was relaxed I had a depression on the top of my head, I called it my ditch, and whenever I strained I got a soft, fleshy lump in the same place. But the hypothesis that I would be better off at altitude would indeed be difficult to verify and it seemed now to be proving to be the other way around. I was becoming weak beyond belief.

Once, in the Garhwal region of the Himalaya in northern India, we were attempting a mountain called Bhagirathi III. At Nandaban, our 4500-metre base camp, nausea and dizziness overtook me. Staying in my tent all day long, I only poked my head out to vomit and couldn't keep any liquid down.

Everybody is different and some people acclimatize better than others. It seemed that I had climbed up to base camp too quickly. Joe Simpson, who was on the trip, had some experience of high-altitude medicine and he roused me to ask if I could walk heel to toe for three metres. On the second step I fell flat on to the grass. This balance test is a sure-fire method of diagnosing cerebral oedema, which he recognized straight away. If I had stayed at that altitude I would have quite rapidly deteriorated and it would, sooner rather than later, have become fatal. The team members tossed a coin and Johnny Dawes was chosen to piggyback me down to the guesthouse at Bhujbasa, 1000 metres below, where, on arrival, my wellbeing had much improved.

Phil, Grids and I arrived at a spring in which two Berbers had constructed the most fantastic display of bottled drinks. They had tapped the water and had it running through a sprinkler system so that the effect was of a fine mist drifting across our path creating a rainbow spectrum. Through this mist one could make out red, orange and green bottles all arranged in banks and pyramids. For a desiccated trekker arriving here virtually on his hands and knees this mirage seemed almost spiritual. These guys had it sussed. No one could pass by here without buying at least one bottle. It was impossible.

At the spring I found my resolve to continue walking had collapsed completely, so feeble had I become. I made the very difficult decision to climb on to the back of the mule. It wasn't an easy decision because it spelt the end of my climbing Jebel Toubkal under my own steam, which was the most important thing for me. I wasn't one of these people who would be happy taking a cable car to a summit.

So, unhappily, I climbed up on to the colourful saddle, which also had all our bags strapped to it. With me the mule must have been carrying 250 kilograms, nevertheless his agility impressed me. I didn't have any stirrups, so every time the beast climbed up a step of above a metre's height I nearly got bucked off. In this manner I rode past tottering pillars, vast cliffs and a meadow with a matrix of streams running across it and dark boulders dotted here and there.

Grids and Phil mucked around on the boulders, trying to climb up them. I think Grids got up one, though I wasn't very interested, preferring to travel deep into my thoughts on why I was getting so ill again. If it was the altitude then I should be descending not climbing higher. I was torn between my ambitions and my increasing weakness.

I was angry at the swiftness with which we were travelling, how hard we were working, the altitude we were gaining but, because I was ill and steadily declining, I didn't say much about it. Sid was gesturing that we should climb the mountain in three days up and down like everyone else and he was rushing me. He said in halting French, '*Un jour au Neltner, un jour au sommet et un jour pour decendeur.*' Which would kill me.

Every time he saw our sleeping mats and bivvi bags Sid would shake his head, as if to say, 'Don't you people know there is a refuge up there?'

When we finally arrived at the Neltner refuge I was somewhat saddle sore but I wore a beaming smile of satisfaction. It was my first attempt at riding since my accident.

At the hut doorway I had my path blocked by Sid, who pointed to my feet and then to a box of slippers outside. Evidently he wanted me to wear the slippers before I entered but because of my splint I could not. With the splint I have to wear my shoe. I motioned to him pointing to my right foot and then shaking my head saying, 'No.'

'No', everyone can understand that, I thought.

Sid grumbled and grunted and stopped me from entering. After a few minutes I realized that I wasn't going to get in without the slippers. So I took off my shoes and, on stockinged feet, struggled through the dark passages of the refuge, twisting my ankle violently, painfully, and often.

My wellbeing deteriorated at dinner and I should like to draw a veil over the rest of the evening and the night that followed, except I have a lurid memory of vomiting copiously into my favourite hat that a good friend back in Wales had made for me. The other two all enduring friends who were nearer to hand took it away to empty and brought me a cloth. Later, staggering down three flights in the dark, I wet myself and disturbed the guides' sleep. During that night I plumbed new depths of misery.

At 5 am Phil and Grids arose and came to see whether I was up to doing the hill. I wasn't. The last thing I wanted,

or was able to do, was climb a mountain. I had an unhealthy grey pallor and I kept on retching painfully. A
deflated balloon, that is how I imagined myself. Not just
physically but mentally deflated too.

There was a discussion about taking Sid but Phil and
Grids decided to play a cruel trick and left him with me. I
had a rant into my Dictaphone about my friends abandon-
ing me and going up the hill when I was probably suffering
from altitude sickness and should have been descending
urgently.

I was homesick for the first time in my life and I had only
been away from Wales for three days. When I was seriously
injured and locked away, in the hospital and then in my
own body, for three years I had become accustomed to
comfort. Everything else was hurting, so I reasoned, why
not make myself as comfortable as I could.

But this had backfired on me. I was used to sleeping
anywhere, from a hammock 1000 metres up a cliff face to
behind filthy rubbish bins in the centre of Grenoble, but I
had evidently become too soft. I was missing Jane; we had
only been married three weeks and I wanted my
comfortable bed with her in it. Wouldn't it be nice to have
her mop my brow and bring me hot drinks? Why on earth
did I come to this godforsaken rubble pile in the middle of
the desert? If it was a slag heap I'd asked for I might as well
have gone to the local slate quarries and saved myself
hundreds of pounds.

Kingdoms of Experience, Andy Grieg's Everest book,
just happened to be lying around, left by one of the
Toubkal climbers no doubt. Friends and acquaintances
populated its pages and reading this made me even more
homesick. I openly wept as I talked into my Dictaphone;
my guide and the muleteers mustn't have known what to

144

make of me. They were probably thinking, we've got him up but how in Allah's name are we going to get him down again?

About midday Grids burst through the door looking as if he hadn't even been a walk in the park. But then Phil virtually crawled into the refuge on his hands and knees a good half an hour behind.

He muttered, 'You're lucky you didn't come with us. That was bloody awful.'

'Don't say that, Phil. I'm really depressed.'

'I'll tell you what, I wish I'd stayed here with you.'

'But that was my dream just extinguished. I'd been planning this for ten months.'

But it wasn't just the time spent planning. It was something else. It was a blow to my self-respect and it raised all sorts of doubts as to whether I could continue on this course in my life.

'Perhaps I should just give up trying to climb mountains. It won't do anyone any good anyway.'

The child in me wanted my friends to bolster my ego, for them to say, 'Don't give up, Paul, it'll all be OK next time, on Mount Kenya, just keep fighting.'

But they weren't like that. They cared for me in their own way. These were hard men. I wanted Jane there to stroke my hair. That's what I wanted. But I wouldn't get any of that from these friends. All the shoring up of my ego had to come from within. When I got home I was actually glad of this.

Grids exploded, 'It's like you said, we might as well have walked up a slag heap and burnt a thousand quid.'

He was a funny bugger.

'There must have been something good about it.'

'Not really. It was just a giant 1000 metre scree slope,'

offered Phil. But did he not realize that I would have given anything to go through what they had just experienced? How I would have relished the pain of a 1000-metre slag heap, the burning that I knew so well, like my muscles were on fire. How I would have cherished the freezing cold in the early morning, the dry thirst in my throat as we ascended, the glare as we contemplated the horizon of late morning from up high. I would have given my right arm, literally, to climb to the summit of Jebel Toubkal. It only got in the way anyway.

After the guys had eaten lunch we headed on down. Worried as I was that I was still suffering mountain sickness, I wanted to descend as quickly as possible. I mounted the mule with the help of my two friends and once again, less than twenty hours after arriving at the Neltner refuge, rode down the narrow path in the direction of Imlil.

The descent was much worse than the ascent and the only way I had any chance of preventing myself being bucked off was to lie on my back all the time, almost resting the back of my head on the mule's backside. It must have looked very strange to the other trekkers, a man, seemingly of good health, lying down on the back of a mule with a look of horror in his eyes. In this manner I rode for a few hours until what I had most feared happened.

Grids and Phil had run ahead to have a cup of tea at Sidi Charamouche, leaving me alone with Sid and Mohamed the muleteer. We were traversing a particularly unstable scree slope which fell away to the right, my weak side. The dead weight of my dense, limp leg coupled with the ever-loosening saddle strap around the mule's belly to effect a disastrous consequence. The saddle spun around the mule's girth and I found myself upside down with my head between the mules kicking legs. There was a vertiginous, ballbearing scree slope dropping off by my shoulder. Looking up, I could see the Mizane River raging several hundred metres below though the rucsacs, on which I had been riding, and which were now strewn across the path.

My head hit the rocky path with a thud. Because of the hole in my skull it felt as delicate as a paper lampshade, brittle like an eggshell. I was lucky to get away with nothing worse than a ten-centimetre gash.

Down at Sidi Charamouche Grids and Phil helped me dismount.

'You could at least have been around when I fell off that bloody horse,' I moaned.

'It's not a horse,' said Phil. 'It's a mule.'

'OK, OK.'

'I apologize. Do you apologize, Grids?'

'Nah. It'll do 'im good.'

They did stay with me from then on though.

That night we were back in Lahcen's guesthouse in Imlil, Grids and Phil tucking into a delicious tajine, licking their plates clean. I endeavoured to eat a plateful but due to stomach cramps that felt like my insides were being tied in double knots, I only picked around.

Grids passed me a bottle of bright orange fizzy liquid, 'Here, drink this. It'll do you good.'

Half a bottle is all I drank before rushing straight to the bathroom to painfully throw up.

But by now I was mildly relieved. The reason for my surprising contentedness was that we had shed a 1000 metres and I was still being sick. I reasoned that this, unequivocally, pointed to stomach illness.

The exact same food as my compatriots was all I had eaten. Or was it? I thought back to that dark railway station in Casablanca and the cheese sandwich. It was painful to accept that my failure on Jebel Toubkal was due to a bad cheese sandwich. Still, better this than altitude sickness, which is what I feared most.

'Only those who dare to fail greatly can ever achieve greatly,' that's what Robert Kennedy said.

I think I get his point but had I failed greatly enough to succeed on Mount Kenya?

7

Mount Kenya for Headway

> But legs come with a high price: the software to
> control them. A wheel, merely by turning, changes
> its point of support gradually and can bear weight
> the whole time. A leg has to change its point of
> support all at once, and the weight has to be un-
> loaded to do so. The motors controlling a leg have
> to alternate between keeping a foot on the ground
> while it bears and propels the load and taking the
> load off to make the leg free to move. All the while
> they have to keep the centre of gravity of the body
> within the polygon defined by the feet so the body
> doesn't topple over.
>
> Steven Pinker – *How the Mind Works*

After arriving back in Wales I knew I had to push that
debacle on Jebel Toubkal out of my mind if I was to
retain any semblance of self worth. I threw myself into
organizing the Mount Kenya for Headway project. I had
decided to raise awareness and money for the head-injury
charity Headway, a cause close to my heart. Sir Chris
Bonington CBE was to act as patron and I got approval
from the British Mountaineering Council; now all I
needed was some money. There was a lot to sort out,
including a national raffle, a book auction via the Internet, the never-ending, but eternally fascinating tinkering

with gear adaptations and searching for a commission to make a film.

Just when I thought all was lost on the filming front, Meg Wicks and Richard Else at Triple Echo Productions came up trumps with a commission from BBC Wales. Meg would direct cameraman Keith Partridge, and my old mate, the alpine guide Brian Hall, would come along on safety. The three of them I knew well, so my plans couldn't have turned out better. Most importantly, we knew we would all gel as a team.

'The short rains have not stopped and will run into the long rains I think,' said the abnormally skinny taxi driver.

But every one knows that drivers of taxis the world over talk rubbish. Nevertheless it was supposed to be the dry season and it was pissing down in Nairobi. What would it be like on the mountain? Would it be deep with snow? Why hadn't I even bothered to bring crampons and ice axe? This rain only exacerbated my disposition to worry.

We were headed for the freight terminal at the airport where, once inside the compound, we were assigned two 'fixers'.

'I'm Dixon,' said the short, very dark man who was impeccably dressed.

'And I am Willis,' said the second, who was taller, lighter and impeccably dressed.

Dixon and Willis were like LA cops from a TV series.

'We are here to make things smooth for you,' said Willis.

And Dixon added, 'Yes, smooth. You need us. Without us you would be here all the day and all the night.'

I surveyed the scene. It was complete and utter mayhem. As a British person I was taught to form an orderly queue;

instead there were hundreds of men all crowding around kiosks, all trying to shout louder than the next man, all waving notes in the air.

'So what will it cost us,' asked Jane.

'For you, only six thousand shillings,' answered Willis.

Jane did some mental arithmetic while my mind wandered; even before my head injury I was never any good at maths.

'That's about sixty pounds,' she deduced.

I looked again at the seething mass of people and said, 'To get our barrel through customs, that's well worth it.'

We handed the cash over and Dixon and Willis set to it, pushing and jostling, shouting to be heard, bribing others with our money.

'How long have you been here?' asked a southern English accent over my shoulder.

The man wore a pair of spectacles with only one arm on them. He was unshaven and looked very weary.

'Oh, we've just arrived,' I answered. 'How about you?'

'Well, don't be disheartened but, and this shouldn't apply to you, three days!'

'Three days! How've you managed that?' Jane asked with a gasp of surprise.

'We're doing marine research and we have bottles of gas that they're not happy with. I guess they think we're smuggling drugs, but why ever would anyone want to smuggle drugs into a place were nobody can afford them?'

The afternoon drifted by as we sat on a bench in the shade, visited sporadically by Dixon and Willis who had reams of paper they needed signing. 'Here on the dotted line please.'

The two of them then approached and Willis asked for more money.

'What have you done with the six thousand shillings you were given,' I enquired politely.

'We had to use it for bribes etcetera,' answered Dixon in a very convincing impersonation of Yul Brynner in *The King and I*.

'How much then.'

'Only thirty thousand,' answered Willis, not to be outdone this time.

We could tell that the pair were out to rip us off but at least they did it with a smile.

Eventually a fellow with incredibly thick lenses on his spectacles beckoned me into a huge hangar. And there it was; the blue barrel, nestled between two crates. It wouldn't be mine for a few hours yet but I was happy to have it in my sights. I had to confirm it was indeed mine by signing on the dotted line, then agree to having the barrel searched by customs. Luckily they found nothing. Then I had to join a long queue to leave through a door which officials in suits kept firmly locked, and sign an exit form to remove the barrel from the hangar.

Just one more signature was needed to leave the compound and that was it. We thanked Dixon and Willis for doing a fine job and finally took the barrel to our hotel.

That evening we were filmed over teriyaki with Mr Mount Kenya himself, Ian Howell. He has climbed more new routes on Mount Kenya than any other person.

'I came to Kenya thirty-three years ago because I wanted to climb Mount Kenya and I never went home,' he said in the precise manner of an English gentleman.

He continued, 'I gained employment in Nairobi with a telecommunications company but now all that is, alas, coming to an end.'

I enquired why.

'Well, you see, I'm retiring, and besides, I can't stay in Nairobi.'

'Why not?' asked Brian.

'It isn't safe anymore. People are getting robbed, burgled and mugged left right and centre.' Wistfully he added, with a twitch of his nose that moved his spectacles, 'I'm going to have to go back to Britain. I have a house and family in Gloucestershire.'

One got the sense that he was lonely but that may have been my writer's brain reading too much into a situation. I didn't question him further on the matter.

After dinner we got around to the logistics on the mountain. He unfolded a map and began tracing the route we were planning to take. 'This is the Chogoria route, the route you are looking to attempt and this here . . .' he lost it for a moment '. . . is what you are aiming for, Point Lenana.'

I feigned ignorance, as it was good to hear that which I had read about for months from his mouth.

'You will climb via Minto's Hut and then here by the Austrian Hut.'

I asked him if it was normal for there to be so much rain in the dry season.

'No, it certainly is not. Ever since that dreadful El Niño we have had the strangest weather here in Kenya. . . unpredictable, unseasonal. You might experience deep snow on the mountain. Are you prepared for that?'

'No, not exactly.'

'And the roads might be impassable due to deep mud.'

All this doom and gloom was beginning to get me down. It wasn't his fault. He was quite bright about the whole trip.

'You'll have a fantastic time whatever happens, summit or no summit. Mount Kenya is a very special group of peaks.'

We paid up, left a BBC-sized tip, and jumped in a taxi.

Early next morning, we paid a visit to the city hawkers' market for Brian to log up some local colour amid the plantains and saris and Maasai spears.

'Look at that whip-wielding security guard,' I mentioned to Jane, whilst on camera, knowing that Keith would then have to film my POV or Point Of View.

As Keith was filming the guard he sauntered over to us, all the while tapping the coiled whip on his knee-length boot.

'Were you just filming me?'

'Well, actually I was. Why, do you mind?' retorted Keith.

'Yes, I bloody well do.'

'I'm very sorry. I'll tell you what. I won't use it! How's that?'

'Papers,' demanded the guard, the tempo of the tapping on his boot increasing.

Keith looked at Meg and Meg rummaged around in her briefcase. She waved a piece of paper in front of the guard. It was permission to film in the Mount Kenya National Park and he read as much.

The security guard glared at Keith for what seemed like an age until he finally got out what he wanted to say. 'You give me shillings.'

'Ah, it's like that, is it?' said Keith, who had already showed his skill at surreptitious filming in the freight depot and was now doing the same with bribery. 'How much then?'

'Fifty shilling.'

'No can do, big guy. How about ten shillings?' Keith held both hands up with his fingers splayed.

'I think forty,' smiled the red-eyed guard who had

dropped his aggression a little and was beginning to enjoy the bartering.

'I think twenty.'

'OK, thirty-five or I will put you in jail.'

'Thirty-five it is then,' agreed Keith.

Although we were staying in one of the poshest hotels in Nairobi, on BBC expenses, we were determined to find the cheapest way of getting to the mountain. The local bus was fifty times cheaper than a taxi and correspondingly less safe. While Brian and the bags travelled in a Landcruiser, Jane and I rode to the mountain on the public bus to Chogoria.

On all my travels I have been determined to travel in the cheapest possible mode. This means that you get to mix with normal local people instead of being protected from them with the other tourists.

Clambering onto the bus, a guy called Phineous gave us a bunch of leaves to chew on. Khaat is very popular throughout Eastern Africa and has a natural amphetamine in it. We sped along chattering and smiling. All the while the driver was going for wild, dangerous overtaking manoeuvres as Jane sat with her eyes shut tight and white knuckles gripping the seat in front of her. In the rear-view mirror one could see the orange stained teeth of the chewing driver.

As we ripped along Jane noticed coffin and headstone vendors lining the roadside. Kenya has one of the highest road mortality rates in the world.

When the bus pulled in to collect more passengers, teenagers out to make a few bob would crowd around to sell fruit and sweets though the sliding windows. I bought a bag of passion, as the fruit is engagingly known in Kenya, and gave the lad a minor note expecting him to disappear. On the contrary he went and asked his mate for some change and then gave me a handful of coins back.

We sped past pineapple plantations with barbed wire fencing and lookout towers all around. I asked the man in front of me why there was so much security.

He said casually, 'Del Monte,' and went back to his newspaper.

Corn grew everywhere on the central reservations of the highway. This use of space is in my mind a fabulous lesson for UK governments. How much acreage is wasted on the central reservations of Britain's network of motorways? I suppose combining it might present a bit of a problem though. The more altitude we gained, we began to see tea and coffee plantations.

The Transit Motel at Chogoria was like the *Marie Celeste*. We had to put our order in for dinner two hours beforehand, even though they only had five meals to cook. The moth gracing my omelette I was too hungry to complain about.

A lively team of porters arrived at ten next morning to take charge of the BBC gear, and Jane and I found two for ourselves called Gabriel and Charles. Then there was Bernard Kinyua, our guide, a thickset man who was always smiling, displaying his fine teeth. He had obtained a scholarship to go to America to learn guiding skills and spent nine months in Jackson, Wyoming which was no doubt where he picked up his Eddie Murphy manner.

He said with a sheepish smile that the name Kinyua actually means 'One who drinks a lot of alcohol'.

'So you're telling me that your name means piss-head?' Brian wondered whether to believe him or not.

We were attempting the most beautiful route on the mountain, the Chogoria route on the east side. Most trekkers attempt Mount Kenya from the west side, the

Naro Moru route. But first we had to get to the beginning of the long walk in.

Like skeletons in cupboards the bamboo forest rattled hollow and echoing in the warm breeze as for twenty-three kilometres the two Land Rovers slid about in ruts up the boggiest road imaginable to the Park-gate. Eddie the driver, who with the speech impediment, just grinned as the Land Rover tilted to the point of capsizing.

The number of times we had to bail out and start digging or rocking the Land Rovers I lost count of. When I say 'we' I mean everyone else except me because Eddie wouldn't let me help, while the others were forced to walk for long stretches in the deep in mud. There were also leopard tracks in the mud and maybe, just maybe, one observing us from the bamboo. I guess he knew that big cats go for the lame.

At Urumandi Lodge, at the Park-gate, we erected our tents. We didn't want to taint the wilderness experience up here by sleeping in a house so we slept below the hagenya trees, the leaves of which fell continually like a gentle green snowfall. The Lodge is at 3000 meters and the beginning of the long trek up Mount Kenya.

The team pitched the tents in a circle and we all got an early night but then, 'What was that?' said Jane sitting bolt upright.

'What? I didn't hear anything,' I replied dozily, but then heard it too. . . Heavy footfalls and tearing vegetation. It was the middle of the night and we were trapped in a tent surrounded by wild beasts. A distant howling and a not so distant grunting then began.

'Oh, that! Probably just some antelope or buffalo,' I whispered attempting to remain calm. Unzipping the door of the inner tent, I fumbled with the head-torch.

'Get . . . back . . . in . . . the . . . tent!' Jane now hissed with a terrified urgency in her voice.

'I want to see it, whatever it is.'

'It'll panic if it sees that torch.'

'OK, I won't use the torch.'

I undid the zipper of the fly just in time to see the moonlit rear end of a huge elephant disappearing into the bush. Pulling the tent door shut I snuggled back down into my sleeping bag and drifted back off into a fitful sleep as the distant howling of the colobus monkeys continued.

We arose before the sun and discovered the strangest thing; my walking pole appeared to be missing. I always stick it in the earth outside the door so that I can use it to climb out of the tent, but now it had gone. Huge plate-like tracks were all around the tents and these I followed into the bush. Lo and behold about thirty metres from the tent, in the long grass, was my walking pole. It appeared that the elephant picked it up in its trunk, twirled it a few times like a majorette, and then hurled it into the forest.

'Why do you think there's a path into the bush here?' I asked and then, realizing why with shock, we looked at each other and grinned inanely.

'Oh, my God!' Jane exclaimed putting her hands to her mouth.

We were camped right in a game path. At night scores of elephant, buffalo and warthog would use a track that went straight through our tent, not to mention the leopards and lions that follow to feed on them.

To calm ourselves we strolled down to a grassy clearing with fine views of the peaks where we photographed the mountains as the sun bled over the horizon, a deep red turning to a profound orange before the day, all too quickly, stole the dawn.

I was learning how to use my newly adapted camera, which George Smith, a good friend of mine, had designed. He had put a bracket under the base with a handle going up the left-hand edge of the unit. To this he had attached an electronic cable release. Added to this the camera had an auto-focus, and George had attempted to solve my zooming problem by gluing an arm to the lens that I could push on my thigh.

The weather had changed in the night and the sun was now beating down with some ferocity as we breakfasted and struck camp. We had to be expeditious about this so as to get the porters on their way. The last thing we wanted was for them to be left hanging around. Our entourage of Keith, Meg, Brian, Bernard and the nine porters would walk six kilometres – to get us, but especially me, acclimatized – to the next camp. The fundraising for Headway had taken up so much of my time that I hadn't had time to train or go walking for a couple of months. My lack of fitness was a grave worry to me. What if I couldn't do it? What if I couldn't even make the walk in?

The first step was of immense importance to me. It wasn't just the first step on the mountain but the first step of a new life, a life of adventure in my new-fashioned body. I took that first step:

My brain began to compute . . . The motor cortex, on the top of my brain at the front, kicked into action. At precisely the same time a sizeable area of my brain right in the centre, the basal ganglia, also began to fire. There are usually about a hundred million neurons in a brain, though mine now contains a few less, and the motor cortex and basal ganglia hold a fair proportion of these cells.

All these neurons have up to a hundred thousand dendrites, thin wiry inputs, per cell, and millions of these

159

signalled all at once in my motor cortex. One of these pathways went straight to my legs to initiate the step, whilst the other travelled via the basal ganglia. The basal ganglia helped me with my posture and muscle tone, or anti-gravity control, so that I didn't collapse in a formless heap on the ground.

Once the signal arrived in the cell body a new signal was triggered and began its journey out of the cell via a special exit route called an axon. The electrical signal travelled a metre down my spine at the speed of 400-kilometres per hour. The current then crossed the synapse, a tiny gap containing neuro-transmitters, acetylcholine or dopamine, to the cell next door. This process repeated itself a couple of million times until the weak electrical current, about eighty-thousandths of a volt, reached its destination: the skeletal muscle fibres of my legs. Rectus femoris, quadraceps femoris, gluteus maximus, biceps femoris, gastrocnemius and soleus are just a few of these muscles.

At the very same moment a cauliflower-shaped structure at the back of my brain, the cerebellum, began to receive input from my feet, legs and torso. It then began the unenviable job of keeping me upright. This was achieved by sending out in the same manner, neuron to neuron, electrical signals to the skeletal muscles all over my body, orders to tense or relax, depending on where my centre of balance was. Minute, or in me very large, shifts in position were thus made continually.

My basal ganglia, motor cortex and cerebellum all had to work in consort to initiate the movement of walking. Two without the other make for a complete disaster. The left parietal motor cortex in my brain is significantly damaged so the right half of my body has a substantial task cut out for it to move at all. All these functions have to work together in a cascading system to commence action.

I continued walking as millions of neurons were firing up and down my body, deciding to move, initiating movement, and twitching, more or less, all the muscles in my body, balancing. Electrons were coursing up and down my frame, I could sense it, I didn't just fancy it. In this dynamically charged manner I walked, electrified . . . You can tell whose been studying the neurology textbooks.

We went on until the way was virtually barred by a gigantic pile of elephant dung, which stood over knee-high. In drying mud we then came across footprints of the animal, circular and as big as dinner plates.

Further down the track we came to a bank of clay that had been excavated and I asked Bernard what a mechanical digger was doing out here?

'Not a digger?' he said. 'See the tusk marks? It is the elephants. They are digging for salt.'

The hagenya trees formed grand tunnels and the sun sprinkled a golden dust through the branches, from which lichen was hanging down like grey hair.

Bernard told us the lichen was known as Old Man's Beard. 'It means you do not have to carry toilet paper!'

Two hundred meters before the Roadhead Campsite I was forced to stop and deal with painful abrading and blisters on my foot.

Brian noted, 'You seem to have the worst of both worlds. Your foot is paralysed and yet you have all the feelings of pain.'

This may appear so but it would be a lot worse if I didn't have any feeling. I would just continue walking with worsening holes in my feet and the ever-present probability that they would become infected. At least the excruciating pain was an early warning signal.

Jane and Brian got to work on my toes. Brian thought that the toe area of my splint was too thick so whittled it carefully with his penknife. While he did so Jane wrapped my toes individually in strips of Second Skin.

'That should do the job,' said Brian passing the splint back to me. Why hadn't I done this before, I thought, studying the fine job he had made of it. Then I remembered that I couldn't do things like that on my own any more. I had to ask friends to do tasks like this for me. I thought of a dream workshop I would have one day with vices of all sizes to take the place of my hand. This little task having saved me blisters, I could now walk the last few metres to the campsite.

Jane didn't have the same attitude to the porters as I did. She was used to carrying all her own kit on her back and thought hiring people to do it for you was immoral. I tried to explain how respected porters are in their own communities but I know I hadn't convinced her. She still tried to carry heavier packs than they did. But to save weight she had spent months beforehand dehydrating broccoli, mushrooms, courgettes, aubergines and onions. Brian, on the other hand, was a veteran of many expeditions and used to buying fresh food along the way. Eventually he took pity on us and handed over some fresh potatoes and carrots.

Jane and I carried the same sized rucsacs and at first the other trekkers would look censoriously at her, not realizing mine was full of feathers and hers full of food and cooking and climbing gear. But after only one afternoon Brian convinced me to do away with mine as it was causing me to lean radically and twist with every step. I didn't need much convincing. My back was already paining me. Luckily, as their loads were light anyway (not having to carry fresh vegetables), Gabriel and Charles could share my load between them.

Rucsac off, the first obstacle to be negotiated was a small, icy cold river with stepping-stones across it. With Jane standing on the opposite bank and Bernard and Brian on either side I set off across the slippery stones. From the bank the first stone was a big flat-topped rock, which I stepped onto without any ado.

There were two more strides to the far bank but on most attempts my right foot doesn't behave itself. It lands not where I tell it to but ten or fifteen centimetres to the right, left, forwards or backwards. I stepped my left boot onto a greasy pyramid-shaped boulder and un-weighted my right boot. For a brief moment I was balanced on my left foot, frozen in the image of Eros in Piccadilly Circus. I thrust out my trekking pole to Jane but it was just short of her grasp. I had to take another step.

Perfectly, and unexpectedly, my foot hit the last stepping stone. In one smooth movement I lunged toward Jane, pointing my trekking pole, as a fencer does a foil, as if I were performing a Botta dritta. She grabbed the end of the epée and unceremoniously hauled me onto the far bank.

After sitting in a bush for a minute to get my breath back, we trudged up the hill in single file. The path was a metre deep trench and just wide enough for a boot. White protea flowers grew to head-height, as did the pollen-laden giant heather. I held a cloth over my nose whenever I passed by one of these. Bernard informed us that the giant heather usually grew in forests up to six metres high but there had been a fire on this side of the mountain which decimated all the plant-life. 'That is why the heather is only two metres tall.' He added, 'You should see the other side of Mount Kenya, which was untouched by the '89 fires. It is truly beautiful.'

I found it hard to imagine a place more beautiful than this.

Bernard then pointed over our shoulders: 'There is Mugi Hill and the Giant's Billiards Table.'

Kilingo as the Billiards Table is known in Bernard's tribal language, Kikuyu, is a remarkable hill with the top clean cheese-wired off.

Two tawny eagles circled about, high in the now bright blue sky, as the porters steamed past in a workman-like manner. Nothing could prepare me for what I saw next. As we approached a flat ridge there unfolded before us the most heavenly view I have ever seen. On the other side of the ridge dropped sheer orange cliffs, 400 metres to a flat-bottomed once-glaciated valley. In this, the Gorges Valley, the silver thread of Vivian Falls tumbled down a full 500 metres farther from a green flat pasture. Another smaller fall dropped down into this pasture from the glistening waters of Lake Michaelson.

There were the weird flower stems of cabbage groundsels here and there, as well as a profusion of grey-petalled and orange-stamened helichrysum. This carpet was dotted with alpine buttercups and we could see our distant objective for the first time.

Pondering the scene before me, I believed at that moment that if we all saw such sights every day of our lives, and showed the corresponding emotional response, we would all be so overwhelmed that we wouldn't be able to achieve a single thing. We come across very powerful feelings every day but our brains tells our minds that we've seen it all before and, yes, we are aroused, but not that aroused.

I do not have the science to back up my theory but I think it is the brain's way of dampening down the senses so we aren't in a continual state of over-arousal. And yet that which lay before me was so serene, so ethereal, that it set me thinking if people saw the true beauty in each and every thing they wouldn't have the urge to make war.

The summits of Batian and Nelion had their heads in the clouds, as occurs every morning like clockwork at eleven. But I knew exactly what was up there inside those clouds from the photographs I had so often studied back at home. I knew the shape of the mountain, like a big letter M, with Batian by a trick of perspective appearing lower than Nelion, even though it is the higher of the two.

In front of the two main peaks there stands Point Lenana. Although 200 metres lower than Batian, it seemed almost equal in stature because it was considerably nearer. Point Lenana was mottled with patches of snow and crowned by a darker rock that fell away precipitously.

In the words of Felice Benuzzi, author of that classic of mountaineering literature, *No Picnic on Mount Kenya*: 'It looked imposing: a black violet rock perched on a bright white ice dome.'

This was his first sight of Point Lenana after escaping from a nearby British prisoner of war camp in 1943 just to climb the mountain.

Due to global warming the glaciers on Mount Kenya are retreating at an alarming rate and the ice dome Benuzzi writes of is now no more than a few permanent snow patches. Almost sixty years on, it looks a very different mountain from the photographs in his book. Bernard confirmed this.

'Glaciologists say that in forty years' time there will be no glaciers at all on Mount Kenya.'

In my weary state and so stunned by what I was seeing I fell headfirst into a gap between two boulders. The porters simultaneously jumped up to lend a hand and pulled me out and back upright. One could see visible shock on Gabriel's face. Thankfully I was unscathed.

'First fall,' I remarked.

'Let's just hope it's the only one,' said Jane, who was rummaging about in her pack.

Keith was filming us constantly but I was glad that the camera was momentarily off me. Brushing myself off, I perched on a rock whilst Jane got the lunch bag from her rucsac: mackerel in curry sauce, dried fruit and strawberry-flavoured cheese. The strawberry cheese was a mistake; We hadn't bothered to read the label and threw several packets of the dreadful stuff into our trolley.

During lunch Jane was strangely quiet. At length I got out of her that she had been suffering from stomach cramps the whole day.

'I'm absolutely knackered,' she said, adding wearily, 'I just want to sleep.'

'It does that to you, altitude,' said Brian who was our resident altitude expert.

It may have been something to do with the fact that she was a 1000 metres higher than she'd ever been before and carrying a weight, which even the porters don't like to carry, and they live at this altitude. She agreed to give up some of her load when we got to camp.

As I munched, Brian asked Bernard where the route went from here. 'This place is about halfway to the camp,' he replied and then paused as he proceeded to trace out the route on the landscape with his finger. 'It goes over this hill and down.' My eyes followed his finger.

'Then over the middle hill and down.' My eye fell upon the distant place to which he was now pointing. Surely, I thought, the camp must be there. 'Then across the flat and up the cliff,' Bernard carried on.

'How far then, after the cliff?' I asked impatiently.

'And down to the camp after maybe twenty minutes,' he retorted with a kind smile.

I squinted. Unless my eyes were playing tricks with me, and the camp Bernard was pointing to was actually a hell of a lot closer than it seemed, we still had about ten kilometres of walking ahead of us. I was already feeling giddy with the altitude as I limped off toward that distant place.

We passed a pinnacle, which the guidebook told us was 100 metres high. It turned out to be no more than thirty metres, but beautiful nonetheless. Mentally I traced a route on it that I would have loved to climb in a former life. Across the gap . . . up the thin flake . . . climb the shallow corner . . . and then the crux . . . a helmet of smooth granite right on top. All the while Keith was hovering around us, getting footage of our boots tromping, of us donning our hats, of us eating our dried fruit, of Jane and me doing anything.

At one point, climbing up a winding narrow path through a cluster of dark brown rocks, I overbalanced, toppled off the path and somersaulted down a drop of a metre.

As I went I seemed to have all the time in the world to work out and act upon a whole sequence of movements: put your left arm out . . . Make sure you land on your left side . . . Whatever you do don't damage your right side . . . And watch you don't bang your head because you ain't wearing no helmet.

Fortunately, I hadn't broken any bones and I didn't need any stitches but to risk many more falls had the very real possibility of jeopardizing the whole trip. I castigated myself for being so stupid as to be wearing no helmet.

From then on I vowed to take much more care. If at any time I felt fatigued I would have a sit down and take five.

It would be foolish to fail again. My failure in Morocco through being ill was one thing but here at least I had a modicum of control over this situation.

Finally, after trekking up and over numerous rocky hills, we came to the wall about fifteen metres high with a series of ledges going up to the left. The porters were long ahead. It felt like a ritual, putting on the helmet, snapping together the plastic buckle and tightening the chinstrap.

Giving Jane my stick, I fingered, caressed even, the rock holds. I remembered their texture, not as grainy as granite, yet not as smooth as sandstone. It was a rock I had felt somewhere before. For a moment I was lost in a world of reminiscence. I was a good climber once. I had done things that people thought were crazy and just took it all in my stride. I climbed alone without ropes once, naked, to the top of a mountain in Argentina, because it made me feel alive.

Now I had to have Jane above me, coaxing, me and Bernard on the outside, fielding me to make sure I didn't fall off a ledge. But I was doing it! I was climbing Mount Kenya. I was much more comfortable now that I was actually on my way, instead of feeling the trepidation that comes with intent.

There was water running over a shelf and I wasn't convinced that my foot would stick, not being very good at slippery surfaces.

Even though Bernard was only a single metre away and Jane just above, I felt vulnerable. What if Bernard failed to catch me? I probably wouldn't survive a ten-metre fall, not now that my head was already cracked open. I clambered on to the top of the cliff, surprised and shocked at the difficulty and magnitude of what I was attempting.

While descending another hill, I became exhausted and sensed I couldn't go on. After Morocco I could not endure another failure. It could have spelt an end to my mountaineering endeavours. I slumped on my back on a boulder.

'How do you feel?' asked Jane.

'I'm well and truly fucked,' I exhaled.

My head was swimming in thick glue and I was seeing double. It was already late afternoon and I knew from what Bernard had told us that the camp was at least three kilometres farther. Then a strange let-whatever-happens-happen detachment swept over me: It isn't my problem if we get benighted.

But it was very much my problem. This lazy train of thought was dangerous.

We climbed down through a wonderland of penis-shaped rocks some of them ten metres tall and all of them with a helmet shaped glans atop. Bernard had led us to believe that there was no water in the form of streams or pools for that whole long day. So when we came to a stream at 4000 metres I wept with relief.

'This isn't supposed to be here in the dry season,' offered Bernard, more to himself than to us.

The stream was little more than a trickle; to me, in my dizzy state, it resembled a ribbon of molten silver. The path ahead was obvious as it wound its way across a meadow to the base of yet another cliff, then disappeared over the horizon. Even though Bernard did his best to demonstrate how near we were to Minto's Hut, I couldn't face another rock face and persuaded him to let us camp were we were.

We had entered a hanging valley, the silhouettes of giant groundsel waiting to ambush us on three sides, while the stream fell 500 metres into the Gorges Valley, just a few metres from the tent. We were right on top of a huge overhanging cliff.

Brian went to check out a giant boulder with all the faces overhanging: 'If only we'd brought our slippers with us, that boulder would have given some good sport.'

I was too knackered to study the boulder in detail but, even at death's door, I could summon up enough energy to have a quick glance. Climbing maybe out of the question for me now but that doesn't stop me from remembering how climbing a boulder used to feel.

It was here that I felt the intense beauty of the mountains properly for the first time since my accident. I sat on a rock outside the tent and began sobbing. All those emotions that I had felt when I had been to those wondrous places, they came flooding back into me, all at the same time. Sunsets and sunrises over Karakoram peaks . . . avalanches and rockfalls into deep valleys . . . movement on rock and the glowing texture of the rock . . . the wildness of Patagonia . . . the remoteness of Baffin Island . . . travel to far off lands, Khirgizistan, Baltistan, Borneo . . . or the homely peaks of Wales . . . Too many happenings to mention.

Those memories I had held at bay for far too long for fear of hurting myself. I didn't want to get upset about something I could do nothing about. Getting depressed would have only disrupted my rehabilitation programme. But here it didn't matter, I felt as though I were free again. Free to see, hear, smell and feel all those mountains all at once.

Like Felice Benuzzi I too had been imprisoned, not in a POW camp but in hospitals and in my own body. I too looked out from my prison bars at what he saw: 'an ethereal mountain emerging from a tossing sea of cloud. A massive blue black tooth of sheer rock inlaid with azure glaciers, austere yet floating fairy-like on the near horizon.' And like him I, 'stood gazing until the vision disappeared amongst the shifting cloud banks'.

That night I dreamed of climbing a vertical rock wall. It was the Redwall at Gogarth, my favourite place to climb: it was a hot summer's day. Even though my face was a foot away from the rock I could feel the heat radiating from it. It hummed with the heat. I dreamed that it was almost too hot to touch. There was a fine sand on the holds under my fingertips and I was crawling up (or was it across?), around intermittent vegetation, drifting across lichen and through spider webs. I seemed to be levitating up the wall, watching its folds and creases passing me by. Carabiners were clinking about my harness. I was thirty metres out from my last piece of protection . . . And the heat was suffocating me. I was having difficulty breathing.

I awoke doing battle with my sleeping bag in the dead of night and sweating. It occurred to me, before I drifted back off to sleep, that I had a fever.

The morning of 16 January I awoke to the sound of footsteps crunching around outside. When I stuck my head out of the tent door, I saw Keith filming.

'I can't believe my eyes,' he said with a look of amazement.

Across the whole landscape, as far as we could see, there was full five centimetres of hoarfrost. I had witnessed such phenomena before but never to that depth. It was like a carpet of crystal and, as the sun came over the horizon, the ground glittered as though we were on a sea of quartz. We stood together, like the crew of a boat upon a sparkling ocean, and gasped.

Once, in the Garhwal region of the Himalaya, in the early morning, I had walked amongst a garden of ice roses, those mysterious frozen petals laid one atop the other in a circle, in the manner of a hand of cards. And just as the ice roses had melted in the sun, so our carpet of quartz soon disappeared with the warmth of the day to grow again the coming night.

171

In the twilight Lenana was a dark mass, silhouetted against Batian and Nelion, Lenana's heavies, who were wearing their shades, arms folded, trying not to enjoy the last rays of the sun. The evening was so clear. I was having the opposite experience to the first European to see the mountain.

Johann Ludwick Krapf saw Mount Kenya for a fleeting moment in 1849 during a break in the interminable cloud that keeps this hill hidden from prying eyes. He described it as 'an enormous mountain over which rose two large horns or pillars [Batian and Nelion] covered with a white substance'. When Krapf returned to Europe and gave his news to the Royal Geographical Society they laughed at him. 'How can there be snow on the equator? You just saw calcareous earth!'

Sir Halford Mackinder made the first ascent of Batian in 1899 and Eric Shipton climbed Nelion exactly thirty years later in his coffee planter days before he met Tilman. But nobody knows who laid claim to Point Lenana.

We may never know the identity of the first ascensionist and this is a wonderfully provocative fact. Here is a mountain higher than the highest mountain in the European Alps and nobody can be sure who made the first ascent.

By now I was developing the unmistakeable signs of mild mountain sickness. Even with Brian's Diamox, I still needed an acclimatization day and what more impressive place could one ask for to kick around for twenty-four hours. It was like a set out of *Star Trek*; strangely lit with the weird rocks and plants all around.

Early morning 18 February saw an ant line of porters, film crew and climbers traipsing off up the mountain on what was to be my most arduous day.

Bernard said in his Eddie Murphy-style, 'Look in the distance to the far off ridge. Well the hut is just the other side of that.'

'Yeah, right. How many times have I heard that,' I laughed.

Hanging back with me, Bernard opened from being the professional, thorough guide to being a chatty, friendly and full member of the team. As we walked through this wonderland of lakes and mountains and flat-bottomed valleys, I dug around in this man's life.

Bernard had a wife, Wajira, and a daughter of two years, Idha, whom he missed very much. 'But they are only on the other side of the mountain and are close if anything happens.'

I asked Bernard if he had any difficulties obtaining a visa for the States.

'Well now, there's a story. Yes, they made me jump through some bureaucratic hoops, like they do all Africans, but I got there after two years of trying. My good friend Ian Howell wrote me a reference.'

'They thought you were going to try and move there even though you have a wife and baby back here in Kenya?'

'Yes, yes, but listen to this. I went into Nairobi, to the American Embassy, to collect my visa and that was the day of the bomb.'

'Which bomb?' I asked, momentarily forgetting.

'The Osama bin Laden bomb. Do you not know of that?'

'Oh, yes. Yes. Of course.'

Bernard was thrown though a window and out into the street. He woke up in the hospital with severe concussion and a closed head injury, the most acute form of Acquired Brain Injury (ABI). There not being a hole in the skull, the swelling has nowhere to escape to and so the pressure builds up within the brain, which results in brain damage.

'Apparently I was found wandering in the middle of so

much carnage with blood all over my head but I don't remember anything of that.' He paused, sighed, and then continued, 'And that was the first time I had ever been to the US Embassy.'

That was some story, I had to admit.

Bernard then challenged me to feel his head.

'I'll feel yours if you feel mine.'

Running my fingers across his scalp, I felt the dints in Bernard's skull.

'That's nothing. Feel my head,' I dared him.

'Oh, my God. That is a terrible hole,' he said, reflexively taking his hand away, as I think he thought he was doing me harm.

Walking and talking intermittently, we covered many subjects. One subject I had read a little about but wanted it from a Kikuyu's mouth was the relevance of Mount Kenya for his tribe.

'Kirinyaga is its real name. We will make sacrifices on Kirinyaga; a goat's neck will be slit and we hang it from the branches of a fig tree. Then we leave it over night and if it is gone in the morning, then our prayers have been answered. Usually we pray for rain. We would never cut the fig tree. This will make Mogai angry.'

I asked Bernard who Mogai was.

'Mogai is our God. He made all things. Now most Kikuyu don't pray to the mountain or make sacrifices under the fig tree. The young people go to the church. But there are a quite a few older people who still sacrifice the goat.'

Did Bernard still believe in Mogai?

'Oh, yes,' he instantly replied and then went on, 'But I also believe in your God. To me they are one and the same.'

Trekking for a kilometre or so across a flat bog, I still felt I was being observed by the skinny human figures of the giant groundsels. We then came upon a 400-metre hillside of steep loose gravel and scree which, to my relief, turned out far less steep that it appeared from straight on. I should have been aware of that illusion, having come across it many times before. Mountain faces can seem nearly vertical when viewed from square on. Also the scree, which I had expected to be loose and awful, was relatively solid underfoot.

From high on the hillside I looked down at the way we had so far climbed. In the distance one could see the huge molehill-like feature of Mugi Hill and the planed top of the Giant's Billiards Table with its green tablecloth. I could make out the Bandas, the track as far as the roadhead and the path along the broad ridge. I could see the flat-bottomed Gorges Valley and the steel mirror of Lake Michaelson with the great orange cliff of the Temple plunging into it. On top of these cliffs there was Minto's Camp with Hall's Tarns dotted about.

To my right were three peaks, Macmillan, Delamere and Corydon, with the perfect green penny of Hanging Tarn perched on an improbably steep hillside just below. Directly above us on the ridge where we were headed was a tottering yellow tower called the Tooth. And just behind me the porters were sitting around Square Tarn, eating dried fruit and filling up their water bottles. Above, Point Lenana towered. We had another 100 metres to reach the ridge and, I was promised, the hut wasn't far past here.

So, after four hours of hard sweaty work, we found ourselves milling about on the ridge and beholding another view, which was altogether different from that which we had just climbed up. After the lush Gorges Valley, I turned my head ninety degrees to the barren and desertified Hobley Valley. With hardly any vegetation in sight, this was a moonscape of rock and rubble.

I sighed as I looked around me. The hut was nowhere in to be seen. But then I saw a vague path traversing across a couple of kilometres of loose scree and yet another ridge.

'Is that where we're headed now?' I asked Bernard with some surprise, though it was obviously the only path up here.

'It's only a little distance.'

'And the hut is just the other side of that ridge?'

'Just the other side of that ridge.'

We had to descend to a boulder field to get to the continuation of the path. These boulder fields are my worst nightmare. I could easily break my leg on these sections. At least I had my footballer's shinpad on to prevent my shinbone from being skinned should my leg go down a hole. My strength had left me and my body was working on an alloy of determination and sheer will power. Jane hurried ahead to put the tent up for my arrival. Later she told me of how she took off jogging but, out of sight, collapsed in a gasping heap because the air was so thin.

The leg, which had carried me so far now started to complain, 'Am I not a reasonable leg?' it questioned me. 'But now you've gone too far!'

To prove its point it started to shake violently, throwing me off balance. It was rebelling. I needed to coax it, use all my charm to calm it down. In the end I had to sit on the scree and have a long rest. As I watched the swirling clouds building down in the Hobley Valley, my fear returned. Looking up at the sheer cliffs sweeping down from the summit ridge, now directly above me, I was gripped by sickness and loneliness. How on earth was I going to overcome those precipices? I had got myself in too deep.

When I eventually climbed over the ridge the camp was immediately there, all set up, and Jane was waiting for me with a steaming mug of sweet tea. There was a hut built of wood, which must have been on the same site as the iron hut Benuzzi had seen.

This was the Austrian Hut where the porters would sleep.

I was already on the point of tears when I staggered into Jane's arms.

She gave me a cuddle and, crying now also, she whispered, 'I think you're very brave.'

'We're not even at the top yet,' I sobbed, regardless of the fact we were being filmed in our intimate moment by Keith and his long lens.

Hitherto we had been surprised that this, the second most popular mountain in Africa, was so empty, especially at the height of the tourist season. The west side of the mountain; the Naro Moru route is the busiest route and that is why I left it well alone. A quiet time, that's what I wanted. But here several brightly coloured tents adorned the rough moraine and quite a cosmopolitan crowd was stumbling about the rocks. We had hardly seen a soul thus far and were somewhat put out to have our solitude interrupted.

Snow was falling on the rocks and settling on the hut roof, which didn't augur well for the following day. This just added to my worries. The summit ridge looked less imposing from here and I thought, perhaps naively, that I could climb it. Now I had got this far I couldn't imagine turning back without giving the that ridge a determined attempt, but I couldn't even think of it with the rocks blanketed in snow and ice.

We went into the dark hut to cook our dinner and we met – though the meeting was a little one-sided – an Austrian couple who were rude to the point of absurdity.

'How are you doin'?' I said to the heavily bearded man by way of a pleasantry.

He looked down his moustache at me with a look of scorn, as if to say, 'Who do you think you are, talking to me?'

'Hello,' I said with a little more persistence.

This heavily logo-badged man just snorted down his nose at me.

This response urged me on to crank the handle and persist in my enquiry, 'Are you going to climb Batian?'

He looked away and I still received no response. Thinking, perhaps, that he was deaf I put an end to my questioning.

Almost immediately afterwards he began telling his porters off. 'When I have been in the Himalaya, climbing Cho Oyu, I had much better service from the porters than I am getting with you!'

I couldn't believe my ears. My arm began to rise up from my side in anger.

The local porters just grinned and talked between themselves in Kikuyu, even though they knew English.

'You bloody ignoramus. It is people like you that make all Westerners seem like idiots!' I wanted to say, but in my weary state I couldn't get the words out.

For a brief moment I also wanted to tell him that I was a famous climber, probably more famous than him, and that I had been told that Cho Oyu was only a snow plod. But what was the point? The outburst would have only made me look pathetic.

Then in came his wife. She was plastered in logos too, the names of the companies that sponsored them. Some climbers, strangely, stitch logos onto their clothes when they have nothing to do with the company to make them look like they are important sponsored mountaineers. I do not know whether this was the case with the Austrian pair who were obviously professional climbers attempting Batian or Nelion.

I cringed. It was painful to see how others must have seen me once. OK, so I was never so rude but I still thought I was more important than many other people just because I could climb better than they could.

Bernard had already enquired with the porters just what the pair were doing there.

'They are The Austrian Mount Kenya Expedition.'

'What. Just the two of them?'

'Yes. They have just missed the summit because they have been involved in a rescue.'

'Oh, God. Who was rescued?' I now felt I had done them a disservice for being so quick to judge them.

'A porter,' Bernard sighed

'A porter. Up on the rock face?'

'Yes . . . Yes, a few porters can go on the faces. He froze in a crack and couldn't move up or down. The Austrians climbed up 500 metres and got him down.'

'That's a great deed but still, they don't have to be so rude.'

'No, you would think not. But some of the tourists think that the porters, and even the guides, aren't as good as them. They think that they can do everything better.'

Jane trotted down through a building-site landscape to the Curling Pond, which was frozen solid. She had to chip the ice out with a piece of granite and fetch it back in a saucepan before getting a brew on. The two of us ate couscous with dehydrated broccoli, peas and courgette, with fresh potato and carrot from Brian, a real carbo-load. Apricots straight from the can topped off a meal that one could never order in any restaurant.

The Curling Pond is at the snout of the Lewis Glacier, the only glacier left on Mount Kenya. There used to be more than eight glaciers on the mountain but in the past sixty years these have dwindled so that now there are just a few hectares of permanent ice. In another twenty to forty years there will be no ice at all on Mount Kenya, so bad has global warming become.

The much-famed Diamond Couloir has totally disappeared, as has the Ice Window route. It had been my ambition to climb the Diamond Couloir ever since I read about the route in *Mountain* magazine at the tender age of sixteen.

Wandering and tripping into the starry moraine, my breath condensing in the head-torch beam, I retired at eight in the evening to be as well rested as possible in the morning. Before crawling into the tent I stopped and, for the first time in days it seemed, gazed up into the dark, pinpointed heavens until I saw a shooting star. Then, happy I had seen one, I retired into my nylon turtle shell.

Sleeping through the freezing night was not difficult in my snug chrysalis of down and when the alarm sounded, at 5.15 am, there was rime ice all over the inside of the tent. We had put the stove in the doorway so that we could make our sweet milky coffee from the warmth of our sleeping bags. Jane then made us instant porridge which I choked down, almost puking once.

As the sky lightened in the east, I struggled to dress myself, squirming on my back in the tent. I slid both my elbow pad and shinpad on, which made me picture briefly a warrior preparing for battle. Then I struggled with my boot and splint and, after shunning the offer of help from Jane, finally laced them using the Paul Pritchard patented toggle system.

I had devised a system for putting my boots on alone; holding a length of string in my mouth with a plastic karabiner attached to the end, I have a spring-loaded toggle on my laces. Getting the laces round the hooks of my boots is a job but after completing this I hook the karabiner in the lace and hold it tight. This allows me to slide the toggle down my lace.

Finally I stood, unstable, on the piles of rock as the vague red on the horizon turned to a glowing ember.

Threading my hand through the wrist loop of the walking pole, I took the first step of the final 250 metres to the summit of Point Lenana. The first hundred or so steps of a day's walking are always the most strenuous for anybody, but for me especially and in particular when the going is on unstable rocks. My leg takes a while to warm up and find its place on my unbalanced body and my torso remains asleep, twisted and stiff. This is just until the tendons and ligaments stretch. There was not a cloud in the sky and as the last star was fading, so another perfect day began.

The nine porters, including Charles and Gabriel, would not climb with us to the summit. They would stay at the Austrian Hut and hang out in the sunshine. This particular trip will have been casual for these guys, strolling about in a relaxed fashion. Other porters on the expensive tourist 'expeditions' we had seen were weighed down with chairs, tables and even toilet seats. It was surreal to say the least, watching tourists having dinner brought to them while they sat on chairs at neatly laid tables amidst the piles of rubble.

Shortly after we had left the hut the golden ball of the sun crept over the horizon and the six of us stood stock still on the ridge. Like devotees of Islam we all faced east basking in the sun's warmth. After about an hour we came to the first difficult section, a loose scramble of perhaps ten metres to ascend back up to the ridge. As my feet dislodged stones, I watched them tumble and bounce 400 metres to the less-steep hillside below my feet. Around my waist I had no rope and felt the exposure, the void below me, with a dizzying pressure from above.

Almost immediately after the rubble scramble there was another obstacle, a projection on the sharp ridge were I became fast for a full thirty minutes. In frustration I tried just about everything to overcome this. I attempted hopping and flopping my torso onto the shelf but, on looking down, I became cradled in fear and couldn't commit with any conviction. In intense concentration I perched awkwardly on the ridge.

'Perhaps you should use your bottom,' suggested Bernard.

'Oh, yeah. I'd forgotten about my bum.'

With help, I jumped in the air and spun my backside around so that I could balance on the ledge. Once there I walked my bum-cheeks backward onto the projection and with my hand swung my leg up on to it. Teetering over the void I lifted my other leg up on its own and then powered up on just one leg. I was shaking with the effect of the adrenaline coursing through my veins and I informed Jane that I would need a rope from now on.

As Jane tied the rope around my waist with a bowline, a group of tourists coming back down from the summit crossed our path. The guides like to get them to the top for sunrise, which means getting up at 3 am. Anyone who knows me will realize that, if there was a way of avoiding this sadistic ritual, I would have taken it. There were two English women, an Australian couple and their guide.

I asked the holidaymakers if they could see Kilimanjaro from the top but they shook their heads, 'Too much cloud.'

'And what about the difficulty?'

'Oh, there's a pretty steep wall in a hundred yards,' said one of the English women. 'I thought that was the hardest bit.'

At least I had a rope on now. I wouldn't say I wasn't struggling but I was much more relaxed now I was getting to grips with that summit ridge. It had been my ambition for two long years, this mountain, and now here I was on the last leg.

Meanwhile Bernard chatted to the guide in Kikuyu. He had been teaching Jane and me some Kikuyu phrases and the guide was impressed when Jane greeted him with, '*Ninatcha.*'

The guide answered, '*Nequerda,*' as one always does.

Not to be outdone I waved and said, '*Tu town na na,*' with briefly confusing my Kikuyu Swahili, as they carried on their way down the ridge.

Once tied in to the rope, with Jane using her short-roping technique, I was more confident and felt as though I could take risks with slippery footholds or loose handholds. At times, in my excitement, I was climbing up the steep path too quickly for Jane who had to jog to keep ahead of me. But this proved to be a poor strategy, as I would then collapse, gasping for oxygen in the rarefied atmosphere.

A little further along the ridge was the wall that the English woman had mentioned, about five metres high and moderately steep and difficult.

Brian took over my protection and, after ascending the wall, put a sling with a karabiner on a rounded rock spike and, clipping the rope into it, braced himself, should I fall. After the first move, where Jane had to hold my big boot on a small rounded knob, I climbed unaided, belayed up an open groove in the wall, bridging in my hiking boots. My right leg still wouldn't do what I asked of it but the joy of actually climbing again, on a rope, was overwhelming. Even with only one arm and a leg that wouldn't behave itself, I could climb. I had made it easily, if strenuous, and straightaway my mind was occupied with pretensions of harder climbs.

Sitting on top of that wall I surveyed the landscape below and above me. A party of three was climbing on the lower section of the South Ridge, the normal route, up Nelion. Batian and Nelion were just on the other side of the Lewis Glacier and we could see the summit hut glowing in the sun. Ian Howell built that hut by soloing up to the summit of Nelion thirteen times with pieces of the thing. Determination counts for a lot, I think.

The rock on Nelion looked unstable, like a shattered limestone quarry, but Bernard insisted it was excellent rock.

Down below, nine brightly coloured, beetle-like tents clustered around the Austrian Hut, now bathed in sunshine. The dirty carpet of the Lewis Glacier was just fifty metres below us but ten years ago we would have been sitting on the ice, so far had it shrunk and receded. There was an impenetrable band of cliffs between the summit and us and these set me to worrying once again.

'How the bloody hell are we going to get up those things?' I asked Brian, not really expecting an answer.

Pulling myself to standing, I once again wound my way around the several gendarmes on the ridge and then discovered to my relief that the path went off to the left and joined the west ridge rather than attack the cliff band head-on. Steaming up this final section of snow-patched ridge, I was feeling great until stopped in my tracks by a wall, just one last step, of about three metres. This time there was no way around. The crown of basalt, so difficult to scale, sits on top of a bulk of kenyte lava, which is in essence rubble.

Jane climbed up on to the top first and I followed her on

the rope. I remember the sharp holds cutting into my hand. I remember Brian having to hold my boot on the ledge. I remember finding the perfect hand-jam and milking it for all it was worth. I remember getting one knee on top of the mountain. I remember throwing the other knee on to the top of the mountain. And I remember Jane giving me her hand and I taking it, and accepting her help to stand precariously.

Walking up the final few metres to the summit, tied to Jane, after all the planning, worrying, fundraising and hard work, it was as if I was in a trance, numb. Had I been hypnotized by this mountain? No. I was approaching my first of many more summits.

Jane hung back to let me be the first to touch the summit. On the very top, painted on a sheet of steel, were the crossed Maasai spears on the vertical eye-shaped shield, the symbol of Kenya. Bolted on to a rock was a bronze plaque dedicated to Johann Ludwick Krapf with these beautiful if devotional words:

GO SAFELY FRIEND, FOR HERE IS HIGH, GO DARINGLY,
WHERE EAGLES FLY, GO ETERNALLY, WITH JESUS NIGH.

As the summit photos snapped and flashed and amidst the hugs from Jane and Brian, the peck from Meg and the handshakes with Keith and Bernard, I felt strangely detached and deflated. After two years of planning, scheming, designing, training and fundraising, I now had to search for new ambition. I was lost again, adrift again. This was a feeling that I knew well.

And as with all my climbs that went before, the enjoyment and fulfilment is never on the summit and only comes in retrospect when one is safely on the ground. We were only halfway through our journey and still had to get down what had taken us five days to climb up. I think I hid my concerns about the descent well, apart from asking what the time was about four times while we were on top.

'Nine thirty,' answered Jane.

'Nine thirty-two,' answered Jane again.

'Why don't you just buy a watch?' she finally answered.

I'd proved to other head-injured people that they could still follow their dreams, whatever they may be. I had awareness raised in the climbing community of head injury issues. Most climbers don't know just how devastating a head injury can be and ninety per cent had never heard of Headway. Now they had. And I'd raised several thousand pounds for Headway. But, by undertaking this climb perhaps the most important personal demonstration was that I could still get out there and see the beauty of wild places, look down on the world, just like I used to.

'How do you feel?' asked Meg.

'I thought I would have been an emotional wreck on the summit but I must be all cried out,' I answered, paused, and then added some banal statement; when the camera is on you, you have to say something.

As we began our arduous descent I saw a picture of Moel Elio in my head; that soaking and stormy day now seeming so very long ago. How far I'd travelled on the journey of recovery and how much I had discovered about myself, how I fit into the world around me and the nature of my relationships with others, and how they have changed, since that first climb in my new body. I had experienced the highest highs and the lowest lows. I had failed and I had achieved and been just about everywhere in between.

This had been the most severe test of my life on the most

beautiful of mountains. Yes, closer, more precarious, more of a balancing act than any of my previous extreme rock or ice climbs. And more difficult than any of 'my' mountains, more tortuous than Mount Asgard, after twenty days of sled-hauling, more painful than Trango, on which I had suffered pulmonary oedema, and requiring more staying power than the Central Tower of Paine, on which we slept for three weeks in hanging tents.

Why do I do it? I had asked myself this question many times as an able-bodied climber and here I was asking myself the very same question again as a disabled one. I had only one answer. To feel alive. And at this moment I felt more alive than I had felt in a very long time.

And I was sated again . . . For the time being.

After all I had been through I was still a climber at heart.

8

Scar Tissue

Nothing in life is so exhilarating as getting shot at
without result.

– Winston Churchill

Jane and I moved to Tasmania in December 2001. Apart
from Jane wanting to go home – she had spent two years
in Wales and wanted to see her family again – it was
important for me too. Not being part of the climbing scene
any more, I felt it was time to move on and begin a new
life. Not many people get the chance to re-invent themselves. It was as though I had died: the professional climber
was being re-incarnated as a crippled Tasmanian writer.

We settled in a rain forest on the slopes of Mount
Wellington, or Pooranettaraa as it is known to the Nuenonne
people. Tasmania is a cosmopolitan place compared to rural
north Wales. Added to the 16,000 indigenous Aborigines
and the Anglo-Saxon settlers are Vietnamese, Laosians,
Italians and Greeks, remnants of immigrant workers who
were brought in to work on giant dam projects in the fifties
and sixties. Tasmania is powered solely by hydro-electricity
and its scores of dams stand testament to a bygone age.

On 'the Mountain' I spent my days walking, cycling
when it wasn't raining, and writing. If there's one act that
has helped me more than the interminable physiotherapy,

it is writing. Writing about, dissecting and studying my misadventure has aided me beyond reckoning. It has helped me make sense out of what, at first, seemed not to have any sense at all.

It has been over seven years since the life changing occurrence on the Totem Pole. Some would say I am gathering up the scraps of a life torn apart by a terrible accident but I prefer to call it progressing on life's pilgrimage; forging ahead and taking the adventure of being head-on.

In *The Totem Pole*, I poured my life out on to the page and in so doing I saw that I do have mental strength after all. That re-awakening has raised my weakening self-esteem to a new level. Analysing the altered relationship with my family and my ex-partner, Celia Bull, has been essential to my present disposition, as has the whole exploration of my changed mind.

One historical figure who may have found healing in the form of writing is Geoffrey Winthrop Young. That greatest of pre-great war mountaineers lost his leg whilst in charge of an ambulance on the Italian front. Despite the surgeons having to amputate above the knee, he didn't give up and went on to climb the Matterhorn on his prosthesis. This verse from his poem 'Wind Harp' is especially poignant:

> What if I live no more those kingly days?
> Their night sleeps with me still.
> I dream my feet upon the starry ways;
> My heart rests in the hill.
> I may not grudge the little left undone;
> I hold the heights, I keep the dreams I won.

Joe Simpson said of his own book *Touching the Void*, 'Digging up all those skeletons only served to scare the hell out of me but spending twelve years lecturing on the same story, telling it repeatedly, almost fictionalized it, distanced it from my mind.'

But surely writing one's traumatic story down is the first step in a cathartic transformation to distancing and fictionalizing.

Apart from an on-going healing process, there is also a genuine want to empathize, touch or help someone. I had to be totally honest with my fears of not being able to urinate again and all consuming self-doubts about my inability to have sex. Amongst others these are the things that people with head injuries will worry about to all heaven.

Perhaps most importantly, throwing down what happened on to the page has aided me in seeing my place in human kind as no more or less trivial than anyone else's.

Jean-Dominique Bauby, Jaqueline Spring, Christopher Reeve, Helen Keller and Christie Brown are all people who wrote perhaps as a form of healing. Jamie Andrew, Warren Macdonald and Aron Ralston are other contemporary climbers to have written of their own ill-fortune.

Macdonald lost both his legs at mid-thigh when a massive boulder rolled on top of him on Mount Bowen in far north Queensland. His 1999 book, *One Step Beyond*, reads like an ode to his lost legs. At first he consoles himself with the positive memories of having been places that most people have never been.

He also likens himself to a baboon he saw once in an African wildlife documentary on the TV. The baboon is trying to get to a water hole that is writhing with crocodiles. In the end, dying of thirst, the hapless primate risks everything and approaches the pool. He finishes up with his head in the jaws of a crocodile but miraculously wriggles free. Macdonald recounts how the rest of the troupe stare at him as if he were a ghost, 'because it forces them to face their own mortality'.

He likens himself to the baboon as, now in his wheelchair, he feels the eyes of strangers boring into him.

Immediately after the accident he thought the part of his life involving climbing and being active had gone forever. But by the close of the book, just two years later, he has moved on towards an acceptance of what he has become and, mischievously, can't wait to pick up his first hitchhiker in his car. Moving on, he has now climbed Mount Kilimanjaro and Tangerine Trip, a big-wall route on El Capitan.

In an email interview he said, 'I saw it as a chance to tell my story in a way I wouldn't be able to tell in that kind of depth in general conversation. It was mainly a huge relief rather than a purging of my soul.'

Obviously it takes a strong willed person to be on the end of the pen. But plenty of this stuff would have just been buried and forgotten if he hadn't started writing and that may have made healing a longer, more painful process.

Jane was introducing me to a great deal of Tasmania and much of it on foot – bushwalking was one of the few ways I could get exercise. It was on one of those trips, to Mount Eliza in the south-west wilderness, that I first laid eyes on Federation Peak. I could only gaze at the saw blade of the Eastern Arthur's silhouetted against the blue of the Southern Ocean, with one giant oversized tooth, Federation Peak, towering above the rest. To a climber, even a disabled one, this mountain was irresistible.

Jane had already traversed the range and told me it was recognized to be the toughest bushwalk in Australia.

I grinned as I felt a challenge coming on.

'We'll need plenty of help to get you across there.'

It is normal for an able-bodied person to traverse the range in five days but we had no idea how long it would take us. We planned for eighteen days of food.

About a year after the accident, when I sold every scrap of climbing and mountaineering gear, I also gave up my sponsorship deals. Now, for the first time in more than fifteen years, I was faced with having to pay actual money for my equipment. It is expensive stuff, climbing gear.

Deep in the forest we parked the truck by a bridge spanning a lazy river, black with tannin. The diversity of vegetation was precious; myrtle, sassafras and celery-top pine, pre-historic manferns and pandani. This was relic vegetation, present on the continent of Gondwana sixty million years ago.

Beyond a locked gate we entered a country of black devastation. Bulldozed piles of smouldering timber lined the roadside. The contrast was astonishing, from a sub-lunary paradise to the hell portrayed in Hieronymus Bosch's *Garden of Earthly Delights*.

I shook my head. Nearby, one of the last remaining stands of eucalyptus regnans, the tallest flowering plants in the world, was due for harvesting. Many of these hard-woods are sold to Japan for seven dollars a ton as wood-chips to make toilet paper.

With Jane hauling me up by the scruff of my jacket I scrabbled up on to another fallen tree. It was like trying to climb on to the roof of a VW Combi covered in Vaseline. At times I would have to commando crawl under a series of fallen trees, getting Jane to push my sack in front of her.

Bauera, a dense thicket with small razorblades for leaves, ripped our thighs until they bled, a little like fighting through a tangle of razor-wire. This is possibly the weirdest aspects of Tassie bush walking behaviour – they insist on wearing the very shortest of shorts and after a two days of enduring this kind of attack the thighs are left red raw.

On one fight through a bush I got my foot stuck under a root in ankle-deep water and, with my arms windmilling, went down like a caber. Suddenly there was an excruciating pain in my scrotum.

'I . . . I . . . Get . . . Aaagh . . .'

'What's the matter? Do you want a hand?' enquired Jane rather calmly.

'Yes . . . I've . . . There's something in me bollocks.' I forced the words out at last.

Jane pulled on my arm and got me to my feet. There, just under the surface of the water was a sharp, snapped off sapling, about four inches high, on which I had impaled myself.

Jane shrieked as I presented my backside for her to inspect, 'Oh my God, there's something red hanging out of your shorts.'

'What do you mean.'

'It looks like entrails.' I heard a gasp. 'It's just dropped off!'

I peered down warily at the water between my legs. expecting to see my insides steadily sinking. But all I saw was a floating piece of red gum bark.

Climbing up on to the range, we approached the Four Peaks. These involved actual rock climbing and abseiling. When we arrived at the base of the first peak I donned harness and helmet and Jane tied me into the short rope.

Snatching a fingerhold with my only usable hand, I stepped up with my good leg on to an outside edge, whilst smearing awkwardly with my right wooden-feeling foot on the end of a pin-straight leg. Now I was off balance . . . Left forearm pumping . . . The only way I could regain balance was by moving my hand again, which I was reluctant to do, as I would be left with no hands on the rock. Had I not had almost twenty years' worth of dynamic climbing experience I would not have known how to make myself weightless for a fraction of a second. Pulling hard with my arm and letting go of the rock and, at the moment when I was neither going up nor down, latching on to another fingerhold I had seen in the previous instant, I was absolutely in my element. This was exactly the same as the moves I used to do, the only difference being that, while in the past I would have been pulling it off on an overhanging wall, now I was executing the identical response to the rock on a slab. This process I repeated again and again until I found myself straddling the first ridge.

After a brief rest I was lowered down a cliff into a sort of Caspakian jungle of Edgar Rice Burroughs' novel *The Land That Time Forgot*. When some foliage moved to the side of me I half-expected a brutal Neanderthal to be peering through the leaves.

We wandered past soaring walls of quartzite, identical to my treasured Gogarth, white as the teeth of a TV evangelist. I climbed wide chimneys, steep cracks and seams, overhanging faces and sharp arêtes . . . in my imagination.

Lagging behind the others on Thwaites Plateau, I studied the now familiar yabbie holes. These little blue lobsters are also known as 'the crayfish of the plains' and live in burrows to come out at night and roam around the moors in search of food. Really! To a Brit these creatures seem as much a figment of the Aussie imagination as yowies or drop bears.

When we arrived at the high point of the range, Federation Peak, we had been struggling along for ten days.

I craned my head up and saw that it was steeper and more technical than I had ever imagined. A series of leaning, greasy ledges must be traversed back and forth to a summit chimney.

I realized that I had underestimated the climb and would have felt far safer with one of my guide mates. It also started to rain for the first time since we had begun our traverse. So, without histrionics and with a certain relief I have seldom experienced in failure, I wandered off down the narrow track.

Another reason for my return to Tasmania was to get a cranioplasty: in 2000, Colin from Clatterbridge had told me that covering the hole in my skull with a plate would be too hazardous a procedure and would risk further brain injury.

In 2002, James Van Gelder, the surgeon who performed my original operation, sent me an email in which he expressed the opinion that this response only reflected the sorry state of the NHS. The original procedure was done with a view to having a cranioplasty a few months post-op, depending on when I was stable enough to undergo another operation.

It was true that a plate in my head would give me much more confidence when out hiking or mountaineering and perhaps I could even get away without wearing the helmet. Having said that I was finding myself forgetting to wear it more and more often – a sure sign of improvement.

Andrew Hunn, Tasmania's pre-eminent neurosurgeon, was to perform the operation:

I look in the mirror. The shaved head with the grotesque notch cleaved out of it – a flat, horizontal shelf indented into the skull for two inches – looks as though a quarter segment has been chopped out of an orange. 'We shall have to get to know each other again.'

This is the first time I've seen myself bald and I can't avert my eyes. I feel awkward for staring; one shouldn't stare. It is with the unwholesome fascination with which one looks upon a 'cripple' that I now regard myself.

The huge scar makes excessive demands upon my mind, coerces it to take a trip back in time, all the way back to the Totem Pole. Like an indelible, long abiding stamp of misadventure, that ditch in my skull serves the past. I am drenched in memories.

It aids the recollection that I am on the same neuro-surgical ward in the Royal Hobart Hospital that I was brought to on a trolley five years ago. The very same grey view out of the ward window, the same sterile white walls (and I assume the same sterile disinfectant smell, though since my accident I am bereft of that sense), the same sounds: alarms, screams of patients and footfalls of nurses. Drip stand, shower chair, bath hoist, commode, blood pressure sleeve, pulse and temperature monitor. And there, still, Moi, the nurse about whom I hallucinated that she was trying to kill me the last time I was here. Now it's only good to see her. She comes in and asks me how I am. We shake hands.

To stare into my eyes is to look into the past, to that Friday the thirteenth . . . The tyrolean, the long abseil down 'the Tote', the sea water suddenly rushing up to my waist and soaking me, shouting up to Celia, 'I'll have to jumar back up the rope!' Swinging in a pendulum and then . . . the black silence. (I didn't see or hear the scimitar-shaped rock falling.)

As I study that yawn in my skull I am forced to reconsider what I once was: a climber, through and through. It *urges me to evaluate my life over these past years. I don't even recognize that bloke with the paunch and bald head. You are only connected to my past life by a spider-web thread.*

But although my life with a disability is hard, I can't help smiling back at my reflection, with pride etched in my crow's-feet. You really knew how to go for it, didn't you.

But do I still?

As I scrutinize myself, waiting for them to take me down to the theatre, I ponder what my being means to me now. I have traversed mountain ranges with a half-paralysed leg, slept on the ground and scrambled up rocks with one useable arm. Although I am using my body again, the reflections of my past life as a climber, full of agility, keep appearing, all grainy, at the most inopportune moments.

I used to say that the accident was the best thing that ever happened to me, for it put me on a different life course: a one-eighty shift from a predictable existence as a professional climber. In The Totem Pole *I entertained the idea that I had the accident purposefully, subconsciously on purpose, to avoid a humdrum life. I didn't want to go down the road of many of my mates, doing bolder and bolder climbs, maybe getting my own guiding business or, perhaps, coming to a sticky end.*

No, knowing what lay around life's corner was never for me.

But now I realized that this was me in denial. Although my accident gave me a beautiful wife, after five years I was more realistic. Nobody would have wished what I went through upon themselves.

Are not all acts in life eventually predictable? I mean, now as a disabled person I was doing what disabled people did: cooking, cycling, fishing, love-making, driving, oh, and a bit of mountaineering. Again I now knew what lay around life's corner, so if I had suffered my accident on purpose it was a waste of time.

Whatever was to be was to be.

Then, there was the familiar voice of Alexis behind me.

'Paul, it's time to get on the trolley, mate.'

When I came around from the anaesthetic a feeling that I had reverted back to 1998 enveloped me. Actually it was as if I'd never left the hospital in the past five years. Even Jane looked the same, except that she was now seven months pregnant and proudly sporting a well rounded belly. It was like some topsy-turvy dream, good and bad at the once.

The following couple of weeks were spent in a rotation of training and resting. On Mount Wellington there is a road that hairpins steeply all the way up to its 1270-metre summit and I had been attempting to cycle up this for six months. Having acquired a new, sleek racing trike, with a yellow mesh seat, extra low-slung, and fifty-two gears, I was keen to push myself and the machine to the limit.

A Scouse doctor and an intensive care nurse from Oldham, both now living in Tassie full-time, were to accompany me. Up to 900 metres I kept good pace but began to flag as we left the tall eucalyptus forest and entered a world of weird stunted bushes, all pushed in the same direction by the invisible moulding hands of the wind.

My comrades were a kilometre ahead as I approached 'The Big Bend', and I was being overtaken by people out walking their dogs. Four and a half hours later, legs jellyfied, I crept on to the plateau which signalled the highest point of Mount Wellington. Oldham John shared his banana with me; I had foolishly forgotten to bring any food and had hit a massive sugar low.

A geographical smorgasbord was laid out below us from the Tasman Peninsula and Maria Island in the east to Bruny Island and Federation Peak to the west. The whole of Hobart was directly below us. But I didn't even have the strength to get up out of my recumbent tricycle seat and avail myself of this wondrous view. I had to make do with craning my neck.

When it came time to leave the summit we set off together. But almost lying down in my reclined seat I was creating hardly any wind resistance and I soon sped off, leaving my friends pedalling to keep up with me. I was riding the luge in the Olympics as I overtook cars and even a coach. John, who rides fast Yamahas, felt piqued and was pedalling ever harder to keep up.

Scouse Edi couldn't sustain the pace either. 'You might be slower on the way up but we've no chance coming down.'

On one particular hairpin bend I even got the tricycle onto two wheels – memories of the Snowdon Bike Hike.

The wind blasting through my hair was joyous until a bee hit me in the eye, and sent me into a momentary speed wobble. This only served to create in me a great adrenaline rush, as if to let me know what I had been missing the last five years. After a brief stop to rub said eye, it was off down the hill again. That which took four and a half hours to climb up took fifteen minutes to descend.

After a swift shower back at the house I made a grave error. I took the ute out to buy some groceries. With my one good leg feeling like jelly and the other virtually dead this shopping trip was always destined for disaster.

After a couple of kilometres I arrived at my first obstacle, a roundabout, on which I wanted to turn to the right. There where houses and gardens all around. I was making it round the roundabout easily when my left foot slipped off the brake and onto the accelerator. I must add here that I drive a specially adapted automatic with a left-foot accelerator. (More than one person has crashed it and I'd like to see an auto-thief at work on this vehicle.) I accelerated on to the pavement and through a garden fence.

With the section of fence now lying over my windscreen and occluding my vision, I proceeded through the flowerbed and across the lawn. Just as it seemed as if I was never going to stop, the fence on the far side of the garden finally halted the ute. The engine, and I, let out a sigh.

Peering out from the wreckage, the first thing I noticed was how grand was the house to my left. It was built in Georgian style with big bay windows. Then I spotted four faces, each etched with a similar look of horror, in one of the bay windows. In a moment they were beside me worriedly enquiring about my welfare.

Forcing the door to make my escape from the quite mangled cab I remonstrated with myself. I shouldn't have been bloody driving.

When the house-owners saw my disability they thought I'd injured myself in the accident.

'Don't move until the ambulance gets here,' a wiry chap said with a look of concern.

'No, I'm always like this. Honest,' I answered, attempting to allay their fears.

But that only served to confuse them.

One could see the cogs whirring in their worried heads, 'Can he drive at all? Has he even got a license? Insurance?'

Once I'd got my composure back I managed to justify myself a little further by relating how I'd just cycled up Mount Wellington for the first time and my legs were like blancmange.

They invited me inside, sat me down, and made me a cup of tea. What accommodating lovely people I thought. And they were but then there was a knock on the door.

The wiry one stared at me wide-eyed and said, 'Oh, no, it's the landlord. I suppose he'll want to know why there's a car parked on his lawn.'

9

*The Longest Climb –
Kilimanjaro*

My adventure was ending. But I knew something
momentous had happened, which would leave its
mark, and alter me decisively, from now on. A
whole life, a whole universe had been compressed:
a density of experience neither given to nor desired
by most men; but one which, having happened,
would re-fashion and direct me.

Oliver Sacks – *A Leg to Stand On*

Stepping out of the house and into the drizzle, I took off
on another training walk up Mount Wellington. In my
pack were warm clothes, sixty metres of rope, five litres of
water, some food and a sizeable piece of stone from the
garden.

My circuit usually stayed the same as I ramped up the
weight on my back. If I was struggling I could jettison the
stone and tip out as much water as need be.

On this day I broke my record for the 330 metres to the
Springs, the halfway point to the summit; and in mud and
leaf wash. After a brief rest I set off down Radford's Track.
In my eagerness to get back to a dry house I was steaming
downhill when the inevitable happened. The heel of my left
boot slid out in front of me in the slippery mud and my

gammy right leg was left behind. In a sort of scissor splits action I went down, with a scream of agony, in the slime.

My walking pole was bent out of shape and so was my right leg, which also seemed paralysed. I lay there in the grime for ten wet minutes. Pictures flitted through my head of three yet again disappointed climbers superimposed on a photograph of mountain I had not yet climbed – Kilimanjaro. Was I about to scupper my next expedition through my own stupidity?

But then I began slowly to move my leg; it was but a brief moment of paralysis. With the knee in agony, I managed to pull myself to my feet and, after composing myself, hobbled off down the hill on a deformed stick.

The next day Kerri Muir, my physiotherapist, told me that the medial ligament damage I had sustained was usually a six-week injury. Now, I was going to Tanzania in two months so my training regimen was effectively over.

Catrina the orthotist measured the length and circumference of the knee and ordered a neoprene brace with alloy hinges from Sydney.

'If you wear this, especially when you're going down hill you should be OK,' she told me. 'But rest it for now.'

'I will,' I promised.

I had too. Any exercise had me gripping my knee joint in unyielding pain.

I was to attempt Kilimanjaro in January 2003 with 'a bunch of cripples'. Jamie Andrew, Pete Steane and David Lim are all climbers of repute but they are all disabled too. How on earth, you may ask, can a quadruple amputee, a partial paraplegic, a guy who has had a paralysing nerve disorder and a hemiplegic even climb on to a bus, never mind up Kilimanjaro. But this bunch of relative strangers was going to give it a go.

The team was truly international. Jamie is a Scot, David a Singaporean and Pete a Tasmanian (Australian really but folks from the island state like to stand apart). Then there was me; an English man who has lived in Wales for half his life and recently emigrated to Tasmania.

First and foremost, as climbers, our aim was to ascend Kilimanjaro by a glacier route. Our secondary purpose in attempting this climb was to demonstrate that being disabled does not necessarily imply a lack of ability. We would be making the climb without a guide or back-up above the base camp. Thirdly, we just happen to be pretty efficient at raising cash, so why not put something back into a country from which you are taking so many potent and treasured memories.

As a group of mountaineers we have had to claw back our lives following catastrophic accidents or, in the case of David, serious illness. Though some might class them as seriously disabled, Jamie, David and Pete are very athletic and extremely good at what they do; namely climbing rocks and mountains. I felt honoured to be going with them.

This plan had just one sticking point; Jane, we recently found out, was due to give birth on 25 January 2003.

'Don't even think about it,' said Jane, before I had even said anything.

'Don't worry, I'll be back from Tanzania by then, even if I have to rush straight into the delivery suite.'

'Yeah, very funny.'

We talked and together agreed that, if the birth went well, when our baby was one year old Jane would 'give me a permit' to go to Tanzania. Whether I would feel able to tear myself away from this new wondrous creature that was soon to enter our lives was a matter that only time would settle.

So, I cc'd my team-mates describing the awkward situation in which I had found myself and outlined my position; I would have very much liked to have been part of this venture. Doubtfully, I suggested delaying the trip for a whole year, but not if that was going to put the expedition in jeopardy. Luckily for me the team agreed and the trip was put off until January 2004.

Cadi Eliza was born on the first day of the second month of the third year and this single event was possibly the most profound of my life. She was a joy to behold but also confusing. Instantly I felt the pull of home, and the mountains began to fade into the background. What was happening?

This was a radically new experience for me, a man who had been used to doing just what he wanted, going wherever the wind took him each day. (It was only later that I realized a parent, even a disabled one, can still go off on crazy adventures and take their child with them; it just requires a little more organization.)

The idea of Kilimanjaro, with all its attendant dangers and insecurity, began to produce in me a white noise like that from an untuned television. This expedition was to be the zenith of that which my life was now about; going on mountaineering trips with other disabled people was what I wanted to do more than anything else. It was the first time I had felt troubled in this way about any mountain.

But the well oiled expedition machine ground inexorably towards its goal until 5 January 2004 found Pete Steane and me on a plane bound for Singapore.

Airports aren't the best places for Pete Steane who sets off metal detector alarms regularly with the rather large amount of ironmongery in his body. He also has two callipers that support his ankles – his lower legs are extremely atrophied – and two spares that he carries on top of his bag. These 'suspicious' items, which could be shoe bombs, he is often asked to take off and put through the X-ray machine.

His muscular upper body is shown off always by his policeman brother's old blue shirts that he has torn the arms off and his massive thighs are similarly exhibited by a pair of very short shorts, called 'stubbies'. These quads look out of place atop two chopsticks. Security guards check him out with an air of dubiety and he is searched more often than most.

Pete's story is a litany of catastrophe punctuated, at regular intervals, with acts of blinding singularity.

In 1982 this talented eighteen-year-old climber decked out on to the edge of a ledge, 'a trivial 8-metre fall on a scruffy little cliff in Tasmania'.

He broke his back.

From that moment on Pete became an incomplete paraplegic; to the layman that translates as a loss of half the muscle groups below the waist, zero feeling in the feet, meagre circulation in the lower legs and, to top it off, a complete loss of bladder function. In the early days Pete would climb with a leg bag to hold urine, but as he progressed on to the more difficult rock climbs he would do away with this cumbersome bladder and, much to his belayers' distress, would have the odd accident.

Since 1985 Pete has been at the fore of creative new route activity in Tasmania, establishing rock climbs across the state. He became especially interested in one of the remoter cliffs, not only in Tasmania, but in Australia. Just getting to the 350 metre Frenchman's Cap entails wading through the thigh-deep bogs of the 'Sodden' Lodden Plains for up to two days. He would make this trip countless times.

It is also part of every climber's ordainment to make the pilgrimage to the great granite cathedral that is Yosemite Valley in California. So Pete was compelled to go and experience the vast golden walls of sun-kissed rock. But after his ascent of the 1000-metre Nose of El Capitan he experienced renal failure, a side effect of his paralysis.

Many people faced with a similar burden would just say 'bugger it' and take it easy from then on. But Pete sees it differently: 'Any reasonably motivated person is not just going to give up and sit on their arse for the rest of their lives because they become crippled.'

More recently Pete collided with a 4x4 whilst cycling home from work. He broke his neck, sustained multiple fractures to his shoulder, arm, both legs, hand and nose. While he was in hospital undergoing tests he was diagnosed with renal cancer. An operation to remove one of his kidneys followed but this led to internal haemorrhaging.

This accident has left Pete with limited use of his arm. He has found that he cannot climb as well as he used to, so has thrown himself into paragliding. Tasmania, being in the Roaring Forties, is not a place for the novice pilot. Pete has had some wild flights deep in the bush but just as many failed trips due to the vagaries of the weather.

Singaporean David Lim met us at the airport where we were to do a pre-expedition media briefing to keep our main sponsor, drug company Novartis, happy.

David Lim, we were to find out, is a person of contradictions. He is as at home schmoozing with the President of Singapore as he is near the summit of 8000-metre Cho Oyu. I have never had such sponsorship as on this trip and it was mostly down to David's business acumen and contacts.

Afterwards, in the foyer of the swish hotel, we sat entranced by the glass elevators zooming up out of a plastic rainforest.

Pete, who isn't the most forthcoming of people when he's in a strange situation, nudged me. 'When that reporter asked me what I thought was going to be the most challenging obstacle of the climb, I felt like telling her, "this media briefing", but I knew that wouldn't go down well.'

David, Pete and I arrived in Nairobi bleary-eyed. There we met up with Jamie and the film crew, Sheffield-based Slackjaw Productions, which consisted of the supremely relaxed Richard Heap and my old Llanberis friend Ben Pritchard. We also met our man on the ground, Musa Kopwe, and our guide, Safi Mteta.

When Pete asked Safi how many times he had climbed Kilimanjaro, he replied, 'Over ten times.'

Pete nodded. 'What, in your life?'

'No. This season.'

David, not knowing the levels of his three team-mates' indolence, had arranged a tight schedule that allowed no time for dilly-dallying: Land 6 pm – hotel – quick shower – dinner – bed – breakfast at 5.30 am – load up bus – leave Nairobi at 6.30 am.

This itinerary appeared exhausting to me but we did need whipping into shape. The 'camera crew' were also keen sleepers and on more than one occasion a faint pulse was the only sign that Richard was still alive.

About three hours into the drive we left Kenya and entered Tanzania. Crowds of Maasai women with long earlobes and draped in colourful beads prowled around the customs office. These women have a keen eye for anyone who shows a lack of resolve when it comes to bargaining.

They must detect it in the body language of the tourists. Ben, they spotted straight away as a soft touch and he ended up parting with hundreds of shillings.

We paused at Arusha for an artificially bright orange drink called a Chemi-Cola, and presently our bus turned up a dirt track lined with banana fronds and mud huts. Children waved and adults nodded casually from the roadside.

The bus trundled into Upendo Leprosy Centre where we were to make our first sojourn. Our team was raising money and buying equipment for the centre. Jamie, being Scot of the Year 1999, is a one-man fund-raising machine and he and David raised the majority of the funds for the trip.

We had been in consultation with the Rotary Club of Arusha, the group that runs the centre, for over two years by now and were eager to see the place for ourselves.

The centre houses, at the last count, fifty adults and thirty-one children who advised us that they really wanted new equipment for their cowshed. Many times the actual beneficiaries of charity aren't listened to and the donation, however well meant, is misplaced. As well as raising thousands of dollars we had special wooden hand-cranked cream separators being delivered from India – others, made of glass, are easily fumbled and smashed by people with leprosy. We had no target. We just wanted to raise as much cash as we could for the centre.

One of the main problems facing people with leprosy is that, through fear and ignorance, they, along with their families are barred from their communities; they are then unable to work and feed their families. The centre takes the 'lepers' and their families in, encourages them to do their own work and in the process re-attain some dignity.

Local representative of the Rotarians, Faye Cran and Catholic nun, Sister Lucy, led us on a grand tour of Upendo and revealed to us exactly what they were doing at the centre.

A small fish farm, producing tilapia, was the first stop and then Fay introduced us to a cabinet-maker who showed us his latest work, a fine chair. We entered a courtyard where we saw a woman making beautiful textiles on a loom and a mother making exquisite jewellery while attempting to control her two small children. Jamie posed for a photograph with an amputee called Hitler, whilst a little fellow who made crazily painted bowls out of papier-mâché showed me his wares.

Nestled amongst acres of lush vegetables was a shipping container that had been recycled as a schoolroom. Chickens and ducks roamed all around the place, while goats and cows were kept away from the vegetables in cramped pens.

With the new cowshed the families would be able to continue running their own businesses and thereby make their own money. After all lining up for a group photograph, it was back on the bus for the final two-hour drive to Moshi, the gateway to Kilimanjaro. The mountain was secreted behind a dense curtain of cloud but we could sense something ominous there to the east.

Once at our hotel, we chatted over a Kilimanjaro beer about logistics and how we wanted to climb this mountain. I am for the flexible approach, allowing for all things unexpected. But Musa and Safi were more rigid of opinion.

'We will climb from here at three thousand eight hundred,' said Safi, pointing to a map layed out on the table, 'to this camp here at forty six hundred.'

'That seems a bit much,' said David. 'Eight hundred metres in a day.'

Normally above 4000 metres it is recommended that one would climb no more than 300 metres in a day to avoid altitude sickness. If you were going to climb high you would sleep low.

'Yes, but after a night at four thousand six hundred, we will then descend to four thousand.'

This went against my way of thinking – climb high sleep high – but I kept quiet. Perhaps I should have spoken up.

Afterwards, in the hotel, room Jamie made his worries known. 'It all seems a bit rigid this plan,' he ventured, walking into the shower on his kneepads.

'I think that's what you get when you go with any trekking company,' I shouted into the bathroom. I had experience of this type of rigidity in Kenya.

'Yeah, well, it's my first time doing anything like this, trekking companies and all that.'

Jamie Andrew suffered extreme frostbite on Les Droites, a mountain high above Chamonix, in 1999. He and his climbing partner, Jamie Fisher, had just climbed the classic Corneau/Davaille route on the north face when a ferocious storm hit. The pair dug a shallow snow ledge on the Brèche des Droites, a small notch on the summit comb.

On this ledge, no wider than a coffin, they spent almost a week in hurricane-strength winds, mostly without food, bar a couple of squares of Kendal Mint Cake. In the valley, ski runs were shut because of the wind and the sheer amount of snow that had dumped.

The consequent helicopter rescue was one of the most dramatic in French history and made headlines around the globe. Tragically, the rescue came too late for his partner Jamie Fisher, but Jamie Andrew survived, despite hypothermia and having to have his hands and feet amputated.

We did not discuss our disabilities excessively on Kilimanjaro. We were just another team of climbers on an expedition, or that is how we saw ourselves. I had not the inclination nor the energy to decipher the inner workings of my team-mates' minds as I concentrated on the climb.

This expedition was built on the acceptance of help from each other but this went mostly unsaid. It was only on reading *Life and Limb* that I found out what Jamie really thought: 'In the three years since I became a quadruple amputee I have come to accept that I can't do everything for myself all the time. I'm just thankful for all the things I can still do. Constantly being indebted to people isn't such a bad thing either. It brings you closer, builds bonds.'

After his accident Jamie made an astonishingly rapid recovery and was once to be seen crawling, much to the distress of the entrance staff, on his stumps up the steps of an Edinburgh gallery. Within three and a half months he had learnt to walk on prosthetic legs and had re-learnt the tasks that the non-disabled take so much for granted, such as washing, dressing and eating. Jamie still suffered the agony of phantom limb pain but was considered well enough to leave hospital.

In June 2000 Jamie ascended Ben Nevis, the tallest mountain in Britain, and in April 2002 he ran the London Marathon. He also made an attempt that same year on Mont Blanc, Western Europe's highest peak, but was forced to turn back just 300 metres below the summit due to bad weather.

Although the highest point in Africa, Kilimanjaro is nowadays a bit of a circus. The Tanzanian volcano sees 25,000 attempts, in a virtual ant line, every year, although it is estimated that only forty-five per cent of these attempts are successful. The peak also sees twenty-five deaths, making it the mountain with the highest number of fatalities, due to altitude sickness, in the world.

The Marangu tourist path or 'Coca Cola route' is so technically easy that people are able to ascend very high very quickly. Some unscrupulous trekking companies, who look to profit from getting trekkers up and down in five days, dangerously abuse this aspect of the mountain.

The Crane brothers cycled up the 5896-metre mountain and others have flown hang-gliders and paragliders from the summit. Indeed Pete, a keen paraglider himself, nearly brought his 'wing' along. 'Just imagine, you three trekking down a steep hill for days and me having a beaut of a flight down.'

As climbers, even disabled ones, we didn't want to walk up the tourist route; we needed more of a challenge. We aimed to climb unguided, on a remote route, to Kibo, the highest of the three summits of Kilimanjaro. We opted for the distant Credner Glacier, way to the north, which is climbed by very few mountaineers ascending the volcano.

The first day was steeper, hotter, more humid and generally tougher than I had imagined in my most fevered dreams. When we set off Jamie was trailing and I thought we were in for a relaxed time of it. But as the day progressed, and he got into the swing of things, a blistering pace commenced that wasn't to slow until we were off the mountain.

My lack of training, due to my knee injury, was telling already as I lagged far behind the others in a pool of sweat. Consoling myself, I reasoned that the others each had two good thighs while I only had half a body but deep down knew this to be a cop-out.

My lungs felt as if they were about to explode as I gasped like a dying fish out of water. And this at such a low altitude did not augur well, I worried, for the summit day. My only hope lay in my getting fitter as the trip progressed, which wasn't altogether likely during a two-week climb.

Our team of twenty-eight people, guides, climbers, porters and cooks, wandered through the dense bush. The porters each had eighteen kilograms balanced on the tops of their heads, sometimes in the most unmanageable bundles. We would get to know some of these people very well, as you tend to do, living in the mountains, and count them as our friends.

Over lunch smiling Masanje, a diminutive Chagga and our assistant waiter, scratched numbers on the ground and, using simple sign language, made the system known to me. Added to the regulation eighteen kilograms was their personal kit and food, which sometimes brought the total to more like thirty kilos. If they refused to carry it they would be picked out as a troublemaker and wouldn't get any more work.

Eric, the porter manager, hung back with me, as I was the last man and, approaching Machame Camp, we passed Richard Heap from Slackjaw curled up like a foetus at the side of the track.

'What is the matter with him?' asked Eric.

'Nothing,' replied Rich suddenly opening his eyes. 'I'm just catching up on some kip.'

When Eric and I arrived at camp it was already set up. Some of the more acclimatized porters had been there a couple of hours already. The day was coming to an end.

In the west, Meru, the second highest mountain in Tanzania, was silhouetted against a sun setting into the dusty Serengeti. Turning in early, I didn't have any problem sleeping on the fifteen-degree slope on which the porters had pitched our tent.

We awoke to a white frosty world at 3000 metres and bowls of warm water to wash in. We sat on the earth around a tarp and ate an excellent breakfast of eggs and toast. After I fell back attempting to stand up Pete joked that we could do with a table and chairs.

Jamie's leg stumps had swollen in the night and were now too fat for his prostheses. The swelling on one stump went down quite quickly once he was standing but the other persisted.

'It's happened before but not this bad,' groaned Jamie. 'I might have to catch you up.'

He bounced up and down on the titanium poles, which were his legs for a full half hour before the limb sank in to its socket. Now he could eat some breakfast using a fork fastened to his lower arm with a Velcro strap.

The day started as it meant to continue, steep. With 800 metres of ascent in one day I was worried that this would make a member of the team sick. Having been ill with altitude sickness before, I am somewhat paranoid in these matters. But it pays to be paranoid when someone's life might be at stake.

The Machame route is the second most popular route on the mountain. It is prettier, has more impressive scenery and is more challenging than the Coca-Cola route. It also takes longer to ascend, giving a trekker more time to acclimatize but also making it more expensive. People of all nationalities were taking this route by their hundreds and we would only part company with them two days hence. I for one was looking forward to that day. Feeling on show the whole time, I was aware that almost every person that passed us by stared.

Presently we arrived at a crag, from which we had to traverse off the safety of a broad, vegetated ledge and climb up above a leg-breaking drop. Pete, being a natural rock climber, cruised up it with his shades on. Jamie clattered across and up admirably on his specially adapted sticks – attached to cups for his stumps – looking like a quadrupedal arachnid. David was already long past this obstacle.

Nervously, for this was the first real challenge of the trip, I stepped on to the wall. My hiking boots felt too roomy and the left sole deformed when I attempted to smear the outside edge of it on to a sloping shelf. It was as if in slow motion that I observed this; it always is in such situations of stress. Repeatedly I stabbed my right boot against the rock until it found a round hole.

'Eric? Can you hold my foot in that hole, please?'

Eric was immediately behind and fielding me closely.

'Of course.'

Putting my life or at least in this case, my legs, in the hands of complete strangers is something I have had to do many times since my accident and more often than not it makes you famous friends for life. This time, I came to discover, was no exception.

At the end of the traverse I paused and took stock. There was a queue of tourists building up on the ledge behind me and I suddenly became self-conscious. Their eyes, burning into my chest, momentarily broke my concentration, but being used to such situations, I didn't pay them anymore attention.

Pulling on to the top of this crag, I arrived on the Shira Plateau, the place where we were to stay for the following two nights. All that remained was to trundle slightly downhill in a casual manner, for about a kilometre, through mist and drizzle to the campsite.

Staggering out of the bushes into Shira Camp, I was reminded of a Napoleonic campaign. Hundreds of people were all huddled in the mud in their individual groups, the brown canvas tents of the trekking companies here and there in the low patches of mist. There were even an armless Jamie, and Pete and David limping around to complete the scene.

That night at dinner there appeared a heavy wooden table with chairs too.

'Do you think they heard me and thought I was being serious?' Pete squirmed uncomfortably.

Thinking back to Mount Kenya, I recalled with more than a little embarrassment my reaction to the rich tourists who had porters carrying tables and chairs for them. I kept my mouth firmly shut.

To say I was looking forward to a rest day would have been an understatement. We had only been walking for two days but this, added to all the time spent travelling had left me feeling a need to ground myself. When Safi suggested a half-day stroll I was dubious.

As the sun rose I was alerted to the sound of David's enthusing, as he was already up shooting photos – his energy was something to behold. My first view on forcing open my glued-shut eyes was of the intricate, overlapping-circle ice patterns on the fly-sheet. Then, as a reminder, my having-just-woken-up heavy breathing communicated to me that I was close to 4000 metres.

On poking my head out of the tent, I then understood David's enthusiasm. Tumorous white clouds were billowing down below us, then surging heavenwards in tumults.

Rich and Ben, the most unobtrusive film crew in Christendom, greeted me with their camera. We chatted about how I was feeling and about how many pills I took each day.

'Two types of anti-convulsants three times a day and whatever else I can get my hands on.'

After a breakfast of interesting fresh orange porridge, Safi guided us on a walk in the direction of the Shira Cathedral, an impressive spire-shaped mountain of 3900 metres and the third summit of Kilimanjaro. About three hours into the trek, and as we didn't seem to be getting anywhere fast, David and I decided to turn back. It is a close run thing between wearing yourself out and acclimatizing properly.

David and I weren't long back at camp when the others arrived with tales of incredible spires poking out of the mist. We had a lazy afternoon that passed us, well me at any rate, by all too quickly. I think that afternoon was the first time we were to smell the sweet fragrance of marijuana around the camp but could only guess who was smoking it.

'Jane? Is that you?' I was calling Tasmania from David's satellite telephone.

David was doing daily dispatches to a web page using the telephone so that family, friends and sponsors could keep in touch with what was happening on Kili.

'I'm at the Shira Plateau – almost 4000 metres.'

Jane said that it was weird to able to have a conversation with me halfway up Kilimanjaro.

Hearing my daughter squeak was enough to render me a blubbering uncommunicative mess. It was just as well the satellite passed out of range and we got cut off.

The next day, on the way to the Lava Tower, we came around a corner to a round of applause from a group of Austrian tourists. They were applauding Jamie and queued up to have their picture taken next to him. The tourists completely ignored the rest of us and this embarrassed Jamie to the point of him asking us to join in on the impromptu photo session. But the Austrians didn't want us;

they only wanted Jamie for which, Pete, David and I felt thankful. But it raised some interesting questions.

Later I talked this event over with Pete. Having been 'crippled' for more than half his life, he has a more mature perspective on a problem than I, who only had my accident six years ago.

Pete recounted an early bushwalk he went on shortly after his accident.

'I had to wear a full-length calliper all the way up my left leg. And when travelling in a vehicle I had to strap on a spinal brace which covered my whole trunk. With all this junk on me I looked like Robocop.

'However while walking along the overland track back to Lake St Claire, my calliper was covered by over-trousers, and I was not wearing the spinal brace. I was obviously going pretty slowly. Some young smart-arse overtook me and said smuggly as he breezed past, 'Got a blister, have you?'

'I think we've all been there in one form or another,' I agreed.

Pete continued, 'I was nineteen years old, and twelve months earlier could have walked the arse off him, so you can imagine I was not that impressed. Anyway, at the shelter at the end of the track, we were all changing shoes etc, getting ready to drive home. I took off my over-trousers, exposing the full-length calliper, and put on my spinal brace to get into the car. 'This guy's jaw was on the ground as he stared at me. I guess he realized that my problem was a little more serious than a blister.'

I asked Pete if he thought that Jamie had a sexier disability than the rest of us.

'You mean the Six Million Dollar Man image – "We can rebuild him. We have the technology!" and all that. It certainly is more sexy than a floppy useless wasted limb hanging off your body. I think Hollywood might have contributed to that.'

The simple conclusion to be drawn is that Jamie was far more 'different' to the Austrians than the rest of us. The tourists could almost equate with our condition, limbs not working properly, but Jamie was, to all intents and purposes, an alien.

Weaving our way through a maze of curiously spherical boulders, from football-sized to house-sized, we progressed toward the glaciers. Some of these glaciers don't reach the top any more and are left stranded like white ghost ships that have run aground on the mountain. Once they lose their source they become impotent and wither. Their slow melancholy melt accelerates into the un-stemmable bleed of a slashed artery.

In this bizarre igneous landscape of ash and rock we paused for a drink of water and a bite to eat. Rich and Ben were on top of a boulder with the camera, mounted on a tripod, pointing in the direction of Meru.

David was taking photos with his new hi-tech digital camera. 'Amazing, you can even change the ISO as well as the shutter speed.'

'You love all this technology, don't you, David,' I noted with a laugh.

'No, I don't. It's just something you need to know how to do to navigate in the modern age,' he answered, knowing something of British humour and sarcasm from his days in the England.

Cambridge-educated David Lim knows an awful lot about almost everything, from who played the supporting role in a B rated fifties western to the rise of Hansonism (a far right political movement) in Australia. His memory, it seems, was not affected by his illness.

Malaysian by birth, David led the first successful Singaporean Everest expedition in 1998. A week after returning home he was struck down by Guillain/Barré Syndrome. This mysterious nerve disorder can totally paralyse a person in a matter of days and it did.

The first symptom he became aware of was when he went to turn the ignition key in his car and did not have the strength. The following morning he awoke at 3 am with a feeling of dread and near total paralysis of his right arm. The doctors seemed to do every test imaginable but could not diagnose the syndrome: it isn't a disease because it is the body's immune system itself that goes berserk and begins attacking the nerve cells, in what David describes as 'a case of mistaken identity'.

Very soon it shut down David's respiratory system. He became speechless, unable to swallow or move. He had to be ventilated on the intensive care ward of a Singapore hospital for six weeks.

Added to the necessary catheters and the naso-gastric feeding tube was something much more traumatic. He contracted a virulent form of pneumonia and as his respiratory muscles became paralyzed, he began to drown on his own phlegm and mucous. The only way forward for David, who now thought he was about to die, was for him to have his lungs suctioned.

A long plastic catheter, about the thickness of a macaroni strand was inserted down his tracheal tube, directly into his lungs. The other end would be attached to a suction socket in the wall. He vividly describes in his book, *Mountain to Climb*, how in a sword-swallowing circus act the greenish gunk was sucked out before his eyes.

'Soon I was filling four large jars a day and at the peak of my pneumonia I was suctioned every one to two hours.'

At first the doctors thought David had had a stroke. He was only a few days home from Everest and, as every mountaineer knows, the blood takes on the consistency of ketchup above 7000 metres, making it much more sluggish in the veins. Only after a couple of weeks did the medical team diagnose Guillain/Barré Syndrome, which his neurologist described as, 'one of the worst things you can get and not die from'.

The long period of paralysis had led to massive atrophy everywhere. The joints of his legs and arms were bigger than the surrounding muscled areas. He spent many months recovering in hospital – the one experience common to us all – including a long rehabilitation process in which the re-learning of simple tasks such as writing, dressing and walking were enormous challenges in comparison to the Everest climb.

David's legacy from his illness is a paralysed ankle, known as drop foot, one atrophied calve and thumbs that paralyse in the cold. He wears a drop foot ankle splint set at ninety degrees.

David now walks with a curious limp; a sort of cross between liquid and robotic. The hip sags smoothly with every step at the very moment the foot is lifted but, because the ankle is effectively frozen, his body lurches forwards, in a mechanical manner on to his trekking poles.

Apart from sweating up Bukit Timah which, at 164 metres, is the highest 'mountain' in Singapore (the tallest building is 280 metres), David's first post-illness mountain climb was Kinabalu on the island of Borneo. At 4092 metres Kinabalu is the only alpine peak trekkers can ascend to in South-East Asia. About eighteen months after going down with Guillain/Barré David slowly, but relatively easily, made it to the summit of Kinabalu.

Since Kinabalu David has climbed to 7900 metres on Cho Oyu, attempted Everest again and Shishapangma, another eight-thousander in Tibet. He also makes a habit of climbing the world's highest volcanoes from El Pico de Orizaba in Mexico to Mount Ararat in Turkey, Mount Fuji in Japan to Ojos de Salado in Chile. They are not always technical and have a mean angle that suits David's gait and disability.

In dribs and drabs the team arrived at the Lava Tower and by late afternoon we had established our camp. Everyone except David and I climbed up to this impressive tower's summit. The route was too steep and technical for me.

Afterwards Pete came bursting into the dining tent, followed closely by Jamie.

'It's bloody amazing up there,' said Pete.

And Jamie added, 'The climb up was a bit touch and go for a while though.'

I was glad I had left it up to them. The altitude of 4600 metres was making itself known and any movement on my part would set off a fit of gasping.

The very thought of rock climbing produced a torpor, which reminded me of when I was a schoolboy told to go out on a cross-country run: I would always run out of the school gate and straight into a mate's house to smoke a fag and watch some crappy day-time television show for the next hour.

On escaping from the dining tent and staggering down to mine, the whole star-torchlit world was spinning. There was already a frost on the saddle and the dark silhouette of the Lava Tower dominated, like a bully. To the east the dwindling Penck Glaciers, Little and Great, shone in a low hum of luminescence.

I remember swearing at my right leg as it refused to go into the sleeping bag and, as I finally lay there, thought of Jane. Not only of how I loved and missed Jane but how I relied on her in a physical sense as well, for help. To zip me into my sleeping bag, tie my boot laces, cut my meat, tie a knot, zip my jacket up, pack up the tent, cook on the camp stove, fetch water, pack my rucsac, put my gaiters on my legs, carry more weight – the list is endless – I needed Jane to do all these things . . . Or so I thought.

This trip was proving to me that I didn't have to rely on Jane half as much as I had done before. Sure, there were some things that I could never do one-handed but for every one thing that she had to help me with I was discovering there were ten others I could do on my own. Even if I failed on this mountain I had learnt to be more independent, so that is no failure. In fact, this single lesson was possibly the most important I was to learn on Kilimanjaro.

People always say that I must have the patience of a saint, but I felt myself getting frustrated regularly on this trip. Without Jane to do most things for me I was taking longer to get going in the mornings and I felt Jamie, David and Pete were always waiting on me. I had determination by the truckload but felt I needed to possess more patience.

Watching Jamie taught me something about patience. Just clipping the waist belt on his rucsac might take him five minutes, where someone with two hands would have it done in a flash. But he patiently persevered and only by persevering does a disabled person learn how to do anything for him or herself.

The occupational therapists would make all these contraptions for Jamie, like a split hook that fitted onto a shoulder harnesses. And at first he could only see the advantages of these contraptions 'If only for scaring small children.'

But he slowly realized that with his bare stumps he could achieve more than with the hook. So that and a plethora of other prosthetic devices are now sitting in a corner gathering dust in his flat. He has astounding dexterity with his stumps, achieving all sorts of manual tasks; he can even roll cigarettes.

Jamie recounts how each time he goes to a certain Edinburgh shop and pulls out his wallet the shopkeeper snatches it from his stumps and takes the money he needs.

'He doesn't mean to insult me but I just wish he'd give me more time because I can pay for things on my own.'

Jamie's diplomacy was already apparent in the way he dealt with the Austrians and this was another example.

'There's something emasculating about having your wallet taken off you as well, but each time I just let it go. I guess I don't want to make him feel uncomfortable.'

Not being so diplomatic I have snapped at people numerous times.

'I am quite capable of dressing myself,' I said harshly to a person trying to help me with my jacket. Eventually I learned to see the funny side of some stranger wrestling with me for control of my jacket.

In the morning, after breakfasting at the heavy wooden table that a poor kid had to balance on his head to 4600 metres, we descended to Stern Moir Camp. I wandered down after Pete – the others being well ahead – through a desertified landscape like the Martian surface. The only things that gave the game away, and made us believe we were still rooted to planet earth, were the sporadic tufts of grass.

The skull of a zebra was resting on the track at 4500 metres. For me this skull answered Hemingway's question when he found, 'The dried and frozen carcass of a leopard', close to the summit in *The Snows of Kilimanjaro*. He asks, 'What the leopard was seeking at that altitude?' I believe Kilimanjaro could be one of the highest hunting grounds in the whole world.

A silver stream trickled through the middle of the meadow, on which we put up the tents. Changigi, Omari and Charles mooched about, while Bungama and Masanje sang Swahili songs from the dinning tent. Nestled in below a slabby cliff a derelict wigwam-shaped hut – such is the state of many huts on Kilimanjaro but the porters still sleep in them – crowned an idyllic site.

I was interviewed by Rich on my life, attitudes and opinions about disability. Believing now that I might be able to climb this hill, I felt much better after dropping 300 metres of altitude. That night, as I struggled with my pit, I was aware of a contentment that had not been there earlier in the trip.

But in middle of the night, listening to the regular irregularities of Pete's Cheyne/Stokes breathing – deathly silence for what seemed like an eternity, then a monumental gasp – I was encouraged to study my own respiration. On exhaling a definite gurgle emanated from my lungs . . . Again . . . And again.

'Oh, my God, I've got the death rattles.'

I had to go down.

'Pete!' No answer, apart from the monotonous disarray of his breathing.

That was the expedition over for me then.

Pulmonary oedema wasn't an entirely new concept to me. I had had the condition before while descending Trango

Tower in the Karakoram in 1995. That time the bubbles were accompanied by extreme lethargy and my partner, Adam Wainwright, had to escort me down off the mountain. But on that occasion we had at least made it to the top. On this mountain I hadn't had the slightest sniff of a summit.

Again, louder this time, 'Pete!' and I give him a prod for good measure.

He wakes with a great inhalation. 'Wha . . . Wha . . . What?'

'Listen!' I put my mouth to his ear and force my breath out. An audible bubbling again comes from deep down in my lungs.

This being Pete's first excursion to altitude, he asks wearily, whilst coming out of his stupor, 'What does that mean then?'

'That's what you get when you go up too high too fast,' And then I add, 'I have to go down.'

Not until I rose did I have a chance to study my pulse, breathing and general disposition. My resting pulse was over a hundred and my head swam.

At breakfast I demonstrated my oedema by breathing in anyone's ear who cared to venture near me. Safi was most concerned.

'Down,' he frowned in a no ifs or buts manner.

The porters then started muttering about ambulances and evacuation.

Jeleman, a wiry Chagga porter with whom conversation in English was relatively simple, said, 'If you go down to Shira you then be out by stretcher.'

He then added with a smile, '*Nzuri*. Good.'

But it wasn't *nzuri* at all. I knew from experience that I only needed a 500-metre descent to recover, but there was no way I was going to risk being abducted on a stretcher.

It was hard to persuade the porters, whose employment records depended on bringing back as many as they took out. But eventually Safi promised, 'I will not say anything if you do not get any worse because I know what this mountain means to you.' And then he added, 'I'll just radio down that you're coming for a rest.'

Jamie read in his guidebook that Safi meant 'clean' in Swahili, so from that point on Safi became known as 'Mr Clean'.

Pete, David, Rich and Mr Clean set off up an enormous hill of scree on a reconnaissance of the Credner Glacier with Charles, a great big personable porter who smiled a lot and didn't get fazed by anything. He had designs on becoming a guide and this was good training for him. Charles also had more than a smattering of English, which is essential for every would-be Kilimanjaro guide.

As I was only having minimal problems with walking, well, not much more than usual, Jamie and I hiked back down to Shira with Kornelli in his capacity of assistant guide. Kornelli, due to his red eyes and very laid back temperament, was now the chief suspect in the phantom herb head mystery.

We were certainly having a good look at the mountain as our route so far had taken us in a huge loop. Ben said it would be good to put a map of our movements in the film as they would be like the opening credits of *Dad's Army*, when those arrows denoting the progress of the German front are going round in circles.

The plan was always that we should take guides to the glacier snout and then cut loose so that the four of us could climb the glacier alone. Even Ben and Rich were to be banned from climbing on the glacier with us, such was our conviction of purity. Pete and David, having two hands each, would operate a small video camera and take as much footage as they could. We would then meet the film crew and guides at the summit.

The rain began that afternoon . . .

It rained for two days. The radio message from the recce team made dismal listening when we could hear them through the static. They could not reach the snout of the Credner Glacier or even see the route on it for the whiteout. Down at Shira a stream of water ran through our dining tent as we ate eggy bread and 'crucifried' chicken drumsticks, and my lungs bubbled as an accompaniment. The next day would be my last chance to climb this lump if one counted the days required against the number of days we had left in Tanzania. If my lungs were still noisy in the morning I would be forced to call it quits. I was being held to ransom by my own body.

In the morning I opened my eyes and for a while didn't remember where I was or that I was suffering from pulmonary oedema. Then I remembered and took in a deep breath . . . No bubbles . . . I cautiously unzipped my sleeping bag . . . No bubbles . . . Crawled out of my tent . . . Still no bubbles . . . Was blinded by bright fog illuminated by the sun just, it seemed, on the other side. The effect was as if I had passed away and gone to heaven . . . NO BUBBLES!

Not withstanding this seeming miracle, I had to make sure by limping across the camp at speed and getting my heart rate and breathing up. Though there was a sensation of pain, as if I had been beaten in the ribs and my lungs were contused, I couldn't find any sign of the oedema.

Yahoo! Yahoo! Upward bound. My breath became laboured as anyone's would after hopping around like a mad person at 4000 metres.

'The death rattles gone then?' said Jamie, coming back from his morning ablutions, with a grin.

One might suggest that a potentially fatal condition such as pulmonary oedema should be treated more seriously, with more concern. But all along there was a graveyard humour on this trip that I had not known in any other situation.

When Jamie had his first fall, tripping on a boulder, and going down with the metallic clatter of poles and prosthetics, much to the horror of the porters, we other three got our cameras out before any thought of lending a hand. In this way we learnt to laugh at each other's numerous falls and mishaps.

The others hee-hawed at my expense when I described how unattractive I looked in the hospital, bald and gamy-legged, to my future wife.

'But you look just the same now,' said David.

We have all been so close to death, I suppose, that, to use a much clichéd phrase, we have learned to laugh in its face. That isn't to say that we dismissed the seriousness of our undertaking or took unnecessary risks; we all have families or friends that are dependent on us and love us dearly. We have each taken a life's worth of risks and I for one, and Jamie now, have a parental responsibility.

As the mist dissipated the mountain slowly revealed itself. As expected, the summit slopes were now completely white, but as the big hill gradually unwrapped itself, and we got to view lower and lower down from the top, Jamie and I stood in bewilderment as David busied himself taking photos. It was a truly beautiful sight. What had been brown rubble was now white, right down to the Lava Tower.

'How deep do you think it is?' asked David, trying to gauge our chance of success now.

'About a foot,' I reckoned.

'First your rattles and now this,' laughed Jamie.

'But if it wasn't for me we would be up there in that,' I said, half-joking and half salve to my own mind.

'Like Pete and the boys, you mean.'

The porters had had a terrible night. KB, Mukuku, Changigi and Omari had slept in the dining tent in the main flow of the water. They were dripping and shivering. David, Jamie and I felt so embarrassed for being clothed in dry down jackets and fleece jumpers that we immediately gave them every item of clothing we had spare. Unfortunately, we didn't have fifteen outfits, so many had to go without, though these porters seemed to accept this graciously. Bungama, the cook, was soaked also but he refused any assistance. He was a hard silent man and quietly relished being so tough.

While the advance party recce'ed another route over a saddle behind a rock pinnacle known as the Shark's Tooth, we packed up the camp and set off up to the whiteness. The day's weather soon deteriorated into a sleet storm, which served to soak the porters once again. Most of these guys were dressed in plastic bags and shod with cheap gym shoes. Normally there would not have been any storms in this season.

The vertical face of a huge boulder provided some shelter from the wind but little resistance from the sleet, which was seeping into every pore. The porters huddled against the rock much as sheep do in Wales. I was becoming more and more uncomfortable with the situation as we waited for the midday call, which wasn't coming.

'The porters want to do well for you but they have been wandering round in circles now for a week,' said a shivering wet Eric.

He didn't even have a plastic bag. Eric was a computer programmer whom Musa had chosen as porter manager for his excellent command of English. This was Eric's first trip to Kilimanjaro and for a man who didn't know anything about the way of the mountains he was a hardy soul with a big heart.

'When we get the call they will do whatever Safi tells them to do,' he said and added, 'the porters have great respect for Safi.'

David and Eric then climbed to the highest boulder in an attempt to receive a signal, which they did at last. Eric talked to Safi. They had again failed to get to the Credner Glacier's snout and, as we were running out of time, it was decided to change our plans. We would switch to the slightly less remote Western Breach.

The Western Breach lies almost directly above the Lava Tower, so our team retraced its steps through the snow on a track we had previously descended. Pete, Rich, Mr Clean and Charles would catch us up later.

Porters were now strung out over the final two kilometres to the camp and at risk of hypothermia and maybe frostbite in their poor footwear. The situation was getting serious. Pete and the other three in the advance team caught me up and overtook me on the final slope up to the Lava Tower Camp. At least the blizzard had eased but with the onset of dusk the temperature was dropping rapidly.

Between ten and fifteen of us crowded into the dining tent. Safi and Charles were complaining of painful eyes. The pair had become afflicted with snow-blindness for, although they were carrying their glasses, they had neglected to wear them. Because it was cloudy with poor visibility it just hadn't seemed necessary.

I removed a small bottle of eye drops from one of the medical packs marked MISCELANEOUS [SIC], and Rich did the honours, but next morning Charles and Mr Clean were nowhere to be seen.

'They went back to Shira in the middle of the night with Tumainiel and Changigi for their eyes,' Eric told me.

The pair were apparently in such unbearable pain that night that they had to be guided down the path blindfolded.

'Don't worry for them. They are tough guys,' Eric added.

Our trip of a lifetime seemed to be falling apart before our very eyes.

'Are the porters still keen to go on?' I asked Eric.

'They have talked about it this morning and if you are prepared to go up then they are prepared also.' He added with a slight smile, 'Not many clients would have given the porters their clothes.'

We had expected our expensive underwear and fleece jackets back when their other clothes were dry but as no clothes seemed to be appearing we figured there must have been a breakdown in communication. What the hell, we could always get new mountaineering clothes.

The guys definitely seemed in good spirits and we spent the morning drying ourselves out. There were wet garments and sleeping bags everywhere and Rich suspended a climbing rope to use as a clothes line. We ate a late breakfast, mango and weird tinned sausage, at the wooden table, which was brought up for the second time and erected in the snow, in burning sunshine.

At about 11 am we were all ready and packed for the short 200-metre climb up to the Arrow Glacier Camp. Most of the porters were to traverse around Kilimanjaro and meet us after the summit; only six were to accompany us to the Arrow.

By this hour of the day the snow had turned into a soft paste and I was slipping and falling all over the place. Ben offered to break trail for me, which solved this particular problem. As I watched Ben up above me my mind drifted back to good times I had spent in his company.

During the mid-1980s I had lived with Ben in a little terraced house in Llanberis. Our diet was terrible back then; fried eggs, chip butties and lots of alcohol, whatever we could get our hands on. In those days he was known as Manic Ben. This nomenclature wasn't for a tendency towards mania but because he became obsessed with a tough rock climb known as Manic Strain and spent many hours of every day on the route.

In those days Ben sported a flat top, had an unhealthy pallor and wore a 'dead man's coat' from some charity shop. In the early nineties he moved to Sheffield, got a first in Fine Art there, and I saw him only sporadically from then on. It was good to be spending time with him again.

When a boy with our table balanced on his head struggled past, slipping and falling in his shoddy footwear, the pair of us thought we had to say something.

'Bungama, we don't need a table at this altitude. Tell him to go down for his own safety,' said Ben softly.

Bungama said something to the boy in Swahili, the boy turned around and, half falling, half sliding he disappeared back down the hill.

'I told boy down catch others,' said Bungama in a matter of fact manner.

We skated into Arrow Glacier Camp, which at 4800 metres was almost the same altitude as Point Lenana, the highest mountain I had climbed since my accident.

On looking across to the south I saw that which had been my ambition to climb for years, the Breach Wall.

People had been telling me that the Messner Icicle on the this huge face had disappeared due to global warming, yet a trinity of impressive icicles fell down the wall still.

Only the briefest itch of sadness came upon me though, as I looked across at the bright orange face, divided into four by the giant streams of ice, like some psychedelic zebra crossing. I was now comfortable with my body and its limitations, well, comfortable enough not to go torturing myself over something I knew I would never do.

It is true that the pace of retreat of the glaciers on Kilimanjaro is accelerating, and that somewhere between twenty and forty years hence this volcano will be devoid of permanent snow. But at least I can attest that the Messner route is still there, though for how long is anyone's guess.

With my 'new router's eyes I searched for new ways up the wall or variations that were possible. I found several, including a direct start to the Messner Icicle. Once this ability to appreciate new routes was my bread and butter, crucial to my creativity, though now I did this just out of whimsy.

My gaze then fell upon the Western Breach. The route we were meant to be climbing, a supposed Plan B, the alternative to the Credner, looked a daunting prospect.

Because of the deep snow the storm had put down, this mountain had been transformed from a dusty equatorial volcano and assumed Himalayan proportions. At this time Kilimanjaro would not have looked out of place amidst the Karakoram giants.

The route looked steeper than I had imagined and then, about three-quarters of the way up the face, disappeared through gullies in consecutive bands of cliffs. The way could lie through any number of deep gashes in these walls.

However much I questioned Kornelli it was hard to get him to give more than a cursory wave in the general direction of the face. 'Route goes up there.'

The kitchen tent was erected and over a massive lunch we worked out our plan.

After my brush with illness, David suggested ascending 1100 metres direct to the summit, thereby missing out the next camp at 5700 metres. We would then traverse the summit, descending 1800 metres to the Karanga Camp, where our porters were waiting, on the other side of the mountain.

'That way you won't have to sleep at Crater Camp and risk the death rattles coming back again.'

'Which they probably will do,' noted Pete with an ever so slight grin.

'It'll be a huge day,' added an excited Jamie.

'Yes, it will be a huge day but the prospect of getting ill at five seven with not much hope of getting down in a hurry is bloody unappealing.' I pitched in my pennyworth.

Jamie, as usual, was all for it. 'I'm all for it.'

Pete nodded his affirmation.

'The next decision is when to get up,' said David. 'The snow will be frozen in the middle of the night.'

'I was afraid you were going to say that,' pronounced Rich.

'So, you're saying climb a kilometre high mountain face in the pitch dark,' I gasped, adding excitedly, 'I haven't done that for years.'

'Midnight then?' said David.

'Midnight,' Jamie said mournfully, more to himself than to anyone else.

It was decided.

10

The Roof of Africa

I wrestled with a desperate fear that now, with
thousands of heartbreaking miles behind us, the
odds might be too much for us. We were now, more
strongly than ever, in the grip of the compulsive
urge to keep moving. It had become an obsession,
a form of mania.

Slavomir Rawicz – *The Long Walk*

Filling the water bottles, cutting the weight down on
every last item and making sure our boots and packs
were ready to put on and go, we prepared for the climb to
the summit. Pete and I crawled into our tent at 7.30 and
waited. We attempted to sleep but sleep wouldn't take us
so we chatted about Pete's accident and life. As Pete is the
only one that has not written a book, I had to ease his story
out of him.

We were finally enveloped by slumber without our being
aware and the beep-beep-beeping of the watch woke us as
if we had never slept. A shower of ice crystals was illuminated in my head-torch beam as Pete unzipped the door of
the tent. Iddi immediately presented me with a cup of warm
black tea as I emerged into a frozen magical cave of a
world.

As Pete fastened my crampons on to my boots, I looked
across at Jamie. David was doing the same for him.

Suddenly Jamie flinched in pain. 'I just had a needle stuck in my foot!'

David and I gave him a sidelong glance as he explained how his phantom hands and feet still hurt him and how he longed to stretch his fingers out.

As the route was difficult to follow in the dark we had opted to take along a couple who knew the way. Though our cripples-doing-it-by-themselves angle to the expedition was compromised and the integrity of what we were trying to achieve was tainted, safety always had to come first, especially for us, being disabled.

Our excellent cook took over the assistant guide post. A member of the Kisinkasa tribe to the north-west of Tanzania, Bungama dressed in a Maasai blanket with unlaced Vans for his feet and no crampons and no torch. This you must understand was for a 900-metre alpine face covered in ice, rock and compacted snow.

Bungama was assistant to ex-assistant and newly promoted to head guide, Kornelli. Kornelli had red eyes and was a small ferret of a man with rotten teeth whom one could easily mistake for being sneaky, but was actually very competent. He did vague out and lose the way a few times on the face but he always got us back on track.

Pete had me on a leash, roped to him, as we climbed up in our private pools of head-torch light. I slipped in the snow and fell sideways pulling the rope tight on Pete, but he just stood his ground in the dark while Jamie came to my aid.

'Do you want a hand?'

'Why, have you got one spare?' I asked facetiously.

While he planted his trekking pole firmly into the snow, I hauled myself up on his stump-socket.

Bungama came over to me and motioned for me to take my sack off.

Here we go again, I thought, as I recalled Mount Kenya. But there was nothing else for me to do. I had already had a few falls and I was now jeopardizing the success of the climb. In fact it would have been highly problematical and dangerous to down climb from this position and would have required at least one other member of the team to help me achieve this. Anyway, there was no way I was descending from here.

There was no time for philosophizing on what this pitiful act meant. In the torchlight I just shrugged the bag off and passed it to Bungama. He then climbed the final 500 metres of the face with two rucsacs on his back.

When Ben saw Bungama's soaked trainers and enquired after the state of his feet he replied, 'I have two pair socks.'

Whenever I slipped Bungama was always there with a steadying hand; at one point I remember having to sit on his head to reach over an overhanging block. On numerous occasions he held my foot in place while I moved up. Anybody else would have slipped away in the snow, in old unlaced trainers, and fallen to their death, but Bungama was like a silent angel, for wings a Maasai blanket, always there to save me.

The guidebook reads that the climb is 'Somewhat exposed' and 'Trekkers will feel a bit out of place on this route', but in the dark of night we saw no precipices above us to bring about dizziness and no sheer cliffs below our feet to produce vertigo.

My right crampon, which I had had specially adapted, wasn't functioning as it should. The points that were reduced by filing were now too blunt. I had done this to aid my right leg, making it effectively shorter, so that my foot, which has trouble clearing the ground in a step, would swing straight through.

I planted the crampon spikes in steep water ice and, to my exasperation, the boot skidded off. Now I would have to go to all the trouble of replacing the boot . . . And again . . . Every time I lift my lead weight leg it burns valuable calories. And another time . . . No . . . I slumped in the snow, momentarily exhausted.

Jamie resembled a lost Marabou stork picking his way up the rocks in the darkness on his titanium stick legs. What impressed me about Jamie was his remarkable drive whilst preserving a relaxed approach.

I thought I was easy going but on this trip I was sometimes irritated by David's temperament. David is a self-professed incorrigible chatterer, always expounding on some theory or another, or giving you the technical details of, say, a camera which you didn't have the slightest intention of buying.

Jamie always exuded an aura of calm in the face of David's chatter, whereas it sometimes served to agitate me and I showed my displeasure to the others behind his back. Admittedly this wasn't like me, and I knew it could create fractures in the team, but I couldn't help myself. I could only put my rude behaviour down to missing Cadi and Jane and worrying that I might get very ill at altitude. I was looking for something or someone to project my worries on to and David was the first target.

The dawn brought respite from a moonless night and illuminated a number of bands of cliffs three-quarters of the way up the face. These cliffs barred the way to the crater rim.

The Messner Icicle on the Breach Wall was below us now. The darkness could no longer conceal how far we had climbed during that long night. As we sat in an incredible position, on a projection of rock which fell away on three sides, we had our breakfast, a muesli bar.

Way down below us the tents were visible as tiny orange dots and I squinted to see movement between them. There wasn't any this early. Maybe in an hour.

'*Twendy . . . twendy*,' said Bungama.

By now we knew this phrase well. It meant, 'Hurry. Let's go.'

He realized that we were moving slowly, even for a bunch of cripples.

On the third cliff band I let the pole drop from my grasp – it still hung from my wrist – and popped between fingerholds, which were glowing in the beginning of the new day. At times I would stop and brush snow off ledges so that I could see them better and then place my boot with elephantine precision.

On arrival at the crater rim, I limped up to Pete who expected me to hug him and say something profound, 'like a poofter'. Instead, he reminded me later, I asked him for the bog roll.

One knew it was midday because of the blinding brilliance of the light.

From the rim I expected to look down into the funnel of an extinct volcano but that was not the case. Instead we looked up at the ice cliffs of the Furtwangler Glacier. I would have liked to have gone across to the glacier and touched those surreal séracs, standing there like an opponent's ivory dominos, but time wouldn't allow for that. Interestingly, the Furtwangler is a static glacier, which no longer flows over the rim and, like a giant ice cube, it sits, slowly melting away.

As we traversed the crater's edge the snow, which had turned to slush hours ago, was holding my foot back and threatening to trip me. Because I had shortened my crampon points they were balling up with snow every five or six steps, requiring me to attend to it with a quick tap of the pole.

We arrived at a shaded boulder that was evidently used as a camp. The place was littered with plastic bags, food wrappers and tin cans. The Kilimanjaro National Park Authorities have been doing excellent work in the last few years cleaning up the mountain and building footpaths to prevent further erosion. To the park's credit this camp at 5700 metres was the only place we found rubbish on the whole trip.

After some black tea, a muesli bar and a handful of popcorn I wearily studied the looming 200-metre slush slope that led to the summit plateau. It looked reasonable enough but it was too much for me. Knowing that there was an easy way around on the flat, and after some tortured deliberation, I decided it would be best for our team if I was to leave them to it.

'I'm going to keep traversing the bowl and meet you after the summit.'

'We're going to get benighted now anyway, so I think you should come,' said Jamie. 'It doesn't matter how long it takes.'

'No, I've made up my mind.'

'It's your decision,' said Pete.

'Then I'll come with you,' said Ben unhesitatingly.

Dejectedly packing my sack, I was aware that I would regret this decision for the rest of my life. We all say that summits don't matter and that it is the journey that counts but at that moment I disagreed. In Albert Camus's essay, 'The Myth of Sisyphus', he wrote, 'The struggle itself toward the heights is enough to fill a man's heart.'

But surely climbing to the heights fills a heart to brimming over.

I watched my friends for a while moving up the steep hill then turned and, head down, sloped away.

But Jamie's words insisted on entering my head, 'It doesn't matter how long it takes.'

Then, 'It's your decision.'

And, 'I think you should come.'

Before I even had chance to vocalize my change of heart Ben, who was behind me, said kindly, 'I'll do whatever you want me to do.'

'I'm going to have a crack at it then.'

Following our footsteps back to the base of the snow slope, I began ascending as fast as my breath would allow. Dragging my leg through the deep mush, my pace very soon slowed. My head was quickly spinning and I was soon gasping for breath.

On seeing me following, David halted and remarked, 'You're looking a bit ropy there, Paul,' and after a gulp of thin air, 'I think you should turn back.'

It is true that I was looking quite ill but I was incensed by his comment. I thought, maybe foolishly, that there was a high degree of empathy on this climb. The team was definitely compelled to work together far more than on any other expedition I had been involved with. Jamie cannot erect a tent and neither of us can do the buckles up on our crampon straps, but each of us had something to give in the way of experience.

That there was never any thought that we would not all climb this mountain together was, until a few moments previously, my unshaken belief: if one of us failed then we would all fail. This was perhaps misguided by a sense of mateship I had felt thus far. Though no one had actually said so, I felt this to be a tenet fairly central to the climb.

Then this.

I muttered under my breath, 'I hadn't realized it was every man for himself!'

For the harmony of the team, I determined I wouldn't argue with David and held my tongue. This was quite a simple decision to make, as I was extremely weary and couldn't have raised my voice if I'd wanted to.

Then in a fit of silent and self-deluded rage, cheeky bastard, I thought. Just because he's been to 8000 metres doesn't mean anything. I've done way harder rock climbs than he has.'

This last train of thought had no bearing on this particular situation whatsoever and eventually, realizing this, I relaxed.

David, so I thought, sensed something in my silence and didn't push the point any further. In fact he reverted to being his normal bubbly self. Only later, when the fog of indignation had lifted, could I see his concerns. After nearly three years of planning and finding the majority of the funds for this trip, he was naturally worried for the success of the team.

Disagreements such as this arise often on expeditions, especially in stressful situations, so his comment has gone unchallenged ever since. It's history, as they say, and David and I are good friends still. And I was going exceedingly, probably infuriatingly, slowly.

With what felt like a sandbag tied to my right leg I wallowed through the knee-deep viscousness, sometimes having to take my leg in my hand and haul it on to a snowy ledge. Sticky snow glued itself to my crampons, forcing me to stop regularly now and clear it off with the end of my special walking pole cum ice axe.

Jamie, with typical exuberance, seemed to be skipping up the incline with an ease that belied the fact that he was close to a thousand metres higher than he had ever been in his life.

None of the team, including me, used ropes on this final section, though there was some weaving around rocky buttresses to be done. At times the ground steepened and my front-points skidded on bare rock, but the terrain was never as steep as the cliffs of the previous night.

Whenever I turned around and looked down, there was Bungama directly behind me, always prepared, it seemed, to catch me, should I slip. David was moving slowly away from me and, however much I tried, my still bruised lungs wouldn't allow me to catch him. Pete was some distance behind me and, as I lay down in the snow under a rock overhang, he overtook me.

'Not far now,' he said wearily.

'*Twendy*,' said Bungama sternly, making me feel like a little boy for the umpteenth time that day.

Pete was right; it wasn't far, about fifteen metres to the plateau.

Ten minutes later I was there and sat down to eat my third and last muesli bar of the climb. I surveyed the scene around me. The plateau was reminiscent of the Ben Nevis plateau in Scotland but with a much greater area and with the odd sérac. The caldera, with its several sub-craters and cones, lay below me; with the covering of snow it resembled half a giant golf ball. The Ash Pit, Reusch Crater and the inner cone stretched into the distance, almost two and a half kilometres.

This volcano was indeed massive and I tried to imagine it in its splendid prime. It would have been a very different spectacle 750,000 years ago with bursting showers of golden lava that would reduce a human back to his atomic structure in an instant.

It is interesting to note that Kilimanjaro is not an extinct volcano at all, just dormant, sleeping, and it last erupted only a few hundred years ago. The Reusch Crater has smoking fumaroles, around which small ecosystems flourish in this otherwise desolate environment.

Bungama, interrupting my daydreaming and held out his hand to pull me to my feet.

This section of the climb, although on the horizontal, was perhaps the most gruelling. That which I thought to be the summit trigonometrical point turned out to be one of those irritating false summits; a radio transmitter about 200 metres horizontal distance from the real summit. Every four steps required a minute's rest, due to fatigue and thin air – I really had had enough by this time – but I still found the energy to take a photograph of Bungama who kindly posed for me.

It was 3 pm and the clouds, unusually for this time of day, were still below us. In my worn-out mind I had the serene sense of walking on the tops of cumulus.

The others had been there twenty minutes when I arrived at the bizarre summit structure:

'WELCOME TO UHURU 5895 METRES THE HIGHEST POINT
OF KILIMANJARO AND THE SUMMIT OF AFRICA,' it read
on a series of old weathered planks.

David came out a few steps and gave me a slap on the back, 'Congratulations. Welcome to the highest point in Africa.'

As I sat, well fell, down on the ground and let the feeling sink in a profound relief swept over me. I'd made it without getting the death rattles; we'd all made it. There were no whoops of joy or any punching of the air, nothing like that, just a contented bunch of blokes, much the same as any other.

'Jamie, can I borrow your mobile phone?'

'Go for it.'

I called Jane there and then. 'Guess what? I'm on the Roof of Africa.'

But I kept breaking down in tears, a mixture of extreme fatigue and emotion.

This aspect of my lability I was becoming appreciative of as to cry tears, of joy or sorrow, speaks volumes more of honesty and truth than mere talking.

'And how did Bolton do?' I was keen also to find out how Bolton Wanderers did in their Premiership clash with Portsmouth.

'They won, one – nil.'

Kevin Nolan with a fifty-second minute strike. How content can a man be?

That should have been enough; to end my story on the summit of Kilimanjaro but there is a peculiar and tragic postscript.

The descent to Karanga, the first camp down from the peak, lasted well into the night. At about 4 pm we began descending the snowy ridge on the far side of the summit to Gillmans Point. This blip on the ridge, at 5685 metres, is the point were many trekkers turn around on the Marangu route. The snow soon disappeared and gave way to black soil, perfect for growing vegetables.

Mawenzi, the third peak of Kilimanjaro, was glowing in the setting sun. It's serrated profile was far more impressive than Kibo from a climber's point of view, but it was impossible for me now. Then, one here and one there, the stars turned on and familiar constellations filled the bluey-black sky.

The night persisted in a monotonous humdrum of thudding feet and a blur of head-torch light. But we didn't feel the pain we were so obviously experiencing, the blackening toenails, blistering heels and crunching knees, because we were content. The four of us and our entourage skidded down volcanic gravel, descended rock slabs on our bums, climbed down cliffs, waded through streams and picked our tortoise way through boulder fields.

David's head-torch failed at some point in the night; he displayed remarkable tenacity and with every trip, stumble and fall he would pull himself back up with a minimum of fuss. On the track his wrist watch alarm began to bleep at 11.30 pm, the wake-up call for the night before – we had been moving on the mountain for twenty-three hours.

A while earlier Rich had run ahead to alert the camp that we were approaching. Like waiters who had lost their way, Iddi and Masanje appeared out of the darkness with a glass jug of orange juice and a plate of biscuits.

'Not – far – now,' said Masanje.

But it was. Or in my delirious state it seemed to be.

On one corner of the winding path I saw a shrine to the Virgin like those in Catholic churches. Mary had a look of infinite sympathy and was stooped over, shrouded in silk scarves. The whole structure was about chest height and I approached it with fascination: could there be a shrine up here really? But the Virgin grew branches, and the scarves turned into a dome of leaves. It was only a bush. I could have cried.

Then after another hour or so there was a vague light to be made out up ahead. It was a tent. Our tent! I remonstrated with myself, no surely not. It's just another hallucination. But as we drew closer the light intensified and before I knew it, we were metres from the end of this long and, at that moment, abstruse day.

Eric came out to meet me and hindered me into the tent, attempting to hold me upright, but really throwing me off my balance and we careered about like a couple of drunks. Then he brought out soup, which we all drank down greedily, followed by eggy bread and a pile of spaghetti bolognaise. It was all I could do to take one mouthful. All I wanted to do was let oblivion sweep me off these ever-so-tired feet. The last thing I remember was apologizing for my lack of appetite and that was it . . .

When I came round it was daylight and I felt like I had drunk ten pints of strong lager and got into a fight the night before. A raging thirst gripped me, as did a pounding dehydration headache. All the team were up and around unusually early, ravenously hungry and with the thirst of a desert. Fingernails had lifted with the desiccation of the previous day's travails at altitude. Lips were blistered by the ferocious sun and glare off the snow, and we were stiff as boards to a man.

Jamie's lips were one big blister and he reckoned his wife Anna would kill him. 'I promised her I wouldn't get burned!'

After a huge breakfast, with several cups of tea, hot chocolate and Milo, Mukuku and Mohamedi packed up our tents; we were incapable. A long, beautiful but achingly painful day's hike followed, down into the rainforest. The following day, the forest ever increasing in height with our drop in altitude, would bring us to the roadhead. Here we collected our 'I CLIMBED KILIMANJARO' certificates and headed to town.

Back in Moshi we were treated with celebrity status as we had been on local TV. Musa came to the hotel and vigorously shook all our hands, except for Jamie, that is. Amidst the congratulations he told us this story of tragedy.

'You might recall that on the thirteenth of this month, when you were on your way to Lava Tower, there was heavy snowing. The weather did not improve well until eighteenth, the day you summited. During these days a good number of parties gave up due to bad weather and returned down. It was during these days we at MK Safaris heard here in Moshi that two porters lost their lives.'

Apparently the porters were carrying the loads of a reputable luxury travel company from England. We were all aghast.

'How did this happen?' asked Pete, shaking his head.

'This is not the first time to hear porters lost their lives. Last year we had four cases.'

'Is it because they are so poorly equipped?' I questioned.

'Indeed. Poor mountain gear to protect them from abrupt changes of weather. Most tour companies, even the most famous ones, do not take serious care of their porters.'

It seemed the same old story from Pakistan to Nepal to East Africa.

'And what about experience? There seemed to be some very young porters up there,' added David.

'Overloading porters, which makes them exhausted, is a great problem. Sometimes these porters are new on the mountain and inexperienced. In case of any abrupt change of weather they are the most affected.'

Musa was very matter of fact about the whole tragedy, preferring not to surrender his professionalism to anything.

This was a very sad postscript to what had been a climb full of joy. To die mountaineering whilst testing your limits or simply in the pursuit of pleasure is one thing. Dying in an attempt to earn a crust, leaving behind a wife and family to fend for themselves, is another.

In achieving this climb I have realized more than just another of my post-accident ambitions, climbing to almost

6000 metres. Much more than that, I have laid to rest a ghost that hasn't only haunted me the six years since my injury. My insecurity phantom has been urging me on, ever upwards, all my adult life.

Ever since childhood I had never been happy unless I was doing something different. Sports weren't for me, especially team sports, which reminded me, even at school age, of the systematized grinding cogs of the army. I had to excel at jumping off the highest roof, climbing the most dangerous quarry face, getting the Fire Brigade called out the most times for moorland fires or getting chased through the town centre by store detectives, and outrunning them. It was all about acceptance in whichever group I was associating with at a particular period in my life; until recently it still was.

No more did I feel the need to prove my worth to other people. And that felt good. That need might have been altogether internal but nevertheless I had felt its rasping, like steel wool on my body's delicate parts, ever since adolescence.

In carrying this climb through I was coming full circle, or should I say full ellipse – for it was by a fairly oblique route – from my old mountaineering days.

This ascent differed from those pre-injury days in the respect that we had taken guides. But we had only done so because of the storm. Apart from that, Jamie, David, Pete and I had done everything as we would have done before our misadventures, only perhaps more slowly. We could still bask in the warm glow of the achievements of our trip. And we could always attempt the same style on another mountain. After all, there are an awful lot of them out there.

But a career of climbing mountains wasn't for me any more. I knew that much. The paths my life could now take were multifarious. However I did envisage a future where mountaineering had its place amidst other adventurous pursuits; cycling, trekking, pedal-kayaking, snorkelling, fishing and writing.

That night in Pub Alberto, a Moshi night-club, the four of us, much to the astonishment of the local pool sharks, played our own unique brand of the game. Using David's fingers for a bridge, I made the shots with my one useable hand.

When it came to Jamie's shot, he would use the crook of his elbow as a bridge and, tying the cue to his stump with a shoelace, made some fine shots. I remarked to Rich and Ben that it was a shame they hadn't brought their camera along.

After my turn, slumped on a stool, I drifted off momentarily into my own world, thinking how far and by what convoluted route this journey had taken me. Five years previously I came tottering out of neuro-rehab like a toddler learning to walk for the very first time. Six months later I walked the length of a Tasmanian beach. Less than four years ago I had climbed my 'first' hill, Moel Elio in Snowdonia, with the magical rain falling in wands.

And now Kilimanjaro.

I grinned to myself.

'Our shot again,' said David.

Coda: The Stiltskin Shuffle

Even though my body had become used to applying itself in a number of ways, I had not done any serious rock climbing since my head injury seven years past. Sure, I had dabbled in my hiking boots, as in the Eastern Arthurs, but here I was doing it properly, feeling along the wall of a dark cave, not knowing what to expect of my body.

The little bouldering I had attempted seemed contrived in the extreme – a bizarre series of strenuous one-arm pull-ups and hops with my foot up the rock. It bore no resemblance to what climbing a boulder used to entail. In fact that act of bouldering was so alien to me now that I doubted whether rock climbing was for me anymore.

Limp, and leaning heavily on my stick, I sweated up to the Wind Tower in Eldorado Canyon, Colorado. The approach to the climb itself was a steep winding path, which terminated in a shuffle along a narrow ledge. Pausing repeatedly, and craning my neck, I had to take care not to topple backwards, so confusing to my senses was this landscape, which once I would have pranced up with inborn content. Rincon, although a lowly 5.4, seemed dizzyingly high and imposing and I felt daunted. What was I about to get myself into?

'Hey, Cris-Ann, that looks really very steep.' I raised my voice up to her as she drifted over the rock as light as a piece of silk caught in the updraught.

'Yeah, but ya know, there's buckets all over here.'

From where I was sitting the rock face appeared practically smooth, so this information was well received. I was supposed to be resuming my climbing career on a forty-five-degree slab, not an imposing near vertical wall, but – one may say strangely – I was quite calm.

I was expecting my post-serious injury mind to be freaking out. You know, I-can't-do-this. You're-going-to-die, that sort of thing. But being without the emotional sack of fear that one drags up to the start of one's first climb is of great benefit: I'd been through all that twenty years ago.

Dieckhoff lowered Cris-Ann down and tied me in with a bowline. He asked me to check the knot but I declined.

So, with a rope above me and complete trust in Cris-Ann's belay building skills, my climber's mind reassured me. You *will* be safe.

I was used to fluid graceful movement, like a water trickle that had decided to disobey Isaac Newton (though some of my mates would disagree), not this Stiltskin Shuffle. This scraping and scrapping with the rock was interspersed with long, maybe ten-minute, pauses whereby I would be at sea on a ledge no bigger than a cigarette packet that had been jettisoned overboard.

Forearm pumping . . . My forearm . . . My forearm looking like a bag full of worms! After seven years I could not believe how good that felt. That burning sensation. The red-hot forearm nonchalantly gripped in a pair of tongs and slammed onto the blacksmith's anvil. The swollen appendage then agonizingly tempered with blows of the hammer and the arteries achingly extruded.

But the transport experienced belied the reality that my body was about to part company with the rock if it didn't come up with something very soon. As my other, spastic, arm fought to push me from the rock I was unable to release my fist-like grip from its precarious hold, because to do that would be to fall from the face.

The knowledge of complete safety brought only little salve to my conscience. I clung to the rock; a worn old jumper that would not, could not, be disrobed from it.

For several years I didn't want anything to do with rock climbing. I thought I had quit the rock. But the bud of begrudging casual interest – to throw away climbing would be to throw away many close friends – slowly transformed into a hungry rose. It had been almost seven years since my accident and I was famished. If this was to be my first climb, then I was going to give it my all.

Side-stepping the outside edge of my left shoe on to a high foothold, I powered up on a single thigh made strong by all the mountain hiking I had done these past four years. Aiding me in this manoeuvre was the fingerhold my four left digits were crimped on to, and pulling down on, directly in front of my face.

My one useable arm, having to do the work of two arms in daily life over the years, has also seen an increase in strength, as have my fingers and thumb.

Once the leg was straight, and ever so delicately, I let go of the hold now at my waist. Reaching up in a fan like motion I contemplated how students are taught to observe the 'three points of contact' rule at all times; and here I was with my one lonely toe.

My fingers discovered a long, deep sloping ripple, as rough as coarse sandpaper. Blindly massaging the rock in an attempt at finding the comfiest spot, the fingers settled down to a night slouching in front of the telly.

My right leg then realized its turn for action had come. Whilst stabbing at the rock repeatedly with my toe I was mithered by the, 'Eee, eee, eee, eee,' of Bernard Herrmanns *Psycho* shower scene score.

Eventually, with elephantine precision, the limb found its ripple and the foot stayed. Leg shaking like a pneumatic hammer, I stood up.

I wouldn't say this system worked well for me, but it was the only way I could use my new body. So with the rock face always to my left, and mugging it with violent kicks, I found I was actually climbing.

Reading the rock became much more important than it had been in the past. Sure, I was used to studying the rock around me but not a whole four metres above my head. The precise layout of the holds was as important as the shape of each individual layaway, edge, crack. Was it a sloper or incut? A two-centimetre hold or three? The sort of decisions a climber normally has to make, but I was finding a need to force these judgements much further in advance.

The bare knuckle fight with the sandstone – more the texture of rough granite – was leaving a trail of skin and blood behind. I made a mental note (*must wear leather gardening glove next time*).

Being a couple of stone heavier than my pre-injury days, the single shoulder, having to do all the work, was feeling it. (The day after the climb it was in bits.)

But I was loving this. Kilimanjaro was profoundly challenging and brought me back into the circle, the fold of humanity that only exists when you are in close proximity with other like-minded people. But rock climbing was what had always given my life meaning; whether it be in a luminous green gritstone quarry or on the sun-drenched granite of El Capitan. It was impossible to shake off twenty years of tactile memory it would seem.

Dieckhoff soloed up an adjacent route and hung by one arm above me pointing to, 'A great bucket here,' or, 'A killer pocket there.'

And before I knew it, an hour after leaving the sanctuary of the ledge, and sweating in the glare, here I was at the belay.

There were whoops of delight for me from below. A cool 'Good work' from Steve Quinlan and even a delayed 'Right on,' from my eighteen-month-old daughter!

There was still a lot to learn about my new (and unlike washing powder) unproved body and many novel techniques to be mastered. After all, I was moving into uncharted territory.

Now normally I would shed a tear after such an emotional event but there was too much excitement within me.

Rock climbing would have a place in my life again. Only to climb slabs, sure, where I would always be in balance, but there are plenty of those – Lliwedd on Snowdon and Idwal Slabs in the Ogwen Valley. The Cioch block on the Isle of Skye and the Rannoch Wall on the Buchaille. I would be able to achieve endless routes on the gritstone edges of Derbyshire. And then there are the international climbing grounds such as Yosemite in California and Handeg in Switzerland.

Six years ago, when I sold my eight point millimetre ropes, big wall rack of pitons, skis, plastic boots and desert rack of camming devices, I thought that climbing rock would be forever out of the question. But I must have suspected something as I couldn't part with one piece of equipment; my first nut, an original MOAC on rope.

I have realized for some time that I am not going to wring much more movement out of my arm or leg. Correct, the brain never stops healing but does get less plastic and therefore slower and slower. Now I am approaching the end of the road as far as getting better goes and must adapt to what I've got (something I have been doing for the past few years).

This doesn't discourage me one bit and all the striving has not been in vain: it has permitted me to have new adventures such as pedal-kayaking, fishing and caving and allowed me to walk again, write again, cycle again, dance again . . .

. . . And now climb again.